Women of the Conquest Dynasties

Wenji gui Han. Permission of the Jilin Provincial Museum, Changchun. On silk in ink and color.

Women of the Conquest Dynasties

Gender and Identity in Liao and Jin China

LINDA COOKE JOHNSON

University of Hawai'i Press
Honolulu

© 2011 University of Hawaiʻi Press

All rights reserved

Printed in the United States of America

16 15 14 13 12 11   6 5 4 3 2 1

Library of Congress Cataloging-in-Publication Data

Johnson, Linda Cooke.
　Women of the conquest dynasties : gender and identity in Liao and Jin China / Linda Cooke Johnson.
　　p. cm.
　Includes bibliographical references and index.
　ISBN 978-0-8248-3404-3 (hardcover : alk. paper)
　1. Women—China—Manchuria—History. 2. Manchuria (China)—History—To 1500.
　HQ1769.M36 J64 2011
　305.40951—dc22

　　　　　　　　　　　　　　　　　　　　　　　　　　　　2011006613

University of Hawaiʻi Press books are printed on acid-free paper and meet the guidelines for permanence and durability of the Council on Library Resources.

Designed by Publishers' Design and Production Services, Inc.

Printed by Edwards Brothers, Inc.

For Professor An Pingqiu 安平秋

and the members of the All-China Consortium
for the Study of Chinese Classics (Gu Wei Hui)

Contents

List of Illustrations ix

Time Line xi

Maps xiii

Acknowledgments xv

Introduction xvii

ONE

Womanly Ideals in the Liao and Jin Periods 1

TWO

Liao Women's Daily Lives 26

THREE

Jin Women's Daily Lives 54

Contents

FOUR
Sexuality and Marriage   80

FIVE
Widowhood and Chastity   106

SIX
Warrior Women   121

SEVEN
Private Affairs   141

Conclusion   165

Notes   183

Glossary   209

Bibliography   223

Index   241

Illustrations

Fig. I.1.	*Wenji gui Han*, section 1	xxvii
Fig. 2.1.	*Fan ma*, section 1	27
Fig. 2.2.	*Fan ma*, section 2	28
Fig. 2.3.	*Fan ma*, section 3	29
Fig. 2.4.	*Fan ma* detail: yurt and tribesmen	30
Fig. 2.5.	*Fan ma* detail: archers	31
Fig. 2.6.	*Fan ma* detail: taming a camel	32
Fig. 2.7.	Kitan hairstyles	32
Fig. 2.8.	Horse and rider	36
Fig. 2.9.	Wall painting of Kitan carriage with camel from the tomb of Xiao He	38
Fig. 2.10.	Wall painting of women preparing food and drink from the tomb of Hann Shixun	45
Fig. 2.11.	Wall painting of celebration with elderly lady and entertainers from the tomb of Hann Shixun	46
Fig. 2.12.	Wall painting of interior genre scene from the tomb of Zhang Wenzao	47
Fig. 2.13.	Zodiac from the tomb of Zhang *shi*	51
Fig. 3.1.	*Wenji gui Han*, "Tribesmen"	58
Fig. 3.2.	*Wenji gui Han*, "Wenji and Women"	59

Fig. 3.3.	Jurchen door guard	63
Fig. 3.4.	Leading a camel	69
Fig. 3.5.	Servants in Jurchen costume from tomb at Jiaozuo	70
Fig. 3.6.	Women in Han dress from tomb at Jiaozuo	71
Fig. 3.7.	Street scene from Yanshan temple	74
Fig. 3.8.	Theatrical scene from tomb at Jishan	77
Fig. 4.1.	Kulunqi tomb number 1, north wall, wedding of a Liao princess	82
Fig. 4.2.	Kulunqi tomb number 1, south wall, wedding of a Liao princess	82
Fig. 4.3.	Kulunqi tomb number 1, south wall, two women with mirror	83
Fig. 4.4.	Kulunqi tomb number 1, north wall, small carriage with deer	85

Time Line

EMPERORS	EMPRESSES	NOTABLE WOMEN
Liao Dynasty (907–1125)		
Abaoji/Taizu (r. 907/916–926)	Empress Chunqin/Empress Dowager Yingtian (878–953)	
Deguang/Taizong (r. 926–947)		
Shizong (r. 947–951)		
	Lady/Empress Zhen	
Muzong (r. 951–969)		*lienü* Lady Chen (b. ca. 960)
		Yemaotai tomb (956–986?)
Jingzong (r. 969–982)		
Hann Derang (941–1010)		
	Empress Ruizhi/Empress Dowager Chengtian (954–1009)	
Shengzong (r. 982–1031)		
Battle/Treaty of Chanyuan (1004/1005)		
		Hulian (d. 1007)
		Princess Chenguo (d. 1018)

Time Line

EMPERORS	EMPRESSES	NOTABLE WOMEN
		lienü Yelü Changge (1006–1077)
Xingzong (r. 1031–1055)		
	Empress Renyi	
Daozong (r. 1055–1101)	Empress Yide (d. 1071/1072)	*lienü* Xiao Yixin
		Concubine Xiao (d. 1071)
Tianzuo (r. 1101–1125)		*lienü* Nuolan (d. 1115)
Prince Chun/Tianxi (d. 1122)	Empress Dowager Xiao (fl. ca. 1122)	
Jin Dynasty (1115–1234)		
Aguda/Taizu (r. 1115–1123)		
Taizong (r. 1123–1138)		
Xizong (Tan) (r. 1138–1153)		*lienü* Shalizhi (ca. 1144)
		lienü Aluzhen
Hailing *wang* (r. 1150–1161)		
Shizong (r. 1161–1190)		Wulinda *shi*, m. Shizong (d. 1160)
Zhangzong (r. 1190–1209)		
	Wenji painting (ca. 1200)	
Weizhao *wang* (r. 1209–1213)		
Xuanzong (r. 1213–1224)		
		Yang Miaozhen (d. ca. 1234)
Aizong (r. 1224–1234)		*lienü* Nie Shunying (d. 1233)
		lienü Feng Miaozhen
		lienü Zhang Fengnu
Modi (d. 1234)		

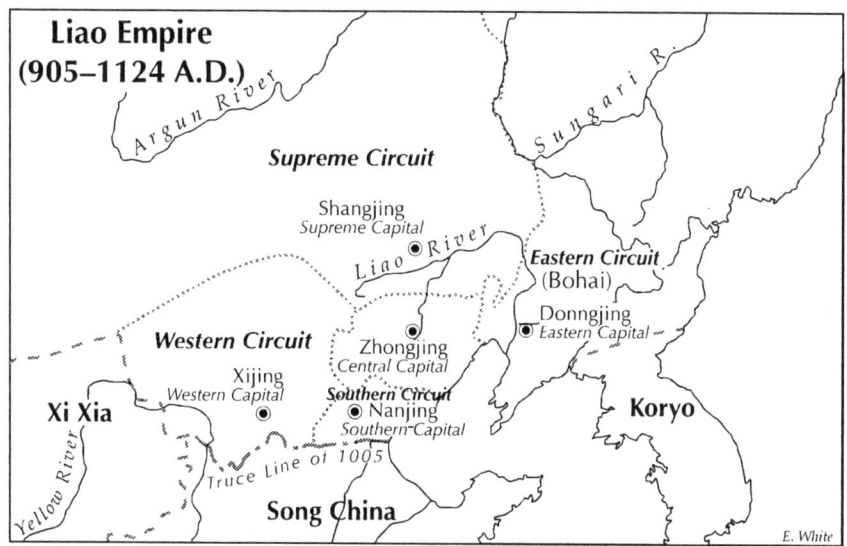

Map 1. Liao state (907–1115; shown ca. 1030). Based on Tan Qixian, *Zhongguo lishi dituji*, 3–4. Cartography by Ellen White.

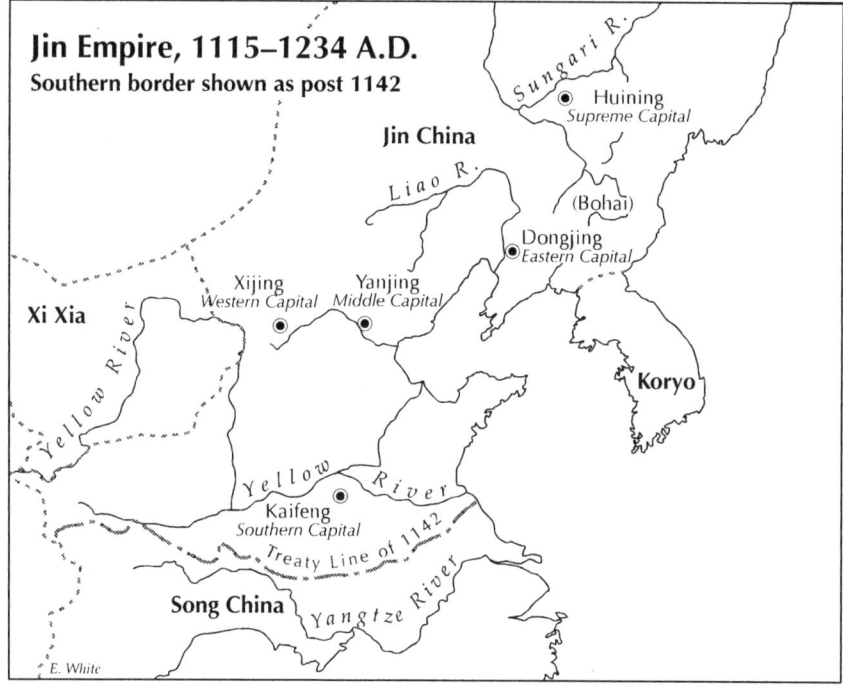

Map 2. Jin state (1125–1234; shown ca. 1150). Based on Tan Qixian, *Zhongguo lishi dituji*, 42–43. Cartography by Ellen White.

Acknowledgments

This book has been many years in the making. My first published paper was on a Liao tomb painting representing the marriage of a princess, discussed in chapter 4 of this book, and my art history master's thesis was devoted in part to the Jin painting of Lady Wenji, also discussed in this book. After a while—a long while—I realized that a common theme in these two early efforts involved representations of women in conquest dynasties and that this was a subject that might bear more research. That insight and the subsequent research it generated over an eight-year period gave rise to the present effort.

I could not have done this work without the help of many people and institutions, chief among which is my own university, which sponsored my research and trips to China through university and departmental grants from the Michigan State University Interdepartmental Research Fund for sabbaticals, and three successive Sesquicentennial Research Grants from the Department of History. Just as important has been the help and support that I have received in China, particularly from the All-China Consortium for the Study of Chinese Classics (Gu Wei Hui), headquartered at Beijing University. I am grateful to Professor An Pingqiu and the members of the Gu Wei Hui. I also want to name and give heartfelt thanks to research assistants, now colleagues, Wang Shuo, Zhao Zifu, Chang Hsiang-hua, and, at Beijing University, professors Yang Haizheng and Zang Jian. I also wish to thank the anonymous reviewers for the University of Hawai'i Press, whose critiques and suggestions did a great deal to improve this book. A special thanks to Patricia Crosby, Asia editor at the press, who showed great patience in herding this manuscript through to completion. Any errors and mistakes are all mine.

Introduction

> The Liao began from horseback and lived on horseback. Both empresses and imperial concubines were good at shooting, hunting, and military affairs.... This custom is unprecedented.

So reported the fourteenth-century chroniclers of the Liao dynastic history, the *Liaoshi*.[1] The Liao and Jin states, on China's northeastern borders, were dominated by forceful, horse-riding, militaristic aristocracies of steppe and forest. Historically, the Liao (907–1125), founded by Kitan tribesmen, and the Jin (1115–1234), established by Jurchen tribes, were the first of four conquest dynasties that originated in inner Asia. Together they successively dominated the late imperial period, which included the Mongol Yuan (1264–1368) and the Manchu Qing (1644–1912). Each conquest carved out a larger portion of China, until first the Mongols and later the Manchus conquered all.

The women of the Liao and Jin conquest dynasties included not only Kitan and Jurchen but also the Han Chinese living under alien rule. Each group had its own history, customs, and distinguishing characteristics and claimed its own identity. One of the challenges encountered in this study was to distinguish among these peoples and discover their salient customs and practices in order to identify and differentiate between pastoralist and forest traits and to characterize the cultural contributions of the Han peoples as well as those of mixed Han identity, known as *haner* (sons of Han), living under conquest rule.[2]

What does examining the lives of Liao and Jin women contribute to our knowledge of China and East Asia? Even though the *Liaoshi* and *Jinshi* are included in the twenty-five canonical histories, they have traditionally been deprecated by China scholars and consequently the women in their pages have been largely ignored. Customs and traditions regarding gender that were established during this period anticipate later social developments. Women living under the conquest dynasties enjoyed agency and power; they forged their own cultural identities. They are important for their own sakes and the stories they tell. They were the true warrior women of Chinese history.

Bred and taught by warriors, Kitan and Jurchen women became warriors themselves. They possessed an exceptional degree of agency, assertiveness, and power, combined, perhaps surprisingly, with Confucian education, literacy, and Buddhist piety. Agency included the ability to make their own decisions about such matters as the selection of marriage partners or alternatives when widowed. Power accrued to empresses who became regents for child emperors and took over direction of the civil affairs of government and to women in other positions of authority in military activities, political situations, or circumstances involving ethical choices. Women living under the conquest dynasties were discriminating in those aspects of Chinese culture that they chose to adopt. Some women from states south of the Liao realm were culture bearers who brought Confucian learning to the northern regions. Those of Chinese background living north of the border preserved their native cultures within their homes, while many Kitan pastoralist women living in yurts proudly followed indigenous lifestyles of herding. The Jurchen, by contrast, rapidly assimilated Chinese culture, language, and literacy. The resulting tension between accommodation and preservation figures throughout the pages of this work. These elements were crucial in shaping women's identities.

The opening *Liaoshi* quotation goes on to single out empresses Yingtian, Chengtian, and Renyi as exemplars of warrior women. Empress Chunqin, better known as Empress Dowager Yingtian (878–953), assisted the first Liao emperor, Abaoji (r. 907–926), in military matters and famously refused to comply with the steppe custom of following in death. Instead she cut off her right hand and placed it on the emperor's coffin as a promise to join him later. Thereafter, as regent, she dominated the selection of the next emperor and commanded her own military division.[3] Empress Ruizhi, better known as Empress Dowager Chengtian (954–1009), ruled as regent for her son, Emperor Shengzong (r. 982–1031), for nearly thirty years and personally led Liao troops to victory at the Battle of Chanyuan in 1004 against the Song.[4] She exerted great power both as a military leader and in administering the state. Renyi, the wife of Emperor Xingzong (r. 1031–1055), discovered and put down a rebellious plot against the emperor. She also accompanied him in battles.[5] This list of exceptional women is not complete without the Jin-dynasty bandit-leader Yang Miaozhen (d. 1234?), who led troops for and against the Song, Mongols, and Jin at various points in the confused border wars in Shandong at the end of the era. Although from a Han Chinese family, she adopted the conquest identity. She is remembered as a traitorous villain in Song-dynasty sources and a heroine in Jin history.[6]

Many conquest-dynasty women adopted selected aspects of Chinese culture and Confucian ethics. For example, Changge, one of the women described in the chapter on virtuous women in the *Liaoshi*, used her literary skills to rebuff unwanted suitors and wielded moral authority when she accompanied her brother in exile, an example of loyalty. Other women were able to make independent contributions to Buddhist temples, indicating that they had sufficient independent income to manage their own resources and money. Still others were themselves well educated and brought up their children in the Confucian classics to become emperors and statesmen.

One of the main themes in this book is the interaction between the cultures of Kitan and Jurchen women and the culture of the Han Chinese living in Liao and Jin territory, examining how these cultures interacted in women's realms and how each affected the other. In asserting agency and power and in their adoption of Chinese values or preservation of indigenous culture, Liao and Jin women to a large extent shaped their own identities. This book examines the ways in which women's identities changed over time as they negotiated between cultures, adopting and adapting certain cultural characteristics while discarding others.

Gender roles were constructed differently among conquest peoples of the north compared with the Han population of the south. Historians have long recognized that women in steppe and pastoralist societies enjoyed more authority than their counterparts in the sedentary and urban settings of China. Marriage customs, female sexuality, and the fates of widows contrasted markedly with the conventional standards for feminine behavior in the Chinese realm. As early as the fifth century, one Chinese scholar noted that among the barbarians, "married women are chaste and virtuous; unmarried women are promiscuous and loose in morals."[7] Such behaviors were closely tied to steppe

Introduction

conventions regarding women. A seminal 1978 article by Herbert Franke identifies a number of the salient characteristics of Liao, Jin, and Mongol women in the dynasties of conquest. Franke and later authors have noted that women in conquest dynasties had more autonomy and authority than women in neighboring societies. No seclusion was practiced, and women had public roles in military, government, and economic activities.[8]

Scholars who examine marriage customs and widow chastity in the Yuan and Ming periods, for example, might ask whether the origins of these customs go further back, to the Liao and Jin periods, where following in death and levirate marriage practices obliged women to turn to Buddhist retreat and chaste widowhood as alternatives.[9] Discussions of marriage, tombs, and joint burials in the Song are similarly incomplete without considering Liao and Jin examples.[10] This study relates women's individual stories and sets them in the social and cultural context of the period. Thus, the Liao empresses Yingtian and Chengtian and the Jin heroine Yang Miaozhen are placed in the context of contemporary conventions regarding sexuality and widowhood for the first time here. The success of the Liao and Jin empires lent legitimacy to Mongol rule in the thirteenth century and Qing rule in the seventeenth century. Women of the conquest dynasties are important for the ways in which they offer an alternative model of feminine history in China.

This study examines the unique characteristics of these women of the Liao and Jin states in the context of social and gender history from the tenth through the thirteenth centuries, seeking to determine how such traits applied to individual women and how they negotiated between cultures to establish their own identities. Their attainments refute the conventional derogatory stereotypes, in evidence since the days of Sima Qian, that "barbarians" were inferior, illiterate, and primitive.[11] In addition to feats of martial heroism, women were also singled out as role models and commemorated in biographies for honoring steppe customs. But at the same time, they were praised for their education, literary achievements, and Confucian ideals. Women of the conquest dynasties combined the *wu* (martial) side of steppe culture with the *wen* (cultural) side of Chinese tradition.

The women of the Liao and Jin states populating the chapters of this book had identity and integrity in their own right and deserve to be better known. These women were energetic and respected participants in their own societies. Kitan and Jurchen women present a model for the famously elusive myth of the warrior woman.[12] The customs Kitan and Jurchen women followed and the precedents they set were echoed in the succeeding conquest dynasties. Cultures in these different groupings were malleable and in constant change. Although indigenous culture might be established at birth or learned during childhood, women shaped their own identities through marriage, education, and religion, sometimes unconsciously, sometimes deliberately. As women of the frontier, they lived in the transient zones between societies and negotiated skillfully among steppe and forest customs and Han Chinese values.

The Setting and the Peoples

The inner Asian frontiers where the Kitan, *haner*, and Jurchen lived had historically been inhabited by many peoples, whose movements spanned hundreds of thousands of square miles.[13] This zone was a middle ground where goods, services, language, and cultural artifacts were exchanged, modified, and returned to be assimilated in new forms, and where no single orthodoxy prevailed.[14] The Liao and Jin territories included the steppes of Mongolia and the rolling plains and forests of Manchuria as far as the northern edges of the Korean kingdom of Koryŏ. The geography ranged from semidesert in the west to grazing pastures in the eastern areas, agricultural lands in the river valleys, and summer pastures in the mountains. In Sima Qian's celebrated words, pastoralists in these regions "move their abode following the water and the grass."[15] Tribal peoples had contended over these lands and fought with one another for millennia. Borders were fluid and transient. As Owen Lattimore has observed, the inland borders of China can be visualized as a "series of frontier zones, varying in depth from south to north . . . and stretching away indefinitely into the plains and mountains and forests."[16] Conquest dynasties occupied, seized, fought over, defended, and extended their control over these lands. No Great Wall existed to fix a border in the tenth to twelfth centuries, as it would in the Ming dynasty.[17] People spoke in colloquial terms of "north of the mountains" or "east of the [Liao] river" or the "Yan-Yun" (referring to two of the famous Sixteen Prefectures) but not of "within" or "beyond" a wall.

These lands had been home to the Xiongnu in Qin and Han times, were taken over by the Xianbei, occupied by the Kitan and Jurchen, and by the Mongols and Manchus in centuries to come. Kitan tribesmen had been active

Introduction

since Tang times. By the tenth century, tribal peoples included the Huihu, Kitan, and Xi in many separate tribes in the western territories, and the Moho, Wugu, Nüzhen, and others in the eastern regions. The Kitan in particular were exquisitely sensitive to distinctions between clans, tribes, and states; the *Liaoshi* lists over three hundred nations and peoples that sent tribute missions to the Liao court—more than in any other dynastic history. Tribute states included Song China, Japan, Korea, and even Persia.[18]

In these societies, both men and women rode horseback, lived in easily portable yurts or tents, and herded livestock, living off their flocks and herds. They moved across the rivers, valleys, mountains, and grasslands, contesting for control of grazing rights and sometimes invading the agricultural territories to the south. Pastoralists and forest dwellers belonged to a broad stratum of outsiders the Chinese disparagingly called barbarians. But this term is an inadequate translation for a more nuanced set of expressions, which identified outsiders according to north, west, east, or south. Horse-riding pastoralists from Mongolian and Manchurian lands were "westerners" (*hu*). Few Chinese dynastic histories recorded the actual names of such tribes or their affiliations, an omission signifying Chinese disdain. Song envoys routinely used the disparaging term *lu* (caitiffs) when referring to them.[19] Conversely, persons of Chinese background living in the frontier zone adopted many aspects of the conquest people and came to be seen by their compatriots to the south as no longer fully Chinese. They were variously known as Han, or *hanren* (Chinese), *fan* (foreigners), or *haner* to the Kitan, Jurchen, and Song alike, depending on their geographic origins and cultural identity, and thus indicating their subordinate status vis-à-vis the conquerors.[20]

The identities of conquest peoples were as shifting as the landscape. Different groups sometimes merged or made alliances, while at other times these same groups were in conflict. People adapted to cultural and environmental conditions, variously reacting against Chinese states to the south or embracing Chinese culture. Always there existed a tension between indigenous cultural characteristics and accommodation to "the other." The process worked in both directions as Kitan and Jurchen women embraced different aspects of Chinese culture and the Han and *haner* residents in the conquest states accommodated to the culture of their rulers and became more "barbarized."

Distinctions between the Kitan and Jurchen are perhaps best illustrated in terms of their successors. The Kitan were related linguistically to the later

Mongols, who founded the Yuan dynasty, whereas the Jurchen were the direct ancestors of the Manchus, who established the Qing dynasty. Language is an important cultural indicator, and insofar as it can be reconstructed, the Kitan language, known mainly from stele inscriptions, had no close cognate language. Some words were similar to those in Middle Mongolian, and many loanwords from Chinese have been found.[21] Joseph Greenberg groups Kitan with the Mongolian branch of the larger Altaic language group.[22] Thus, both in language and in their pastoralist lifestyles, the Kitan resembled the Mongols, although the degree of such linguistic connections has not been established. In addition to his work translating Kitan inscriptions, Daniel Kane has also identified a variant of Chinese employed by the *haner* residents in Liao territory and by members of the Liao court he calls Liao Chinese.[23] Chapter 2, which investigates Liao daily life, also examines aspects of these languages in greater detail.

The Jurchen originated as hunters and fishers in the eastern Manchurian forests, combining herding with basic agriculture in a semisedentary lifestyle. They emerged as a major force in the eleventh century. The Jurchen language stemmed from the southern Tungusic branch of Altaic and was the direct precursor of Manchu.[24] The Kitan and Jurchen peoples differed in respect to agriculture, urbanization, burial customs, hairstyles, dress, and degree of adoption of Chinese culture, but in other respects, such as mounted warfare and marriage practices, they were quite similar. The Kitan maintained and celebrated their pastoralist traditions to the end of the dynasty. They adhered to customary governance by tribal aristocracy in the Northern Circuit but maintained a separate, Chinese-style administration for the Southern Circuit, which was made up of the Sixteen Prefectures obtained from the Latter Jin state. The Jurchen, by contrast, followed Bohai and Chinese traditions and rapidly evolved into a Chinese-style state—so rapidly that the fifth Jin emperor, Shizong, instituted a revival effort to capture the old Jurchen vigor and language, a topic discussed in chapter 3.

Modern historians have sometimes used the term "ethnicity" in describing the tribal groups of inner Asia. There is a danger, however, in using a modern construct to describe a premodern society. "Ethnicity" invokes indigenous, immutable qualities such as ancestry, environment, tribal affiliations, customs, religion, clothing and hairstyles, and language.[25] But the term has modern overtones relating to race and can be pejorative, implying that ethnic groups are inferior or more primitive than a more "civilized" group. In the ever-shifting landscape and malleable identities covered in the present study, this term is too broad and too static. Distinctions among these peoples and between the northern and southern residents of the Liao and Jin states were subtle, transient, and too elusive to be captured by the term "ethnicity." A more flexible and nuanced approach using the general term "culture" better serves the needs of the present examination. Following the lead of the chapters on tribute states in the *Liaoshi*, the steppe peoples are called by their proper names.

"Culture," a term that occurs frequently in this study, is often taken to involve acquired aspects of Han Chinese culture, among which are literacy and philosophy and can include religious beliefs and customs. "Culture" is used in this sense in the current study but also in a broader sense. It can include both inherited and acquired aspects; it can be constructed and is easily transferable. It is both integral to a given people or society and highly mutable. Kitan women's culture, for example, could encompass steppe practices such as following in death and levirate[26] while also embracing selected aspects of Confucian learning and ethics. A woman like Concubine Xiao, whose story is told in chapter 1, could be adept at riding and hunting and at poetry and painting at the same time without being exceptional.

At a time when in Song China the sexes were separated from childhood and women were increasingly becoming sequestered inside their homes, as shown in Patricia Ebrey's classic work *The Inner Quarters*,[27] Liao and Jin women were hunting from horseback and conducting military campaigns. In spite of the acceptance of certain Confucian moral virtues, women in the *Liaoshi* chapter on exemplary women (*lienü*) were singled out for following their husbands in death, and heroines described in the *Jinshi* chapters were also honored for their military leadership and personal courage. Liao and Jin women shared some customs, including bride-price payments in lieu of dowries and levirate for widows. Judging from their tombs, Kitan women maintained pastoralist traits throughout the dynasty. Jin society, however, readily adopted Han culture, a process that was greatly aided by Jurchen leaders who married acculturated women from the former Bohai state.[28] But the chapter on feminine virtue in the *Jinshi* nonetheless honors martial women who defended cities and raised the flags of fallen male leaders; indeed, the bandit-leader Yang Miaozhen was considered a heroine. Kitan, Jurchen, and

Han women each mediated between cultures in different ways. Many of these traits passed into the Mongol and Manchu cultures. The birth of a girl was not a matter for regret in Liao and Jin society, in which daughters carried no dowries but were married out in return for generous gifts from the new spouse and his family. The prominence of women in the Liao period is marked by the large number of elaborate tombs in which a woman is the only occupant or the more important member of a couple.

Women crossed geographic and cultural borders simply by living in place while borders shifted or through marriage or abduction. Marriages between Han and Kitan, Kitan and Xi during the Liao, or between Jurchen and Bohai were designed to secure allies and advance political ambitions. Meanwhile, many Han Chinese from border states such as the Latter Tang and Latter Jin joined the Liao and served loyally.[29] When southern women married northerners, they, like the legendary Lady Wenji, brought with them the Han literary culture. Confucian philosophy and other customs of the "civilized" south were transferred to the north—although, it must be emphasized—selectively.

Culture Bearers

The martial skills for which Liao and Jin women were celebrated invite comparison to the celebrated tale of Mulan, a girl who fought in the army while concealing her gender. Although numerous variations exist, including today's Disney version, in the original tale, Mulan was a woman of the borderlands. She fought for a khan, not an emperor, and after the war was over, the khan rewarded her with a fast camel to ride home.[30] Appealing though this image may be with its reference to steppe customs, it does not seem to have been relevant in the Liao and Jin periods. For one thing, Mulan of the story disguises herself as a man rather than adopting a military persona in her own right. Instead, the inspirational tale at this period was that of the late-Han-dynasty heroine Wenji, which has long been recognized as symbolic of Chinese relations with alien pastoralists. I have found no references to Mulan in Liao or Jin materials.

Wenji's story comes from the chapter devoted to exemplary women in the *Hou Hanshu* (History of the Latter Han Dynasty).[31] Named Cai Yan, she was the daughter of a Han-dynasty scholar and court official, and she became known as Wenji (Cultured Lady) for her education and literary skills. During the chaotic political situation during the last years of the dynasty, the Xianbei of the northern frontier repeatedly raided inside the passes.[32] On one such raid Wenji was abducted, carried off to the steppes, and forcibly married to a barbarian chieftain. Desperately miserable and bewailing her fate, she wrote she "wished to die, but found no way." Although she mourned her homeland, she eventually became reconciled to her fate and bore two sons to her chieftain husband. Twelve years later, she was ransomed and returned home but was forced to leave her sons behind. She mourned their loss even more bitterly: "my spirit shattered, my mind crazed." Back in Chang'an, she wrote, "Home, I found my family all gone. . . . I felt as if my life had ended."[33]

To the Chinese, Wenji was a heroine who never wavered in her loyalty to China, and her story was celebrated in paintings and poems throughout successive dynasties. The Wenji legend was revived in the eighth century by the Tang poet Liu Shang and again in the Song in a poem by the famous statesman Wang Anshi (1021–1086). In pictorial representations of the poems, tribesmen in the nomad camp where she was taken strongly resemble contemporary Kitan.[34] Wenji enthusiasm reached a new high in the twelfth century, when the Song empress dowager, who had been captured by the Jin at the fall of the northern capital, was allowed to return to the Song court—giving rise to more paintings and poems recalling Wenji's story.[35] Clearly, for the Song the main motif of the Wenji story was her loyalty and eventual return.

To the horse-riding pastoralists of the northern frontiers, however, the Wenji story had a different meaning. Wenji and women like her mediated between the two worlds of the steppe and China. A short Jin-dynasty hand scroll depicting Wenji's return is illustrated in figure I.1.[36] The scroll is dated between 1200 and 1209 and was executed by a Jin court artist, painted in color on silk.[37]

In the painting, Wenji is shown on her way back to the capital accompanied by servants in Jurchen costume.[38] She is portrayed as a middle-aged matron riding with the ease of experience and a firm foot in the stirrup. The wind that forces the other figures in the work to shield their faces is welcome to Wenji, who alone faces it without protection.[39] The Wenji of this painting is a heroic figure, emotionally and physically courageous. She was also a mother who had been forced to leave her two sons behind. Her loss is poignantly suggested by the foal accompanying the lead mare; even so lowly a creature as a horse could bring her child with her while Wenji was alone. Courage—as well

Introduction

as good horsemanship—were qualities that characterized Liao and Jin heroines, as shown in the succeeding chapters.

Wenji is depicted in Jurchen attire, with a fur hat, ribbons, a belted jacket, skirt, pantaloons, and high boots. She wears the Jin imperial color yellow (now faded).[40] By the date of the painting, the tribal or "raw" Jurchen had become so peripheralized and alien in Jin society that they could stand in as the "barbarians" who had abducted Wenji. As art historian Susan Bush has pointed out, the painting may have been intended as a moral exemplar for women in the imperial household.[41] Wenji's depiction as a mounted warrior woman reflects the martial roles for women in Liao and Jin cultures, while the implicit messages she bears, loyalty and filial piety, can be understood with reference to the twelfth-century Jin state, which in this representation allegorically represented the Han state, the epitome of a civilized Chinese cultural entity, to which the Jin considered itself equivalent.

The Wenji tale resonates with the women discussed in this book on a number of levels. As a woman who crossed boundaries from civilized China to pastoralist society and back, Wenji was a culture bearer and paragon of Confucian virtue. Her kidnapping parallels the Kitan and Jurchen practice of abduction marriage (a topic discussed further in chapter 4). She anticipates Lady Chen in the *Liaoshi* chapter on virtuous women, who came to the Liao from the Latter Tang state, and Lady Zhen, who was "obtained," or abducted, from the Latter Tang capital by a prince who would become the Liao emperor

Fig. I.1. *Wenji gui Han*, section 1. Permission of the Jilin Provincial Museum, Changchun.

Introduction

Shizong (r. 947–951), later becoming his empress.[42] Wenji's literary skills were embodied in Changge, a Kitan noblewoman, who wrote poetry and prose and advised government officials, and by Concubine Xiao, who composed literature and paintings that were displayed in her home. Concubine Xiao was also a skilled horsewoman who "excelled at hunting . . . who always held her shot until certain of hitting her prey."[43] These women negotiated between cultures and adopted selected aspects from Han culture to create new identities.

Contents

The chapters that follow examine women's daily lives, marriage and sexuality, the choices open to widows, warrior women, and aspects of education, religion, and even the romance of one prominent empress. The first chapter begins, however, at the end of the story by examining models of virtuous women described in the Liao and Jin dynastic histories, whose exemplary behavior reflected contemporary social expectations. But these formal dynastic chronicles were compiled by Yuan historians in the mid-fourteenth century, two to three hundred years after the events and people they describe.[44] Thus, these brief biographies were compiled at a time when values for feminine behavior might have been more heavily influenced by aspects of Confucian culture. For example, the biography of the virtuous woman Changge praises her for voluntarily accompanying her brother in political exile. Her devotion is a clear example of Confucian filial piety. But her epitaph, preserved elsewhere, omits this passage, although it agrees on the other points of her life.[45] Perhaps the best course is to consider that the dynastic histories describe not individuals but behaviors that were admired among the conquest peoples.

Chapters 2 and 3 address the daily lives of Liao and Jin women, distinguishing between Kitan, Jurchen, and Han, each of whom embraced a different culture. The formal histories are silent on matters of daily life, but archaeology in the People's Republic over the past thirty years has provided a wealth of materials, especially from the monumental underground mausoleums in which the Kitan elite buried their dead.[46] Archaeological reports reveal many aspects of daily life, ranging from household artifacts to wall paintings representing contemporary persons and events, and including even the remains of the deceased as an object of study. Certain very rich archaeological resources,

Introduction

such as the tomb of Princess Chenguo, tomb number 1 at the Kulunqi cemetery of the Xiao family—which contains a wall painting depicting the marriage of an imperial princess—and the tomb of an unnamed lady at Yemaotai are discussed in this volume for the first time in the context of women's history. In addition to the tombs of the Kitan, burials of persons with Han surnames contain a wealth of information on the daily lives of the Han and *haner* living under Liao and Jin rule.

The Jurchen, discussed in chapter 3, lacked a monumental tomb tradition, and the few Jurchen burials that have been excavated are no more than rectangular graves containing few artifacts and no wall paintings. The imperial Jin tombs located outside present-day Beijing, which might have contained more information, were systematically destroyed in the Ming dynasty (1368–1644). Jurchen daily life must therefore be reconstructed largely from literary sources and extant temple or scroll paintings. Tombs of people with Han surnames, however, offer more information; though smaller than Liao tombs, *haner* tombs contain artifacts and paintings, which reveal aspects of daily life, including clues to social class and depictions of tea in both Buddhist and secular settings. Interestingly, such tombs from the end of the Jin period contain representations of dramatic performances that anticipate theatrical developments in the Yuan dynasty.

Chapters 4 and 5 investigate aspects of betrothal, marriage, and widowhood, beginning with premarital sexuality, which earned Kitan and Jurchen women a reputation for promiscuity. Marriage patterns are examined, with attention to both major and minor forms of marriage. Conventions pertaining to widowhood and chastity are the subject of chapter 5. Beginning with the ancient steppe custom of following in death, it examines the practice of levirate remarriage and other options that slowly developed for widows, including chaste widowhood and retreat into Buddhist sanctuaries.

Chapter 6 explores the lives of warrior women, focusing on the Liao empresses Yingtian, Chengtian, and the Jin-dynasty bandit-leader Yang Miaozhen. The primary sources from which these stories are drawn are often quite vivid and have the ring of authenticity. Women were warriors in both the Liao and Jin periods, but their activities varied according to cultural identity. While Kitan and Jurchen women led armies and fought battles, women with Chinese names defended their honor in more personal ways. Chapter 7 is devoted to a discussion of women's private affairs dealing with education, religion, and ro-

Introduction

mance. It addresses how women were educated and explores women's involvement in Buddhism and ways in which they contributed to Buddhist institutions. Private histories and Song reports allude to an affair between Empress Chengtian and her chief minister, Hann Derang, that lasted for nearly thirty years, until her death. Examination of this romance in the context of women's sexuality and the constraints on widows, plus new archaeological discoveries, suggest that the rumors may well have been true.

The concluding chapter returns to a chronological analysis and examines the changes in Liao and Jin women over the three-hundred-year span of this study. It is not a history of steadily increasing sinicization, as earlier historians have implied, but rather a history of negotiation in which some aspects and values of predynastic life were maintained and aspects of Chinese culture, such as certain Confucian ethics, were adopted. It is also a story of the tensions between cultures. Moreover, the story widens or recedes much as the geography of Liao and Jin territories expanded and contracted historically. At the very end of the Jin period, just when we might expect to see increasing if not full adoption of Chinese characteristics, a warrior woman–bandit-general emerges to carry on the martial tradition of Kitan and Jurchen women.

Dynastic histories, private histories, travel accounts, literary works, epitaphs, and archaeological materials all contributed to the research informing this book.[47] Each source has required different degrees of caution and interpretation. The facts that emerge show women's lives in the Liao and Jin states to have been extraordinarily rich. Imperial Liao and Jin women enjoyed high status and many privileges unknown in the south. There is no evidence of foot binding. Women rode astride, hunted, and, on occasion, led armies. They appeared openly on the streets and were not sequestered in the home. In short, women's lives in the north contrasted in many ways with those led by their southern sisters in Song China. But were Liao and Jin women truly unprecedented?

Note on Romanization

Chinese names and terms are given in pinyin romanization throughout this book. However, "Kitan" is used for the name 契丹 rather *qidan* because it has been shown to be the closest equivalent to actual pronunciation.[48] On

Introduction

the other hand, the generally accepted term "Jurchen" is used instead of the pinyin *nüzhen* 女真 and "Mongol" rather than *menggu* 蒙古. To differentiate between Han 漢, the title of the Han dynasty (used as shorthand for things Chinese and the Chinese people), and Han 韓, a surname, the surname is spelled Hann. I have used Uygur rather than the Chinese *hui* 回. One problem that continually crops up in studies of Chinese women is how to handle their surnames. Unmarried women were usually referred to using both given and family names without a suffix. Married women did not assume their husband's surname but kept their natal family name followed by the suffix *shi* 氏. I have chosen to simply keep the Chinese terminology, *shi*, rather than attempt to insert the anachronistic "Mrs." or "Miss" or the unwieldy "née."

A Brief Survey of Liao and Jin Geography and History

A short outline of Liao and Jin history is useful in situating the synchronic discussion in the chapters that follow.

The Qidan and Xi tribes became prominent during the Tang dynasty, when some emperors married princesses out to tribal chieftains in order to keep the peace. The Liao state was established in 907/916 by its first emperor, Abaoji, at the end of the Tang period. Although 907 is the traditional date for the establishment of the dynasty, it probably marks Abaoji's accession as the Kitan ruler, although the state was not fully established until 916.[49] The primary capital, Shangjing, was established early in the dynasty. In 938, Liao territory expanded with the acquisition of the celebrated Sixteen Prefectures on China's northern borders (later reduced to fourteen) in forfeiture from the short-lived Latter Jin state, thus extending its southern reaches into modern Hebei and Shanxi provinces and including the site of modern Beijing, where the Liao built their capital Nanjing (Southern Capital; modern Beijing), which presided over the Southern Circuit.[50] This city was more poetically known as Yanjing, after the ancient state of Yan in that region. The territory of the Liao state was organized into circuits, modeled on those of the Tang dynasty, each with its own capital. The capital of the Eastern Circuit, Dongjing (modern Liaoyang), was incorporated during the reign of the third emperor. The Liao government consisted of two parts. The four northern circuits, centered at

Introduction

Shangjing, were ruled by the emperor and preserved the pastoralist way of life with large principalities (fiefdoms) handed out to the Yelü and Xiao nobility. The Southern Circuit, in contrast, had a Chinese-style administration, headed usually by a Liao prince. It functioned as a bureaucracy and collected taxes.

Liao armies, led by the redoubtable Empress Chengtian and her son, Emperor Shengzong, defeated the Song in 1004/5, and the resulting treaty of Chanyuan, signed in the first month of the new year (February in the Western calendar), stabilized the border. The capital for the Central Circuit, Zhongjing, was constructed in the early eleventh century, and the Western Circuit capital, Xijing (modern Datong), was established in 1044, completing the capitals and circuits of the Liao state.[51]

The Jin originated with Jurchen tribes in eastern Manchuria, north of the Bohai, who became their allies in the conquest of the Liao. Jin armies, led by the first emperor, Aguda (r. 1115–1123), with help from the Bohai and the Song, conquered the Liao in the early twelfth century. The Jin then turned on their former Song allies, took the Southern Capital in 1127, and between 1123 and 1142 completed the conquest of the northern half of Song China. The Bohai remained staunch allies and were incorporated into the Jin state. By 1142, when a truce line was finally established at the Huai River, the Jin state included modern Hebei, Henan, Shanxi, and Shandong provinces, parts of Shaanxi, and even some of modern Jiangsu. It also included a large Han Chinese population in these territories. Unlike the Liao, which had two separate governments for the two regions, the Jin government, at Zhongjing, administered both Jurchen and former Song territories.

The Jin maintained circuits along lines similar to those of the Liao. The original Supreme Capital in the Shangjing Circuit, located in modern Heilongjiang province, was soon neglected in favor of the Central Circuit capital, Zhongjing, which had replaced the Liao Southern Capital on the site of present-day Beijing and became the state's administrative center. In addition, the former Song capital at Kaifeng became the Jin Southern Capital, and the Western Capital was located where the Liao Western Capital, Xijing, had been. The Supreme Capital was briefly revived under the fifth Jin emperor, Shizong, as part of his effort to recapture Jurchen culture.

The Jurchen who lived in the southern regions acculturated rapidly to Chinese culture and customs. Under the first four emperors, the Jin state extended its borders to include much of northern Korea and deep into the

Introduction

Chinese south but gave up territory to the Xi Xia state in the west. Jin armies suffered a stunning defeat by the Song in 1160. The fourth emperor was deposed and killed as a result, and his successor, Shizong, undertook a campaign to revive Jurchen culture and, with it, Jurchen military prowess. This effort, although ultimately unsuccessful in stemming the tide of sinicization, left important remnants that would ultimately link the Jin to their descendants and successors, the later Manchus. One such souvenir is the painting of Lady Wenji accompanied by Jurchen warriors. The Jin state was attacked by the Mongols under Chinggis (Genghis) Khan as early as 1211, and sporadic attacks persisted, eating away chunks of Jin territory until 1230, when the Mongols, under the sons of Chinggis Khan, invaded en masse. The Jin finally capitulated in 1234. The Jin imperial cemetery lies outside modern Beijing.

ONE

~

Womanly Ideals in the Liao and Jin Periods

WELL-BEHAVED WOMEN did indeed make history in the pages of Chinese texts.[1] Since the publication of the *Hou Hanshu* (History of the Latter Han Dynasty) in the fifth century, biographical sketches of virtuous women have been featured in the dynastic histories in a special section titled *Lienü zhuan* (Biographies of Exemplary Women). Women in these pages are praised as good mothers and wise counselors, for practicing filial piety, or for other examples of conspicuous virtue. A number of histories published between the fifth and tenth centuries contain *lienü* chapters. In addition to the *Hou Hanshu*, historian Richard Davis lists the *Weishu* (History of the Wei dynasty, sixth century) and *Suishu* (History of the Sui Dynasty, seventh century), plus the privately compiled *Beishu* (History of the Northern States, eighth century). Among Tang histories, the *Jiu Tangshu* (Old Tang-Dynasty History) has thirty-one entries for exemplary women, and the *Xin Tangshu* (New Tang-Dynasty History) features fifty-two.[2] The *Liaoshi* chapter, which contains only five examples, stands out for its brevity. The *Jinshi* chapter has twenty-two. An explosion in *lienü zhuan* came with succeeding histories; the *Songshi* (History of the Song Dynasty), composed at the same time as the Liao and Jin histories, has 374 entries. The *Yuanshi* (History of the Yuan Dynasty) lists an astonishing 742 exemplary women in a dynasty that lasted less than one hundred years. The *Mingshi* (History of the Ming Dynasty) and the draft history of the Qing dynasty have even more.[3]

1

Examining the ideals of womanly behavior as represented in the *lienü* chapters of the Liao and Jin histories and some inscribed epitaphs is a fruitful place to begin this study of Liao and Jin women. The *lienü* chapters cannot be taken as accurate biographical accounts of individual lives; rather, these stories have a didactic function, celebrating the virtues valued by the respective societies, or indeed by the Yuan compilers of these histories, as models of feminine behavior.

Exemplary women in the *Liaoshi* brought Confucian culture, gave sage advice to emperors, and demonstrated loyalty to their husbands by honoring the ancient steppe custom of following in death. Jurchen women led troops in battle, fortified cities against the enemy, and raised the battle flags dropped by their fathers or husbands. Other Jin women fought to preserve their husbands' names before defending their own chastity. Han Chinese women in the *Jinshi* displayed more conventional virtues, such as committing suicide to avoid dishonor or remarriage. One woman, a prostitute, climbed the city walls to exhort the defenders to attack the enemy before plunging to her death.[4] The selections in these chapters reflect particular behaviors that these societies valued in women, including courage, physical bravery, military action, loyalty, and—surprisingly—education in the Chinese classics.

These biographies depart from examples in previous *lienü zhuan* in ways that shed light on the values of their respective societies and reflect contemporary ethical standards for women. Neither of the more recent histories that might have served as models for the compilers of the Liao and Jin histories such as Ouyang Xiu's *Xin Wudaishi* (New History of the Five Dynasties), published in 1077, nor the earlier *Jiu Wudaishi* (Old History of the Five Dynasties), by Xue Juzheng, published in the tenth century, have chapters on virtuous women, although biographies of empresses and imperial concubines are included.[5] We must therefore look for possible precedents in earlier histories.[6] The question of models and departure from precedent is important in probing the contents and conventions of the Liao and Jin chapters.[7]

Lienü zhuan

The *lienü* chapter in the *Hou Hanshu* followed the precedent of an earlier work, attributed to the Han-dynasty writer Liu Xiang. *Lienü* was an intentionally didactic category that included both models of approved behavior and cautionary tales depicting women who behaved immorally. Lisa Raphals, who has compared Liu Xiang's work with entries in the *Hou Hanshu*, argues that women are presented as intellectual and moral agents, which implies that they exercised agency in determining their actions.[8] These tales were designed to counsel rulers and provide guidelines for women's conduct. Virtuous women's biographies tended to concentrate on certain types, including mothers who sacrificed to educate their sons, wives or concubines who were prescient counselors in matters of state, those who sacrificed their lives rather than suffer dishonor, filial daughters-in-law who cared for their husbands' parents, and chaste widows who refused remarriage. Obedience, chastity, and virtue were emphasized in positive stories, while the consequences of immoral behavior were illustrated in negative ones.

The pastoralist lifestyle and martial values of the Kitan and Jurchen, according to which women led armies and followed husbands in death, did not coexist comfortably with Chinese conceptions of dutiful daughters and chaste wives. As a result, Liao and Jin *lienü* tales present in effect a series of negotiations between Han Chinese values and values of the steppe and forest. These brief biographies can thus be read on several levels to reveal personal traits and skills valued in Liao and Jin society. A salient question remains whether these chapters truly reflect the values of contemporary tenth- to mid-thirteenth-century society or that of the later fourteenth-century Yuan compilers of these volumes. However, evidence from burial epitaphs and other independent sources where similar attributes are described suggest that these chapters indeed reflect contemporary values.

All the exemplary women among the *Liaoshi lienü* were from the Kitan nobility, reflecting the high degree of class consciousness permeating Liao society. Exemplary women selected for the *Jinshi* list came from a variety of class levels; they included Jurchen women, those with Han or Bohai names married to government officials, and women with Han names. A second aspect of biographies in both the Liao and Jin *lienü* sections is that the women in them seem to have been selected for actions and attainments that complement or balance feminine characteristics described in other sections of the dynastic histories. Imperial Liao women from the chapter on empresses and concubines, for example, are renowned for martial skills and physical bravery, but those in the *lienü* chapter exhibit literacy, Confucian ethics, and loyalty—and they followed their husbands in death. Jin women are described in the *Jinshi* as good mothers and wise counselors, but many of those selected for its *lienü* chapter demonstrate military skills and courage in the face of adversity.

Liao *lienü*

According to the introduction in the *Liaoshi lienü* chapter, the featured women are divided into two categories: *xiannü* (worthy) and *lienü* (virtuous). *Xiannü* were considered superior to *lienü*. Of the two women selected as *xiannü*, one was the Han Chinese wife of Yelü Jian, a member of the ruling clan, and the other was a woman born into the Yelü imperial clan. The *lienü* category features three women from the noble Xiao clan who were married to members of the imperial clan.[9] A strong aristocratic class consciousness is reflected in this selection.

The first *xiannü* is a Han woman, Chen *shi*, wife of Xing Jian, whose father had served as a high minister repeatedly during the Five Dynasties period. She was noted especially for her Confucian learning:

> From the time she put up her hair [about age fifteen], she was known for her skill in the classics and celebrated for her virtue. She excelled at chanting [verses] and reciting the classics, so that no woman of her time was more celebrated. She was praised by being called a female *xiucai* [talented scholar].[10]

Upon marrying, she was praised for promoting "harmony in the women's quarters through filial piety and virtue." She bore six sons and educated them in classical literature; the two youngest, Baopu and Baozhi, were especially deserving and went on to hold high government offices.[11]

Chen *shi* is identified as a woman exemplifying Chinese cultural achievements, including a literary education, a quality that—while admirable for males—had not been prominent among women's virtues in earlier biographies. Her father likely joined the Liao, as did a number of Latter Tang officials, early in the tenth century.[12] She was therefore probably born on the Liao side of the border. In raising exemplary sons, Chen *shi* conforms to the established model of a virtuous mother. Hearing of her attainments, Empress

Ruizhi (r. 969–982) presented her with the title of *Luguo furen*, referring to the state of Lu, where Confucius was born, and had a stele engraved in her memory so that her virtuous conduct could serve as a model for all women. This stele was so revered that even after being moved to a new site it still received worship.[13]

The biography of her son, Baopu, is listed under the surname Xing in the *Liaoshi* section on honorable officials, which notes that he originated from Yingzhou, attended the Hanlin Academy, and served during the reign of Emperor Shengzong (r. 982–1031) as a military official in Shanxi. These facts suggest he was born sometime in the 950s and his mother probably during the reign of the second Liao emperor. Baopu later worked as an assistant to the celebrated minister Hann Derang. When Baopu wished to resign to observe mourning rites for his mother, Hann persuaded him to stay in office. He later rose to a key position as prime minister of the Southern Chancellery.[14] Baozhi also held distinguished government positions.[15]

Chen *shi* is the *lienü* exemplar who most closely recalls Wenji's role as a culture bearer, a resemblance that is reinforced by her sons' successes. She represents a strong element of Han Chinese culture, which was respected by the Kitan. Indeed, the many Chinese collaborators from border states like the Latter Tang were essential to the Kitan rulers in constructing the state. While Chen *shi* may have had little personal choice in her marriage or residency, she clearly exercised agency in maintaining Han culture and educating her sons.

Another standard *lienü* type was a wise woman who possessed skill in argumentation. The second *xiannü* featured in the *lienü* chapter was a member of the imperial family, (Yelü) Changge (1006–1077), who displayed her literary skills against an evil official and was deeply loyal to her brother.

> Changge was the younger sister of Grand Preceptor Shilu.... As a young girl, she was very accomplished. She was learned in the classics and well read in historical works to such an extent that she was consulted and gave advice on political matters. She was adept at poetry and wrote prose in an elegant style.

Thus far she is a model wise woman in largely Confucian terms. Her biography goes on to say:

She was so pure and virtuous that she had sworn not to marry. Because of her wisdom, Yelü Yixin fell in love with her and wrote poems to her. She refused to answer him. Yixin lied and plotted against the heir apparent. Yixin was arrested but spared, [but] Shilu was accused as an accomplice and therefore disgraced and exiled. Changge followed him in exile and shared his poverty, wearing rough clothing and eating coarse food. When people inquired why she did this, she replied, "Shilu was falsely accused. How could I sleep easily knowing his suffering?" Seventeen years later, Shilu returned to favor and the family was reunited.[16]

Changge faced moral and political problems. She was able to reject the overtures of Yelü Yixin, who, as revealed in a later chapter, treacherously accused Empress Yide, wife of Emperor Daozong (r. 1055–1101), of adultery and brought about her death. When her brother was exiled, Changge was caught between her familial duty and loyalty to the state. How could she fulfill her obligation to her brother without betraying the emperor? Neither could she reject Shilu without violating filial piety. The solution attributed to her as a *lienü* was to remain pure and loyal while following her brother in exile and sharing his hardships. Changge showed her wisdom by skillfully negotiating this political dilemma.[17] Through her education and literary skills, she constructed an identity that according to the *lienü* text included selected aspects of Confucian culture and literary achievement. If Changge read the classics and wrote poetry and prose, one would like to know the language that was used. She might have read the classics in Kitan translation, since some classical Chinese books may have been translated into Kitan. However, more likely she read and wrote in Chinese, since many Chinese loanwords appear in Kitan inscriptions, and a northern Chinese dialect was widely spoken in Liao territory.[18] Kane suggests that educated Kitan spoke and read the language of the Song capital.[19] Changge's literary talents were therefore probably in Chinese.

Changge is the only *lienü* exemplar for whom there exists a second biographical source, her funeral epitaph, written in Chinese. Epitaphs are among the very few genuine primary sources we have on the Kitan or Jurchen. On it, she is identified as a member of the high nobility and the younger sister of Grand Preceptor Shilu. Here too she is noted as a serious scholar. According to the epitaph, she was virtuous and chaste:

Since she was a serious poet, she did not frequently make her poems public but sometimes composed verses on special occasions. Yelü Yixin was fond of her talent and asked her for poems. She refused to give him her real poems but sent him joke poems written backward to tease him. Yixin, ... knowing that she looked down on him, was dismayed.[20]

The epitaph and the *lienü* entry are remarkably consistent regarding Changge's wisdom and learning. Both refer to an encounter with Yelü Yixin in which Changge succeeded in refusing his attentions and embarrassing him. But her epitaph, written shortly after her death, says nothing about accompanying Shilu in exile. That part of Changge's story, which emphasizes filial piety and loyalty, is thus missing from the epitaph. Certainly its omission from the epitaph does not mean that she did not accompany her brother in exile; the entire family may have been exiled. But this incident might also have been a later insertion by the Yuan compilers meant to comply with Confucian ideals current in their time.[21] The entry specifically notes that Changge never married, and the epitaph mentions no husband, which suggests that marriage may not have been universal among Liao women. Liao tombs with only a single deceased female occupant also speak to the possibility of unmarried women. Some women, like Changge, appear to have avoided marriage and led blameless lives.

Each of the three subsequent biographies reference the ancient steppe custom of following in death, a practice that the first empress, Yingtian, famously refused to follow and instead cut off her hand and placed it on the emperor's coffin.[22] Historians have argued that after her action, following in death was no longer considered obligatory.[23] No later empresses seem to have followed this custom. While, as shown in later chapters, widows in Liao and Jin society had other options, the three Xiao women in the *lienü* list all committed suicide. Their acts demonstrate that even late in the Liao period, following in death still constituted virtuous behavior, to the extent that the Yuan compilers preserved this custom in these pages.

Among the three Xiao women featured as *lienü*, the first, Yixin, was "the daughter of the finest horseman in the kingdom." By mentioning her father's horsemanship, Yixin is immediately identified with Kitan values. "She was loyal to her husband, [Yelü] Nu, unto death and was honored by her sons and grandsons for generations. She was beautiful and accomplished and renowned for filial piety."[24] When Nu was accused in the plot against the crown prince and, like Shilu, was exiled, Emperor Daozong wished Yixin, the daughter of an imperial princess, to renounce her marriage. But Yixin refused, saying, "the relationship between husband and wife must be followed in life or in death." Further, she argued, "I have followed Nu since I first put in hairpins. If, in a moment when he has fallen into trouble, I should suddenly desert him, how would I be different from the birds and the beasts? I pray that I may be favored with Your Majesty's compassion and that I may go with Nu. Even in death, I shall feel no regret." The emperor was moved by her plea and consented.[25] Yixin demonstrated skill in argumentation and the prime virtue of loyalty, both consistent with Confucian values. However, her plea "must be followed in life or in death" is a reference to widow suicide.

Erliben and Nuolan are two more Xiao women praised in the *lienü* section.

> [Erliben] was of an upright and diligent disposition, one who followed all the ancient customs, a rare treasure among women. At the age of eighteen, she married [Yelü] Zhuzhe. She was generous and respectful to her elder sisters-in-law, who esteemed and honored her. Zhuzhe died young, and she mourned him excessively. When people reproached her, she replied, "The way of man and wife is like yang and yin, without yang, yin cannot exist. Without the external display of grief, that within would be without value.... Zhuzhe had but a short life, he did not reach old age. [I] must see to the proper rites or heaven will reproach my spirit after death." She then took a knife and so died.[26]

In the beginning of the story, Erliben's behavior is consistent with Confucian virtues. She was loyal to her husband and filial to her in-laws. After Zhuzhe's death, she referred to the Daoist principles of yin and yang to defend her mourning. But in taking her own life, Erliben followed her husband in death, a profoundly Kitan action.

Xiao Nuolan is the most traditionally Kitan of the three *lienü* heroines. She was noted as clever, dutiful, respectful, and diligent. She married Yelü Zhong and served his parents obediently. Zhong praised her, saying, "You may read books to learn the examples of former virtuous women," so she studied very hard and read many new and ancient books.

A rebellion broke out [1115], and the rebels plotted to assassinate Zhong. ... Zhong said to Nuolan, "If I should die in the attempt, would my wife follow me?" She replied, "I respectfully heed what you say." When the Jin soldiers invaded, Zhong was killed in battle. Nuolan grieved secretly without outward display so that others thought her unnatural. Suddenly she mounted a horse and rode off to the site where Zhong was buried. There she killed herself.[27]

Nuolan observed the Confucian virtue of filial piety in serving her husband's parents, but in the end she opted to follow Zhong in death, as he had bid her to do.

It can hardly be accidental that all three of the noble Xiao women married to members of the imperial clan were associated with the steppe tradition for widows. Were these women in particular selected for *lienü* status and so included in the text because they followed their husbands in death? While the *lienü zhuan* section in the *Liaoshi* was a standard Confucian category and praised Chen *shi* as a good mother and culture bearer and Changge for her learning, cleverness, and piety, at the same time it also conspicuously honored traditional Kitan customs.

The authors of the Liao and Jin biographies did not resort to miracles, as was frequently the case in earlier and later *lienü* texts, nor did they feature tales of bodily mutilation, as did the compilers of the *Xin Tangshu*, which was published in the eleventh century and therefore almost contemporary with these accounts.[28] The two *xiannü* exhibit largely Confucian values. Chen *shi* conformed to the ideal of virtuous mother and Confucian *xiunü*, while Changge was a sage counselor who was filial to her brother. The three women selected as *lienü* exhibit mixed cultural identities. Yixin, Erliben, and Nuolan demonstrated filial piety but also negotiated between Kitan and Confucian virtues and opted to make the final sacrifice in Kitan style.

In a statistical study of the various types of "exemplary women," Dong Jiazun has identified two standard models: (1) *liefu*, a widow who sacrifices her life to preserve her chastity and (2) *lienü*, a married or unmarried woman who sacrifices her life either to avoid rape or to die as a martyr for her country. As far back as the *Hou Hanshu*, dynastic histories include both types. Dong recognizes no *liefu* in the Liao and Jin chapters and classifies all five Liao entries and twenty-two Jin women as *lienü*, even though Chen *shi* and Changge did not give up their lives and the suicides of the three Xiao women had nothing to do with avoiding rape or becoming martyrs.[29] In following their husbands in death, all three Xiao women responded to indigenous cultural values.

Before pastoralist women could follow Confucian virtues, they had to be educated, which meant learning the classic works. The selection of Chen *shi* as a culture bearer at the head of the short list of Liao heroines is instructive. Because Chen *shi* herself had been educated, she could teach her sons. Changge too was educated and was skillful in both prose and poetry. Yixin and Erliben argued persuasively with the emperor by quoting from the classics, and even Nuolan had studied books. Their attainments were appreciated and noted in their biographies. Even more ordinary women commemorated in funeral inscriptions are praised for having read the classics. The high value placed on female education may seem surprising for a frontier society, since Chinese conventions about barbarians routinely depicted them as uneducated. Only oral traditions had existed prior to the invention of written, character-based versions of the Kitan language in the tenth century. The Jurchen followed suit by inventing Jurchen script in the twelfth century. Both Kitan and Jurchen had two types of writing, known respectively as large and small script.[30] But existing examples of Kitan and Jurchen scripts are rare, limited to stele engravings and epitaphs. Judging from the quantity of prose and poetry either described or extant, literacy in Chinese was a standard for the elites in Liao and Jin society, both men and women. We have little concrete evidence regarding how girls were educated, no mention of schools, and only occasional references to tutors or to being taught by their mothers, a topic that is addressed in greater detail in chapter 7. Education was no doubt limited to the elite. Apart from entries in the dynastic histories, much of our knowledge of women's education comes from funeral epitaphs and is therefore limited to those whose families were important or wealthy enough to afford funeral steles. What emerges most clearly is that elite Liao and Jin society, including Kitan, Jurchen, Bohai, and Han families, placed a high value on educating women, especially education in the Chinese classics and Buddhist scriptures.

If the *lienü* chapters show how a society wished its women to be remembered, funerary epitaphs reveal how their contemporaries remembered them. Both are idealized. But the Liao and Jin *lienü* are certainly not unreflective copies of received models in which women's lives are forced into conventional boxes of Confucian behavior, good mother, wise counselor, or evil seductress, as is true in both earlier and later histories, including those of the Song, Yuan, and Ming dynasties. Instead, these biographies celebrate behavior unknown in previous accounts, including a combination of martial leadership, Confucian ethics, and following in death that, from a Chinese perspective, would seem highly improbable. Martial leadership and following in death were both obviously at odds with conventional Confucian norms and appear in no previous *lienü* chapters. True, when the *lienü* entries in the Liao and Jin histories are organized chronologically, they reflect an increasing awareness of selected Confucian ethical precepts, especially in the area of education. Their accounts correlate sufficiently with funerary inscriptions that together they offer credible reflections of Liao and Jin ideals. A second source of information on virtuous behavior is found among the funerary epitaphs for Liao women.

The epitaph for Liao princess Qin-Jinguo, the daughter of an emperor, notes that she "liked books and reading, and her behavior followed all ethical precedents."[31] A second imperial daughter's epitaph remarks that "she understood [political] matters quickly and thoroughly. She wrote colorful and beautiful prose articles, was of mild temperament, very smart, a devout Buddhist, and enjoyed reading the sutras."[32]

These epitaphs and others like them clearly link education and virtue, a theme frequent in the memorials for upper-class women. Emotional fortitude was another attribute considered worthy among Liao women. Kitan women were praised in *lienü* chapters and in epitaphs for their beauty and discretion. Empresses and imperial concubines (as discussed in chapter 6) added to these virtues skill in government administration and military leadership. Missing from the *lienü* chapters but often present in epitaphs are examples of Buddhist piety.

One Kitan woman who deserves mention is Concubine Xiao, known as Xiao *fei* (d. 1071) (the suffix *fei* indicates "concubine"). She was the consort of a different holder of the title of Prince of Qin-Jinguo and combined nearly all the virtues the Liao admired, as recounted in her epitaph:

> From an early age, Xiao *shi* was well educated and very intelligent. She read all the classics and histories, and she herself owned several thousand volumes. She wrote poems and prose and transposed her poems into songs that she sang. Her prose writings and poetry were so beautiful that everyone at court enjoyed them. . . . She rode horseback ably, was adept at

archery, and enjoyed hunting. When hunting, she withheld her shot until she was certain of hitting her prey.

She was also good at painting, and she herself painted all the scrolls and wall screens in her home. Whenever she discovered someone to be intelligent, whether male or female, she recommended that person. So many officials requested recommendations that her home was always full of guests discussing history or politics together. [They] criticized people both ancient and modern.... The only pity is that she had no children.[33]

Xiao *fei*'s literary gatherings remind one of the salons of eighteenth-century French women savants, where politics and history were discussed. Xiao *fei* held the Kitan equivalent of salons in her home and "often recommended persons whom she found to be talented to the prince for official positions."[34] She combined admirable traits from the Kitan and Chinese cultures in nearly equal proportions. Along with women like Changge, she exemplified the class of *cainü* (talented women), who excelled in composition, calligraphy, and other arts. Concubine Xiao even painted scrolls and used them to adorn her home. One recently discussed precedent from the Tang dynasty was Xu Hui, concubine to Emperor Taizong (r. 626–649), who was renowned for her poetry and other writings, some of which she used to admonish and advise the emperor, and unlike the cases of the Liao women mentioned above, many of her writings have been preserved.[35] *Cainü* was not a new category in the Chinese lexicon of feminine accomplishments, but the combination of literary talent with horse riding and hunting, not to mention the martial leadership shown by Liao women, was entirely novel.

The tomb of an elderly woman who in many aspects resembles Xiao *fei* was found near the town of Yemaotai in 1974.[36] Several features attracted immediate attention. The tomb is large and well furnished and had not been robbed. Consequently, it had all its original contents. Among other items, it contained a finely constructed wooden funeral house. Inside was a white marble sarcophagus carved with garlands and Chinese-style directional symbols. The tomb's contents included many gold and silver artifacts, lacquer trays, white *ding* ware and pale-green *qingbai* porcelain, and two exceptionally well-preserved hanging scroll paintings that had been rolled and placed in the coffin. Photographs of the tomb's interior, on display in the Liaoning Provincial Museum, also show piles of scroll books lining the walls. The deceased woman was dressed in Kitan style and wore finely worked gold embroidered boots.[37] Several items suggesting Buddhism were present, but the woman's body had not been cremated. An elegantly decorated saddle and other horse equipment were discovered in one of the tomb's side chambers, attesting to her horsemanship.

Archaeologists have dated the tomb to the period 959 to 986 and speculate that the woman was related to the imperial family. However no gold mask or gilt-wire casing, markers of imperial nobility, was found, suggesting that while she may have been from the high nobility she was not a member of the Yelü clan.[38] Assuming tomb construction to have taken place shortly after the woman's death, the dating suggests that she must have been born in the late ninth or early tenth century, a contemporary of Empress Yingtian.[39] She was clearly a talented lady. The horse equipment, boots, and other accoutrements, including weapons, indicate that she was skilled in riding and hunting, but the books in scroll form and paintings suggest that she was also well educated and appreciated art. She must have admired Chinese culture and been adept in the Chinese language, as evidenced by the tomb's contents, if the books are indeed in Chinese, as seems likely.[40] Although the porcelain and pottery items also found in the tomb have received extensive scrutiny, the books and scrolls seem to have been overlooked. The Chinese-style carvings on the sarcophagus suggest that her interests were accommodated in death as well. Two particularly fascinating and unusual scroll paintings were discovered inside her coffin in excellent condition.

These paintings are unique; they are the only such paintings discovered in any Liao tombs to date. One is a landscape in the blue-and-green style, with towering peaks. The other, in a naturalistic style, shows charming rabbits nibbling on dandelions and flowers, with birds and bamboo above, a combination for which no precedent exists in Tang or Five Dynasties art. Neither scroll has a date or signature. Yet critics have noted that the painter was clearly accomplished and that these are works "of a mature development."[41] Their presence inside the sarcophagus suggests that the deceased lady had some special attachment to them. Based on the notation in the epitaph of Xiao *fei* that she painted her own artwork, I suggest that the two scrolls, so carefully preserved at Yemaotai, may well have been by the lady's own hand. If so, the fact that she was not a professional artist may account for certain anomalous aspects, including the rather stiff style of the landscape that critics have noted and the unusual subject matter in the case of the rabbits.[42]

Wall paintings in other Liao tombs show Kitan figures of both men and women in the typical Kitan style with dark outlines and filled-in color and are of a very different style from the hanging scroll paintings. A rudimentary hunting scene was sketched on the wooden sides of the inner coffin at Yemaotai in this Kitan style. The wooden funeral house where the coffin was found is also remarkable. It is about the size of a child's playhouse, with a three- and two-bay structure that Nancy Steinhardt links to Buddhist temple construction. Similar but less well-preserved examples have been found in several other Liao and Han Chinese tombs.[43]

The Yemaotai burial immediately brings to mind Xiao *fei*, noted above, but Concubine Xiao lived nearly a hundred years later and died in the eleventh century.[44] Like Xiao *fei*, this unknown lady combined the pastoralist skills with literary and artistic achievements. She united both sides of the Liao character, pastoralist and scholarly. The Han cultural context is as strong in this tomb as its Kitan identity. The marble sarcophagus, for example, was carved with typical Han Chinese–style leaf garlands, peonies, and flowers and has reliefs on all four sides depicting the Chinese directional cosmology of dragon (east), phoenix (south), tiger (west), and dark warrior (north). One would like to know more about the books found in the tomb. What was her taste in literature? Could some of them contain the lady's own writings? Given the description of Xiao *fei*'s literary output, it is entirely plausible that some of the literary works stored in her tomb could have contained the lady's own compositions. Such a confluence of Kitan and Chinese elements—if we can attribute the selection of items in the tomb to the deceased's own tastes and accomplishments—suggests that she too mediated between Kitan and Han cultures, selectively adopting aspects of each, as did the women featured in the Liao *lienü* selections.

The tomb is located in Faku county in present-day Liaoning province about 137 miles north of Liaoyang. Today the location is remote and difficult to access. In the tenth century this area was in the principality of Dongtanguo but still quite a distance from the capital Dongjing (modern Liaoyang).[45] Given the location of the tomb, it would be difficult to argue that the Han acculturation observed in its contents was the result of close contact with the Latter Tang or other Han border states. More likely, acculturation stemmed from contact with the Bohai. The Liao eastern capital had been the Bohai

Southern Capital. If the tomb is as early as the mid-tenth century, one might speculate that the lady had some relationship to Prince Bei (900–937), son of the first Liao emperor and prince of Dongtanguo, who was said to have been of an artistic nature and a great admirer of Han art and literature. The lady's tomb provides evidence of Han acculturation early in the Liao dynasty, combined with Kitan culture and skills. It anticipates trends noted in the *lienü zhuan* and epitaphs.

This discussion of the virtues attributed to Liao women based on the *lienü zhuan*, epitaphs, and archaeological data demonstrates how steppe aspects were combined with selected Han Chinese elements. The combination differs from one example to another, as shown in the varied descriptions in the *lienü zhuan*. Two aspects stand out. First, education: Kitan women were often educated, and women's erudition and literacy were valued social achievements. Second, steppe customs and values were deliberately preserved, as shown in the *lienü* entries of the three Xiao women (and in subsequent chapters of this book). Perhaps the most abiding impression of Kitan women from the *lienü zhuan*, reinforced by many later historical examples (discussed in the following chapters of the present work) is of women who had the agency and ability to act on their own initiative and on their own behalf. Such assertive qualities might be expected of women who could ride horseback, go hunting, and lead armies. What is unexpected is that so many were educated and adopted selected Confucian principles.

Confucian principles and literacy would be more typical of women of Han background. This expectation is borne out, according to biographies and epitaphs, by elite Han and *haner* women living under Liao rule. Though I cite only one example here, it is nonetheless representative of a number of such epitaphs for women with Han surnames. According to this epitaph, Hann *shi*, who came from the celebrated Hann family of government officials who had received the honorary surname Yelü, was the wife of Geng Yanyi. She was praised in traditionally Confucian terms as

> kind, intelligent, and skilled in debating. Her beauty was like the blossoming peach flower in early spring. Well educated from an early age, she was considered the finest lady in society at the time; she stayed in the inner quarters. [She] always followed the proper rituals and was on good terms

with all the imperial relatives. She respected the elders and gave loving care to the younger ones. No matter what happened, she hid her feelings behind a placid face.[46]

A number of epitaphs recorded for women with traditional Chinese surnames follow similar lines, praising filial piety, proper conduct, literacy, and often Buddhist devotion. If Wenji's purpose among the Xianbei can be interpreted in one sense as bringing Han civilization to acculturate the barbarians, the women of the Liao and Jin periods may be seen as the beneficiaries of Han learning and Confucian ethics, but they adopted these aspects of Han culture selectively.

Jin *lienü zhuan*

The *Jinshi* chapter on *lienü* contains twenty-two women, who are presented in chronological order, as are the entries in the *Liaoshi* chapter, rather than by the type of virtuous deed, as was usual in earlier histories.[47] Imperial clanswomen and commoners alike appear among the entries. For purposes of analysis, I have grouped the women by name or surname in an attempt to elucidate cultural affiliation. Five women with Jurchen names and two others with indeterminate surnames married to members of the Wanyan imperial clan make up the first category. Ten women bearing Han names and married to Han officials in the Jin government make up the second category, while five with Chinese names but unrelated to any government official make up the third. A Han name does not necessarily indicate Chinese origins, since certain names, such as Li or Shi, were common among the Bohai. Other apparently Han names such as Zhang, Hann, Luan, and Feng may have belonged to women from that stratum of the population known as *haner* who had been longtime residents of the northern borderlands and who may have come from mixed ethnic backgrounds. Still other Chinese names probably belonged to the Han or *nan* former subjects of the Northern Song state.[48] The virtues celebrated for women in the different categories accord closely with their cultural affiliations.

Women with identifiably Jurchen names were celebrated primarily as warriors. For example, Shalizhi collected 500 local residents to build a barrier to protect the city when a rebellion broke out in 1144. When more than a thousand rebels attacked, Shalizhi, "using a blanket as her armor and her clothes as a flag, organized the people to fight." After the rebels were defeated, she was honored by the emperor, who presented her with a ceremonial sword and bestowed an honorary title on her.[49]

Aluzhen, of the Wanyan imperial clan, married Jiaguhushan (a Jurchen name). After her husband died, she "had several thousand troops under her command. When her father fought the rebels, she constructed a wall, obtained weapons, and stored grain for the war. . . . She wore men's clothing and supervised operations together with her son. They killed several hundred of the enemy and captured more. [The enemy's] troops were totally defeated."[50] Unlike Shalizhi, Aluzhen acted only after her husband had been killed and might therefore be considered what historian Joan Judge terms a "surrogate male," a woman who wears male attire and acts in a male role.[51] As time went on, Jin women seem to have adopted values that were more consistent with Confucian ethics, but in a crisis, they rose to the occasion with martial acts.

Some of the stories below take place late in the dynasty, during the reign of the last Jin emperor. This was a chaotic time when Mongols were invading and destabilizing the country, and rebels took advantage of the immanent collapse of the Jin state. Both Mongols and rebels such as Cui Li attacked at will.

Pucha Mingxiu was the daughter of a Jurchen general, married to a member of the imperial clan. Her husband was in command of the guards when Emperor Aizong moved the court in flight from the Mongols, and Mingxiu was left behind. As her husband was leaving, he said, "remember only that you should not disgrace yourself whatever the situation." When Mingxiu realized the city was about to be captured, she arranged for her son to be cared for by the maids. Saying, " 'I can only die so as not to disgrace my husband,' she hanged herself. She did not consider death to be suffering."[52]

Wugulun *shi* was the wife of a Jurchen nobleman, prefect of Lintao, who laid down his life for his country. Her brother too was a hero among government officials. Knowing the rebels' reputation, she said, "my husband and brother did not bring disgrace on our country. How can I disgrace them?" Then she strangled herself with a scarf.[53] A third woman (name unknown), the wife of Wanyan Shulan, was also stranded in the city when the rebels attacked. To avoid disgracing her husband, she too hanged herself.[54] Although hanging to avoid rape was a standard Confucian action, these women seem to have been more concerned with avoiding disgrace to their husbands' names.

Another courageous woman was (Wanyen) Zhongde's wife (no personal name given), who cared for her two sons and her husband's concubines during the turbulent years of the dynasty's collapse. When the rebel Cui Li surrounded the city, the entire male population was called to fight. She said, "Men in such circumstances can fight for their country, but what can women do?" She organized the women of the city as a female army to carry stones and weapons to the front lines. But finally when the city fell, she committed suicide. Zhongde's wife might be considered a surrogate male since she behaved like a warrior in defending the city with an army of women. She combined Confucian values of caring for her sons and the concubines with the steppe values of warrior women. Her death and the suicides noted above can be interpreted either as examples of following in death or as the Confucian-style suicide to avoid disgrace.[55]

Duji *shi* married Jurchen general Sahenian. She too was "well educated and understood Confucian ethics since an early age." When enemy troops surrounded the capital, Sahenian was ill and unable to command his troops. Fearing the city must soon fall, Duji *shi* urged her husband to get up and fight to his last breath. She then said to her maids, "I am going to die. Please incinerate my body after my death because I do not want to show my face to the enemy." She closed the door and took her own life. Upon seeing her body, Sahenian lamented, "My wife refused to bring disgrace on me; how can I bring disgrace on my country?" He went forth and fought to the death.[56] Duji *shi*'s suicide shamed her husband into fighting the enemy. She conformed to the Confucian virtue of "women who observe their husbands' faults of character and reform them" as well as exhibiting personal courage in battle.[57]

The cases cited above all pertain to women with Jurchen names or who were married to members of the elite. Two more women, with Han or Bohai names, were also married to members of the imperial clan; they committed suicide to follow their husbands in death. Yin *shi* was the wife of Wanyan Zhuer, who was killed in battle. Upon hearing the news of his death, she hanged herself.[58] Li *shi* was a concubine of Emperor Aizong's. When the government fell to the Mongols in 1234, she, together with other concubines, hid in a Buddhist temple, where they worshipped the Buddha day and night. When she heard that the emperor was dead, she strangled herself in front of the Buddha statue.[59] Pucha Mingxiu, Wugulun *shi*, Yin *shi*, Wanyan Shulan's wife, and Li *shi* all followed in death, an action that needs to be understood as quite different from the conventional Han Chinese suicide to preserve chastity. However, the method of death by hanging parallels later suicides in a Confucian context, where women typically died by hanging or drowning. Death to avoid remarriage was a point where Jin and Han values coincided, since the steppe pattern forbade widow remarriage.

The four examples below belong to the second category of six women with Han (or Bohai) names who were married to Jin officials with Han names. Although they were not overtly martial, their deaths were heroic and the reasons that they gave for their actions involved avoiding shame to their husbands' or the families' names. Zhang *shi* was the wife of Li Ying, an official in the capital. When Mongol troops raided the city, she willingly gave them all she possessed. But when they tried to abduct her, she refused and so was killed.[60] The wife of Hann Qingmin, prefect of Yizhou, was captured by the Song. After Qingmin was killed, she preferred death to rape and so took her own life.[61] Luan *shi*, the wife Xiang Qi, an official in Yixian, was known for her beauty. When rebels seized Yixian and killed Qi and his son, they attempted to rape Luan *shi*, but she cursed them, saying, "how can I [allow myself] to be stained by you dogs and pigs!" The rebels then killed her.[62] These women acted heroically. Their deaths can be seen as preserving their chastity or as following in death, or indeed as a combination of the two. Feng Miaozhen was the daughter of one Jin official and wife of another, Zhang Zao. When Yuan troops attacked, Zao went to Pingliang, where Miaozhen's father lived, for military supplies. Zao urged his wife to come with him to see her father, but Miaozhen refused, saying, "[your parents] are elderly . . . my responsibility is to see that they are happy." When the enemy captured the town, Miaozhen and her family all hid but were discovered. Miaozhen lamented that she could not fulfill her duty to Zao. Having seen to her in-laws, she and her three sons threw themselves into a well and drowned.[63] Miaozhen's actions were more conventionally Confucian. She refused to accompany her husband, opting instead to care for his parents, an example of filial piety. Then she killed herself and her sons to avoid capture and dishonor at the hands of the rebels. Any such dishonor would have reflected badly on her father and husband, especially in light of their high government offices. Her actions, while heroic, are also consistent with both Confucian and steppe values.

The remaining women in this group, who are designated as "officials' wives," maintain the themes of filial piety and suicide. Nie Shunying was the widow of an official. She returned to her parents' home. Her father, an official at Bianzhou, was wounded in the fighting against the rebel Cui Li. "[He] suffered so from his wound that he wished only to die." Shunying visited various doctors and even cut off some of her own flesh to feed her father, but in spite of all her efforts he finally died. Cutting flesh to cure an in-law of illness was an extreme act of filial piety, but doing so for one's own parent involved a violation of the body that one's parents had provided and hence a lapse of filial piety. It was done under only the most extreme circumstances.[64] With husband and father both gone, and knowing the rebels would soon take the city, she took her own life the day after burying her father.[65] Shunying demonstrated filial piety by her care for her father, but she was then free to follow her husband in death.

Death by hanging or drowning links these women with *lienü* exemplars in both earlier and later Chinese histories who committed suicide to preserve virtue using similar methods, but in the context of Jin society, their motivations appear more problematic. Women in this group of officials' wives took their lives not only to avoid possible rape but also, as several entries specifically mention, to save their husbands' names, rather than to preserve their own virtue.

Four of the women on the Jin *lienü* list have identifiably Chinese or Bohai names and are without Jin government connections, a small number for a state with an overwhelmingly Han Chinese population. Their stories revolve around questions of remarriage for young widows, a contentious issue since Jin custom required widows to observe levirate and remarry only inside the family, while Chinese custom allowed widows to return to their natal families and marry again.

Lei's wife, Shi *shi* (possibly Bohai), took care of her husband's parents after his death. Once when her mother-in-law was ill, she cut off a piece of her own flesh (to make a soup) for her mother-in-law, who recovered at once. After her parents-in-law died, her husband's relatives coveted the property and deceived the local officials by saying that Shi would soon remarry. But she threw herself into a well rather than be forced.[66] Under Jin law, her husband's nephew could have married her himself, but the Chinese regarded levirate marriage as incest. Since the nephew wanted to keep her property, he had lied to the authorities. In cutting off a piece of her own flesh to cure her mother-in-law, Shi *shi* was performing an act of filial piety in the correct Han manner. She committed suicide to avoid a forced remarriage, which could be interpreted as an act of chastity or of loyalty.

Also in this third category is a woman with a Han name, Kang Zhuzhu, a young widow who wanted only to return to her husband's family. She may have wished to make a levirate marriage or perhaps to act as a dutiful Confucian daughter-in-law. But her father prevented her. So she jumped from a cliff and died. A fourth woman wished to remain a chaste widow, and when her father forced her to remarry, she refused the marriage bed. Her husband assaulted her and had her arrested. But before she could be returned to him, she managed to strangle herself.[67] Refusing to remarry at the cost of death and suicide by hanging or drowning were common Confucian tropes indicating extreme piety that appear in *lienü* chapters of many later histories.[68] But refusal to remarry was also consistent with Jin laws forbidding the remarriage of widows, although this provision was often waived or ignored for Han Chinese. However, as I discuss in chapter 5, since Liao and Jin laws forbade remarriage, the alternative of chaste widowhood in lieu of following in death or levirate developed in these dynasties well in advance of the Mongol conquest.

Zhang Fengnu, the final entry, is in a category by herself as an example of a patriotic martyr. When the Mongol army attacked the (unnamed) city, Fengnu mounted the city wall. She shouted, "I am a prostitute. I was captured when Xuzhou fell [and served the enemy]. I know that the Yuan will withdraw their troops soon, so you defenders must hold your ground. Don't be deceived by the enemy!" Then she threw herself into the river and so died.[69] Fengnu is an example of a patriot who gives her life for her country. If a lowly prostitute could act with such patriotism, women of a superior class or background who did less would be shamed.

Dividing the women eulogized in the *Jinshi* to discover their cultural identity reveals that Jurchen women were noted especially for personal courage and military leadership. Shalizhi and Aluzhen both led troops and succeeded in their efforts. Duji *shi* knew her husband's faults and acted to correct them. In shaming him into battle, she joins other martial Jurchen heroines. The women in the second category, who were married to Jin government officials, committed suicide or provoked rebels to murder them. Their deaths can be interpreted in different ways, as conforming to steppe custom by following their husbands in death or as protecting their husbands' reputations. Often the two coincide. Only incidentally were they preserving their own chastity. Whether by engaging the enemy or by suffering valiant deaths, these women can all be grouped as heroic. The suicides of Shi *shi* and Kang Zhuzhu had to do with avoiding remarriage, which is usually given a Confucian interpretation; however, at this period, avoidance of remarriage was not yet a common custom even in the south. Bettina Birge, in her study of marriage customs in the Song and Yuan periods, points out that widows commonly remarried into new, exogamous households in Song China and argues that the concept of the chaste widow avoiding remarriage achieved currency later in China as the result of Yuan dynasty laws.[70] The Han widows in the Jin *lienü* chapter who sacrificed their lives to avoid remarriage appear to predate that development and may have been motivated by more complex emotions.

The five Liao women and a number of the Jin women all clearly possessed agency in constructing their own identities and acting on their own initiative. Several of the Jurchen martial women, although in one sense acting as surrogate males, nonetheless had the power to act on their own behalf. Aluzhen took the initiative to defend the city when she supervised military operations; Wanyan Zhongde's wife organized a female army but did not command men; Duji *shi* by her own suicide shamed her husband into fighting. In conventional Confucian discourse, such actions were temporary and the women involved subsequently reverted to feminine roles. Pucha Mingxiu, Wugulun *shi*, Yin *shi*, Wanyan Shulan's wife, and Li *shi* all acted to save their husbands' reputations and so may be seen as subordinate to males. Suicide was interpreted as an act within the feminized sphere.[71] Military action seems to have been regarded by Liao and Jin society as the natural arena for women like Shalizhi and Aluzhen as well as for Liao empresses. (The topic of martial women is addressed in chapter 6.) Whether the portrayal of Jin women as male surrogates reflects the understanding of their own time or is of a construct more Confucian in nature remains a question, one taken up at various points in this study.

Returning to the question of language, while the Jurchen elite may have spoken Jurchen early in the dynastic period, it was rapidly replaced by Chinese during the reign of the first four emperors. The Jurchen language, and with it Jurchen martial prowess, had all but disappeared by the mid-twelfth century, as shown by the efforts of Emperor Shizong in the 1160s. The situation was so dire that the emperor made a special effort to re-create the Jurchen language by having Chinese classics translated into Jurchen script and setting up special Jurchen-language and military-training schools. Although the emperor's efforts at a Jurchen revival were ineffective in the long term, his concern shows just how widespread sinicization had become among the Jin elite.

Negotiating Cultures: Frontier Values and Confucian Ethics

Characteristics evident in the *lienü* chapters and the virtues attributed to women in epitaphs must be viewed as those that society valued at the time rather than uniquely individual achievements. The question might be asked whether these values were consistent with the standards current in the times in which the women themselves lived or whether they became more relevant in the Yuan dynasty, when the histories were composed. But since the Liao and Jurchen *lienü* are inconsistent with the exemplars in the *Songshi* composed at the same time, or those in the *Yuanshi*, compiled in the Ming dynasty, my belief is that they represented the values of the Liao and Jin periods rather than those of the Yuan dynasty, although of course there may have been a good deal of overlap. Elsewhere in the *Liaoshi*, women appear as able administrators and military leaders, but in the *lienü* section, they are praised for their education and wisdom, for raising excellent sons, for skill in argumentation, and for following their husbands in death. Loyalty to state and family occupied a prime place in the values of Kitan women, while conserving the old traditions such as following in death was conspicuously honored. Class status was a major denominator, since four of the five women in the Liao *lienü* chapter were members of the imperial Yelü or the Xiao marriage clans. The Jin *lienü* selections, by contrast, highlight values that included military action, personal bravery, and patriotic loyalty as well as filial piety. Elsewhere in the *Jinshi*, empresses and imperial concubines were praised for Confucian virtues and Buddhist piety. Epitaphs of women in both dynasties reinforce these attributes.

The Jin class structure, based on cultural or more broadly ethnic identity, is reflected in the *lienü* selection privileging the twelve Jurchen women, followed by those married to Han officials serving the Jin government, and concluding with women with Bohai or Chinese names. The deaths of a number of these exemplars link the steppe custom of following in death to the virtue of chastity that emerged in the Yuan period and the cult of widow suicide that appeared in the Ming period, thus mediating between shifting steppe and Confucian values.

These *lienü zhuan* chapters also demonstrate how new values diffused across the frontier zone. Steppe and forest women adopted Confucian culture only selectively. Several recent studies suggest that certain steppe traditions crossed the border in the opposite direction and also made their way into the construction of Han Chinese standards of virtuous behavior.[72] Loyalty to state and family was a cornerstone of steppe life, but filial piety was lower on the scale. Clearly, education was a valued trait for Kitan women, but observance of Confucian rites was less praised. Furthermore, it also seems that marriage was not necessarily universal for women, and some, like Changge, remained single.

We may never know the extent to which negotiating between cultures involved conscious choices by the women involved. No doubt Chen *shi* was following established conventions for Chinese women in educating her sons. That she also acted in the role of a culture bearer may have been entirely incidental. But Changge, although she observed some Chinese values, did not conform to Han conventions regarding marriage, since she remained unmarried her entire life. That Changge and Concubine Xiao adopted selected Confucian attributes may have been expected as part of the elite Kitan culture rather than the result of any conscious decision. In the one case where we have a parallel epitaph, the items on which the epitaph and the *lienü* entry differ are as enlightening as the points where they coincide. Excelling in literary pursuits, however, seems to have been based on women's own agency and in turn provided learned women with greater esteem. Martial actions by Jurchen women were clearly related to the cultural norms of Jurchen society. Quite possibly the editors of the *Jinshi* selected specific women for their martial qualities as the *lienü* entries and attributed Confucian conduct to empresses in a different section. Epitaphs provide more contemporary information since they were composed shortly after the death of the person in question, but even epitaphs cannot be taken literally, since these accounts too tend to emphasize the positive attributes of their subjects and neglect any problematic issues. Furthermore, we must assume that both the biographical accounts and epitaphs were written by men. Nowhere can a woman's own voice be authenticated. The descriptions of women who died at least in part to avoid dishonor or remarriage suggest that the custom of widow chastity was in the process of development, even if at this early date widows' chastity was effected by following their husbands in death.

The increasing number of references to apparently Confucian values shown in the *lienü* biographies parallels other aspects of Liao and Jin society, such as adoption of Han clothing styles, laws, and government structures. Chinese attributes were much more marked in the Yan-Yun region of the Liao Empire and in the former Northern Song areas taken over by the Jin state. Entries in the chapters devoted to meritorious officials in the dynastic histories show more Han and *nan* literati passing the examinations and playing prominent parts in government.[73] The frequency of Chinese-style names and Confucian-style values increase for both men and women in the latter decades of the Jin period. Class status is another possible denominator. Liao empresses and imperial concubines and Jurchen women and women with husbands in the employ of the Jin state were credited with heroic actions. Women with Han names came from less-elite backgrounds, and their actions were less overtly heroic. Thus, the definition of feminine virtue may also have been dependent on both ethnicity and class status.

TWO

Liao Women's Daily Lives

THE DAILY LIVES of the peoples in northern China nearly a thousand years ago are not easily discovered today. While dynastic histories and inscriptions provided the main sources for the discussion of exemplary women in the first chapter, information on daily life comes mainly from tomb artifacts, tomb wall paintings, or a few extant works of the period. This chapter examines the pastoralist lifestyle, daily life of Kitan women, and the lifestyles of *haner* women living under Liao rule.

The lands of the Liao and Jin states were centered in present-day Inner Mongolia and Jilin and Liaoning provinces, with the Xi occupying lands somewhat farther to the west, while the Jurchen were located to the east, in the former Manchuria. The Bohai, Liao, and Jin occupied, successively, the rich Liao River valley. To the south was the Song state after its establishment in 960, and to the west was the Xi Xia state, founded by the Tangut people in the mid-eleventh century. The Liao state maintained a pastoralist-style tribal administration, called the Northern Administration, for the Kitan and their allies the Xi but established a separate, subordinate Chinese-style government, the Southern Administration, to rule the Yan-Yun region, which in Liao times was in the Southern Circuit, located in modern Hebei, whose population was predominantly Chinese. The Han Chinese were sedentary agriculturalists, long established in the region of the Southern Circuit and in the larger cities. The Kitan population was made up mainly of pastoralists, who followed traditional customs and a lifestyle of horse riding and herding in the vast expanses of the Liao northern circuits that covered much of Inner Mongolia and Jilin, Heilongjiang, and Liaoning provinces.

Pastoralist Life

Perhaps the most informative source portraying Liao pastoralist life is a short hand scroll traditionally attributed to Hu Gui. This work, titled *Fan ma* (Barbarian Horses), dates to the late Five Dynasties or early Liao period.[1] Executed in ink and light colors on silk, this painting presents a portrait of life in the Manchurian countryside. It is, to my knowledge, the only extant painting reflecting both the landscape of the grasslands and the range and distinctiveness of Kitan clothing and customs matching those on tomb walls.[2] Internal evidence, both landscape and figures, attest to its authenticity.[3] This work, which has not been published in English-language sources, deserves to be better known.[4]

The landscape resembles the varied countryside of the Manchurian region, with mountainous defiles and open plains. Reading from right to left, it is presented here in three parts. The first section (fig. 2.1) is anchored on the

Fig. 2.1. *Fan ma*, section 1. National Palace Museum, Taipei.

right by a rocky ravine. The center section (fig. 2.2) features rolling grasslands, and the third scene (fig. 2.3) is marked by a single majestic outcropping of rock. The season is early spring. Although the trees are leafless, some horses, still thin from the long winter, are grazing while others roll in fresh grass. Small groups of men and animals are distributed across the landscape. Horses and sheep were the mainstays of the pastoralist economy. In figure 2.1, a group of soldiers are marching into a ravine. To the left are herdsmen; two who have dismounted and allowed their horses to graze are shown seated under a tree beside their distinctive Kitan saddles. One has started a campfire. Another tribesman a short distance away is minding a flock of sheep grazing on the far side of the hillock. A camel caravan emerges from behind the hills in the middle distance.

The tribesmen exhibit typical Kitan hairstyles and hats, and several different modes of dress. Jerkins are pulled up in front and tucked into belts. Hairstyles reveal a shaved forehead and short braids in front of the ears—all corroborated in tomb frescoes.[5] Near the center in the middle distance in the

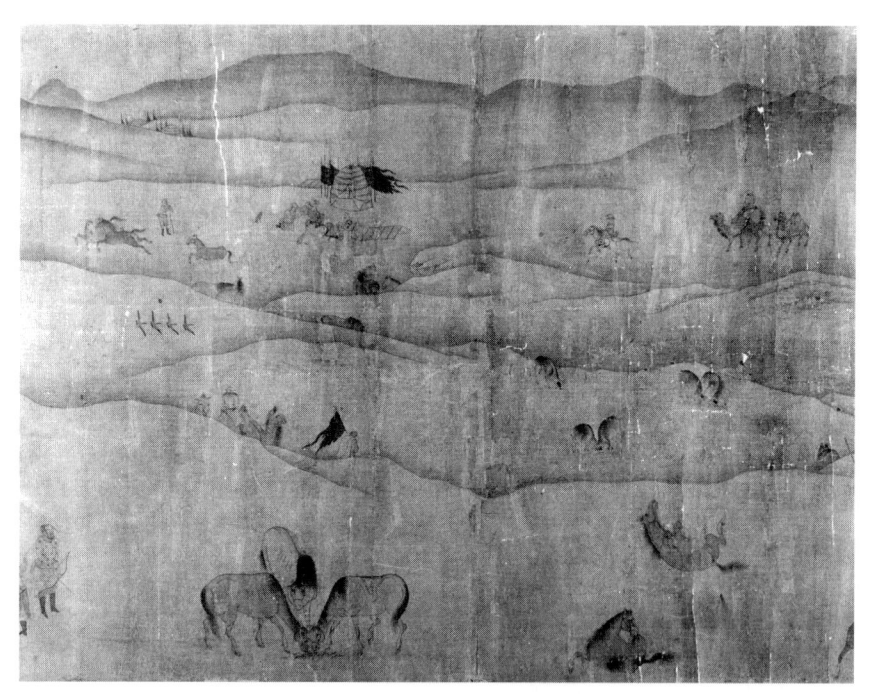

Fig. 2.2. *Fan ma*, section 2. National Palace Museum, Taipei.

Fig. 2.3. *Fan ma*, section 3. National Palace Museum, Taipei.

second section (fig. 2.2) is a beehive-shaped yurt surrounded by flags with two tribesmen seated in front (fig. 2.4). One appears to be examining the other's hair (for lice?). Nearby, another tribesman watches horses frolic. Geese fly north across the landscape. Two hunters stand in the foreground (fig. 2.5). One is dressed in a patterned shirt and is barehaded, with short braids, while the other wears a black cap. Both wear boots, jackets, and belts.

The third section of the painting (fig. 2.3) is dominated by a large, vertical, convoluted rock. In front is a small tableau with two camels, a flagpole, and a sleeping tribesman. More horses graze nearby. In the distance is a mare with her foal—another indication of spring. A truculent camel is resisting its herdsman in the lower left foreground of the painting (fig. 2.6). The camel's knees are bent as he stretches his neck and parts his lips to spit at the herdsman, who raises a whip over his head. These are everyday herding activities in a pastoralist society, where tribesmen lived in yurts, raised livestock, and

Fig. 2.4. Yurt and tribesman, detail from *Fan ma*. National Palace Museum, Taipei.

engaged in military activities. Training a recalcitrant camel was a part of daily life.

The scroll shows only males, but women too participated in the pastoralist life on the grasslands, riding, herding, and administering the family encampment when husbands were away. Kitan tombs, in whose depictions women play a remarkably prominent role, show that women were skilled riders. Their mounts are shown on tomb walls; saddles and horse equipment were interred with them. Their attire, especially boots, were well suited to riding and herding activities. Typical Kitan hairstyles are illustrated in figure 2.7.

Except for this scroll and a few paintings by Song court artists, few traces remain of the daily life of the Kitan and Han inhabitants of the Liao Empire. Tombs, however, offer many insights. Beginning as early as the reign of the first Liao emperor, the Kitan elite abandoned their earlier funeral customs of exposing the dead and began to construct large tombs. Nancy Steinhardt has noted the power and majesty of these underground monuments, which express the imperial might of the Liao dynasty. These monumental tombs of

Fig. 2.5. Archers, detail from *Fan ma*. National Palace Museum, Taipei. Drawing by author.

the Kitan nobility, similar in layout and construction to Tang imperial tombs, already show the degree to which the early Liao were influenced by Chinese models.[6]

Archaeological discoveries from Liao tombs of both Kitan and Han Chinese furnish most of our information on the daily lives of women in the Liao period. Paintings and artifacts in these tombs offer a wealth of information on lifestyles and gender relations unrecorded in written sources. No doubt these paintings had certain meanings to their eleventh- and twelfth-century

Fig. 2.6. Taming a camel, detail from *Fan ma*. National Palace Museum, Taipei. Drawing by author.

Fig. 2.7. Kitan hairstyles. *Wenwu*, 1983, no. 9:15. Permission of Cultural Relics Press, Beijing.

audiences, as I suggest below, but they also speak with different voices to modern scholars about such things as daily life and traditional customs.

Paintings such as the *Fan ma* scroll offer a detailed picture of daily life as it was lived on the steppe, with shifting terrain, a variety of domestic herding animals, and variations in the costumes and hairstyles of tribesmen. The intended audience for such works was the living, whether in the Liao or Song realms, while tomb paintings and artifacts were meant to accompany the dead. To what extent can we say that these murals, horse equipment, and household utensils reflect actual daily reality? One of the main assumptions in the discussion that follows is that these aspects of burial do in fact conform closely to lived life. Tombs themselves are often yurt shaped. Equipment and utensils show signs of use and were thus not replacements made only for tomb use, as was often true in the Tang dynasty. If we posit that wall paintings and tomb artifacts were intended for use by the deceased, they seem to show that the afterlife was envisioned as a continuation of life on earth. Certain aspects of religious belief do appear in tomb art, but they are generally limited to symbols or indications of ceremonies, Buddhist and otherwise, that were performed by the living in honor of the deceased. Other kinds of activities, such as hunting scenes and in one case the wedding of a princess (discussed in chapter 4), are also shown on tomb walls. They were not limited to funerary ceremonies but reflected aspects of daily existence. Given careful consideration, these Kitan and *haner* tombs can be used as sources of information about ordinary life and beliefs regarding the afterlife.

Women in Pastoralist Society

Han Chinese culture had long observed a gender division in all social activities. Distinctions were stressed from birth: boys were laid on the bed while female infants were laid on the floor below the bed and given household items, signifying they were lowly and weak and should humble themselves before others. Boy infants, in contrast, were given the instruments of the scholar.[7] Song customs had boys and girls separated within the household from age six or seven and decreed careers for men and domestic life for women. But women in pastoralist societies had very different roles.

Kitan women rode astride and learned to hunt at an early age along with their brothers. They wore boots and trousers or leggings like men. They took responsibility for the home, herds, and flocks when men were away at war, a common event in pre-Liao pastoralist society and during the Liao border wars with the Song, when nearly all able-bodied men were conscripted. Evidence that women had access to money and property can be found in the long lists of women donors to Buddhist temples (examined in chapter 7). Empresses Yingtian and Chengtian were noted military leaders, but they were not the only Liao women to act in a military capacity. The Kitan inherited the steppe tradition by which women had more agency and authority than was usual in China proper.[8] Liao women may also have received precedents for women's roles from the Tang, where women commonly rode astride, played polo, and—whether one considers her celebrated or notorious—it was not accidental that Wu Zetian (Empress Wu [r. 690–705]), the only woman to reign as emperor in all of Chinese history, gained access to power in the Tang dynasty.

Women are also prominent in Liao burials. Perhaps as many as a third of all Liao tombs discovered to date feature women either as single burials or in burials of couples where the women were the more important of the two.[9] Many women's tombs are as large and as elegantly appointed as any belonging to a man. These burials speak to the importance of women in Liao society, a subject I return to in the chapters to come. In contrast, single female burials were very rare in the contemporary Northern Song state.[10]

The Liao and Jin courts divided imperial women into two categories: inside and outside (*nei* and *wai*), following Tang precedents. The inner court included women who had married into the court as empresses or concubines. The activities of the women of the inner court are described in the chapters in the dynastic histories devoted to their biographies, but women as active participants are also seen throughout the chronicles of emperors. The daughters and nieces in the Outer Court were designated according to their degree of kinship with the imperial family; daughters of emperors by empresses held first rank, emperors' daughters by imperial concubines ranked second; daughters of imperial princes by their wives held rank three, and daughters of imperial princes by concubines held descending ranks.[11] Princesses of the Outer Court attracted little further attention in documentary sources since they left the court when married, but a number of tombs and grave inscriptions of imperial princesses have been discovered that are rich sources of information.[12]

The tomb of Princess Chenguo (ca. 1000–1018), discovered intact and unlooted in 1985, is a prime example of the burial of an imperial daughter. The princess was the daughter of Yelü Longqing, younger brother of Emperor Shengzong (r. 982–1031). The fief of Chen, in the eastern area of present-day Inner Mongolia, was appointed to the princess and her husband, Xiao Shaoju, at their marriage. She was approximately eighteen at the time of her death, and Shaoju was about thirty when he died.[13] The tomb's plan features a corridor, antechamber, two small side rooms, and a large, domed burial chamber somewhat like a yurt in shape.

The typical pastoralist lifestyle attributed to the princess and her husband can be seen on the tomb walls and among the artifacts found inside. Two full-size saddled horses, held by grooms as if awaiting their riders, are shown on the corridor walls, facing outward. The grooms wear jerkins pulled up in front, like the tribesmen in the *Fan ma* painting, and leggings and soft shoes. Goods found in the tomb include riding equipment, weapons, jewelry, and various ceramic vases, bowls, and jars.[14] As in burials of other imperial family members, the deceased were entirely encased in gilt wire; their faces were covered with gold masks and both wore elaborate crowns, as befitted royalty.

The wall paintings in this tomb are executed in what has come to be known as the Liao style. Liao artists created a recognizable figure-painting style, which, while probably based on Tang precedents, was uniquely associated with the Kitan. These works feature rather flat figures of men and animals, outlined with thick black lines and filled with bright colors. A representative example of a horse and rider can be seen in figure 2.8. The plastered walls of corridors and rooms in Kitan tombs vividly portray the Kitan pastoralist life, including hunting, partying, and even the wedding of an imperial princess (discussed in chapter 4).

That Princess Chenguo, like her husband, was clearly intended to be understood as a rider is also supported in literary materials, where women are not infrequently praised for their horsemanship. The couple's bodies were found lying on a funeral platform rather than in coffins. They were dressed in layers of silk and wool clothing, including undergarments, shirts, jerkins, trousers, and leggings. Both wore elaborately embroidered and decorated boots with silver inlays resembling modern Western riding boots.[15] A well-dressed Kitan noblewoman like Princess Chenguo wore a decorated belt from which a number of objects were suspended, including tiny glass and jade bottles, a

Fig. 2.8. Horse and rider. *Wenwu*, 1992, no. 6:7. Permission of Cultural Relics Press, Beijing.

jade container carved in the shape of bamboo, another shaped like a conch shell, a fish-shaped container in amber, and a swan-shaped container in jade. One container held needles; others would have contained perfume or other liquids. Shaoju wore a similar belt, but in his case the suspended ornaments included knives, writing brushes, and pouches suitable for male activities with beautifully worked gold and silver covers.[16] The beads and decorations include gold, amber, pearls, turquoise, and crystal. One piece in amber is carved with a motif of dragons among clouds. These are not specifically funeral items but practical or decorative utensils that the princess would have carried in life. Such small portable items were well suited to a mobile pastoralist lifestyle.[17]

Actual saddles matching those in the wall paintings were found in the side chambers together with bows, arrows, knives, and other weapons. A typical Kitan saddle resembled an American Western-style saddle and featured elaborate silver-gilt decoration on the pommel and cantle and had tooled leather saddle flaps and iron stirrups. A typical tribesman is shown in figure 2.8 holding the bridle of a horse, and the saddle is clearly visible.

The Liao Empire may have enjoyed Silk Road trade, as indicated by glass jars from the Middle East that were found in the tomb, as well as a bowl with an unmistakable Star of David in its center. Some ceramic items were made of porcelain in styles typical of Northern Song kilns, while others were simple utilitarian, dark-brown pottery associated with the Kitan.[18] The entire burial assemblage, including the wall decorations, artifacts, and apparel of the deceased, speaks to a pastoralist identity. This tomb and others like it show how the Kitan nobility wished to be portrayed in death. The princess and her consort were dressed and equipped to mount their steeds and ride off across the steppes of their fiefdom.

The large number of saddles, horse equipment, and weapons found in Kitan tombs reinforces the portrayal of the Kitan as an equestrian culture, while other items, including ceramics and personal accoutrements speak to the domestic side of life. Brown pottery jugs, shown on tomb walls and found inside tombs, are frequently associated with alcoholic drinks. Other items, such as white bowls, spouted pots, and teacups, appear to be of porcelain, which might have come from kilns in the Yan-Yun region, where Song-style porcelains were still produced. Draperies, hangings, rugs, and cushions have usually disintegrated, but such fabrics were probably common in daily life. Tomb artifacts include ordinary items of daily life such as clothing, boots, rugs, ceramics, and household items, even cooking pots. Finds from other tombs show that small tables were in common use but few chairs. Pastoralist Kitan ladies sat on cushions and hassocks.

The Liao traveled by cart and carriage in addition to horseback. The Liao signature vehicle was a large cart with six-foot-tall red wheels and drawn by one or two camels. Whether intended for use in a wedding or ordinary travel, this vehicle with its conspicuous wheels and unusual balance is frequently seen in illustrations of Liao life, in tomb wall paintings and in Song paintings of "barbarian scenes." Such a carriage is depicted on the north wall of tomb number 8 in the Xiao family cemetery at Kulunqi, where the walls of the entry ramp depict the wedding of an imperial princess (discussed in chapter 4; see figure 4.1). The carriage in the painting has two typical red-colored wheels higher than a man's head, is balanced fore and aft like a boat, and has a canopied enclosure surrounded by curtains. In the Kulunqi wall painting, two camels are unhitched and resting behind the carriage. Another, drawn by a single camel, is shown in figure 2.9. The tribesmen accompanying the carriage and on horseback can be identified as Kitan by their hairstyle and costumes.

Fig. 2.9. Wall painting of Kitan carriage with camel from the tomb of Xiao He. *Wenwu*, 2005, no. 1:40. Permission of Cultural Relics Press, Beijing.

Buddhism was the most visible and prominent religion in the Liao and Jin states, as represented by still-standing pagodas and temples in northeastern China. While these impressive structures suggest the dominant role of religion in elite Liao and Jin life, they tell us little about ordinary people. Buddhism is less well represented in dynastic histories, whose accounts of ceremonial events include Buddhist aspects but also reveal another side of Liao belief, invoking gods and spirits through shamanism and animistic rituals, which often required animal sacrifices, to judge by the contents of some of the side chambers in Liao tombs.

Earlier Kitan funeral customs involved exposing the corpse in a tree and returning three years later to burn the bones.[19] No burials of pre-dynastic Kitan have been discovered, but tombs dating from the early part of the dynasty reveal that corpses were dried or "cured" as a way of embalming them and filled with fragrant herbs. In the case of members of the imperial family, the body was entirely encased in gilt wire and had a silver-gilt face mask.[20] This treatment of the body continued throughout dynastic times, as evidenced by a number of undisturbed archaeological discoveries. The same procedure, including gilt masks and gold crowns, was noted in connection with the burial of Princess Chengguo and her spouse. Preservation of the body was inconsistent with Buddhist beliefs, according to which the dead were cremated.

While according to archaeological reports, a few cremated remains, presumably Buddhist, have been discovered in Kitan tombs, the majority of tombs held intact bodies, laid out on funeral platforms, usually without coffins. The idea of burying a husband and wife together displayed on a platform was contrary to Buddhist practice and would also have been morally unacceptable in contemporary Song culture.[21] The *Liaoshi* reports that dual Buddhist and shamanistic ceremonies were conducted at the funeral of Emperor Jingzong (d. 982), at which Buddhist priests officiated together with shamans, who conducted animal sacrifices.[22] Remains from animal sacrifices have frequently been found even in Kitan tombs with a marked Buddhist nature, as seen in wall paintings and artifacts.[23] Thus, Kitan tombs present a mixed religious setting, combining Buddhism or sometimes Daoism with remnant tribal shamanistic ceremonies.

Kitan life was lived in easily transported yurts and tents, as illustrated in scroll paintings and reflected in tomb architecture.[24] Yurts, as seen in contemporary paintings, were typically made on a frame of willow branches interlaced at the top in a rounded shape and covered with skins and felt. Furniture was limited to a few wooden tables but included rugs, cushions, pillows, and hassocks, which have survived in tombs. Celebrations were an important part of Kitan culture and were notorious, according to Song accounts, for the consumption of alcohol—the Kitan and Jurchen, as well as the Mongols, were famous for drunkenness.

The state was ultimately divided into five circuits, each anchored by a capital, but adoption of this model came about only slowly. This practice accorded with both the Chinese custom in previous dynasties and Bohai practice. Liao cities have also begun to receive extensive archaeological attention.[25] The main capital was established by the first emperor in 918. It was first known as Huangcheng (Imperial City) but renamed Shangjing (Supreme Capital) by the second emperor. The city was located in modern-day eastern Inner Mongolia near Balin Left Banner, approximately 124-plus miles north of Zhongjing (Central Capital), established in the eleventh century by Emperor Shengzong on the site of an earlier Xi capital.[26]

The Shangjing Circuit occupied a vast territory around the capital in present-day Inner Mongolia, stretching far to the west across the northern part of the Liao state. The city had two main parts, an imperial sector, or "city," surrounded by its own wall and a "Chinese city" adjacent to it, also surrounded by a wall. Wide roads dissected the city. Other than the walls, however, few foundations were discovered in the preliminary archaeological excavations. Areas of tamped earth inside the imperial city were probably sites for erecting large tents or yurts. The findings suggest that portable housing was probably the norm and that Liao cities, such as Shangjing and Zhongjing, were populated largely with yurts rather than permanent constructions.[27] Even the nobility most probably lived in yurts and tents.

Dongjing (Eastern Capital) was located at present-day Liaoyang on the site of a former Bohai capital. Early in the dynasty, the Bohai state had been absorbed into the Liao realm as the semi-independent state of Dongtanguo, given to Prince Bei, the eldest son of the first emperor. After his death, the region became the Eastern Circuit and the capital was renamed Dongjing.[28] The Southern Circuit, which covered the Sixteen Prefectures, came into Liao possession in 937, when the second emperor acquired the region from the Latter Jin. The capital was popularly known as Yanjing, recalling the name of the ancient state of Yan in the same location, although its formal name was Nanjing (Southern Capital). The Southern Circuit was governed separately from the main Liao state by the Southern Administration, along basically Chinese lines, but was subordinate to the main government of the Northern Administration. The Liao-dynasty Nanjing today lies under the southwestern part of modern Beijing. In contrast to the pastoralist cities where yurts and tents predominated, Nanjing had both walls and houses for the *haner* population. It was constructed as a traditional Chinese city, although the palace and imperial-city sector were in the southwestern corner rather than centrally situated on the north as was customary in China.[29] The wards may have been walled like those in Tang cities, as seems to have been the case with the Central Capital. The population of Nanjing was predominately Chinese. Although the Han Chinese in Liao and Jin territories became, in the words of one observer, "barbarized," they maintained selected aspects of preconquest Han culture and, as their tomb walls show, lived in constructed homes probably in urban settings like Nanjing.[30]

The Central Circuit, administered from its capital, Zhongjing, was established in the early eleventh century in present-day Hebei province, some forty-three miles northeast of the modern city of Chengde and approximately one hundred twenty-five miles south of Shangjing.[31] At first it served as a place where the Liao emperors could meet with Song envoys, who presumably found the trek to Shangjing and back too arduous. The city was constructed during the reign of Emperor Shengzong on the site of the former Xi capital. In 1007, a wall was constructed and the city established as the Central Capital.[32] Like Shangjing, Zhongjing was built in two parts, the northern part was for the palace enclosure and the Kitan generally, while south of this, divided by walls, was a Chinese city.[33]

Despite the pastoralist society commemorated in their tombs, by mid-dynasty most of the elite serving as Liao government officials must have been urban dwellers for at least part of their lives. Some Kitan noble ladies living in cities like Zhongjing and Nanjing may never have placed a foot in a stirrup, preferring instead to travel by sedan chair or a luxuriously appointed camel cart. Nevertheless, the Kitan chose to memorialize themselves in their tombs with reminders and accoutrements of the pastoralist Kitan lifestyle that reflected the traditional values and culture of the steppe pastoralists: riding, hunting, and herding. In so doing, the men and women involved became unwitting preservers of Liao culture.

The most spectacular feature of Kitan burials is the many copper, gold, and silver-gilt masks found in imperial-family tombs. These items are unique; no similar masks have been found in any other tombs in China. In cases where tombs have been looted, the gilt masks and wire suits have disappeared; however, so many undisturbed tombs with gilt and gold masks have been discovered that gold funeral masks have become a hallmark of the dynasty itself.

Both written sources and their tombs suggest Kitan women enjoyed high social status, a condition that reinforces the degree of agency they enjoyed. Han women, in contrast, conformed more to the feminine standards of the contemporary Song dynasty, while *haner* women fell somewhere in between the two social constructs for women.

Hanren and *Haner* Lifestyles

Most literature describing Kitan life and customs is silent on the habits of the Han population of the Liao state, despite their having outnumbered the Kitan, probably by more than two to one. The Chinese population living north of the Yellow River and resident in Kitan territory since Tang times was known to the Kitan as *hanren*.[34] This fact is reinforced by the *Liaoshi* biographies' always indicating a person's place of origin. The colloquial term *haner* was applied to *hanren* who had adopted Kitan customs, at least to some extent. By the mid-Liao period, *hanren* and *haner*, used interchangeably, applied to anyone of Chinese origin living under Liao rule. Chinese from the Song state were called *nanren*.[35] The Liao state made explicit distinctions between the rulers and the ruled.

According to an edict promulgated by the first Liao emperor, Abaoji, in 921, the Kitan and their allies the Xi tribal people assumed superior status, while *hanren* and *haner* were subordinated and discriminated against in legal and other aspects. Han and *haner* were prohibited from intermarrying with the conquerors. Although a law of 994 somewhat raised *haner* legal status, it was nonetheless true that a Kitan who killed a *haner* might be only banished or in some cases excused altogether, while a *haner* who killed a Kitan was subject to execution.[36] Liao prohibitions on intermarriage between Kitan and *hanren* were probably largely ineffective in practice, but they no less underscored the subordinate position of *hanren* and *haner*. This Liao social and legal division on the basis of cultural identity, separating Kitan and from *hanren* and Bohai, preceded by over three hundred years the famous ethnic division of Yuan society.[37]

Hanren and *haner* were further distinguished from *nanren*, Chinese originally from the Northern Song state.[38] Naomi Standen has pointed out how frequently Han Chinese or people of mixed origin with Han names crossed borders and served the Liao state during the early reigns coinciding with the Five Dynasties period (907–960).[39] Most notable were a few favored families such as the Hann and Zhang, who had served the Liao loyally since the days of its first emperor and who had high standing in Liao administrations. Early Liao emperors depended on their loyal Chinese advisers and administrators in establishing an empire, imperial control, and patrilineal succession of sons based on Chinese precedents. While the Liao state by no means replicated Chinese models, such delineation of authority and a stable inheritance pattern were nonetheless necessary. These men, who might uncharitably be called collaborators, and their descendants were richly rewarded with rank and privileges. But, sources indicate, the rank and file of *haner* and *hanren* residents were relegated to subordinate status and suffered various forms of discrimination.

An explanation for the apparent contradiction between the trust and distinctions given these elite families and the subordinate status of the majority of *haner* is suggested by Frederic Wakeman. Although Wakeman's focus is the Manchus of the early Qing and their Chinese collaborators, the situation of the Han and *haner* population living under Liao and Jin rule was undoubtedly the same. "Individual Manchu rulers could not do without the collaboration of Chinese officials.... They were grateful to the most helpful Chinese collaborators for teaching them to rule the empire, ... [but] some Manchu rulers [were] also contemptuous of these turncoats, despising their sense of expediency and condemning their moral compromise."[40]

Manchu and Kitan rulers both were aware of how easily they could become too sinicized to retain the loyalty of their own people. The Kitan countered this possibility by maintaining their pastoralist identity in the Northern Administration and imposing Kitan customs and law onto the subordinate Chinese.

Conquest rulers distrusted *haner* because they lived in territories that frequently changed hands and showed themselves willing to serve so many masters in turn. The legal distinctions between the conquerors and their subjects continued in the Jin period, as will be seen in chapter 3. The Jin ruler Shizong (r. 1161–1190) expressed his distrust of the *haner* officials who served in the government when he remarked, "*Hanren* ... are crafty and slippery and have no loyalty. They run away and keep themselves safe.... *Nanren* are more straightforward and ambitious."[41] Shizong preferred the southerners of the former Northern Song to the Han residents of the north because he considered them more reliable since in serving the Jin they had changed allegiance only once. Denigrating the mass of *hanren* and *haner* and subjecting them to harsher laws was also a strategy for keeping control of the possibly restive majority.

These distinctions are reflected in the smaller tombs of even the most elite *haner* families. These tombs, found in the Southern Circuit region, were typically constructed of brick, usually with a single chamber, a small antechamber, and a short, steeply sloping entry corridor. Wall paintings and artifacts portray a lifestyle that was quite different from that of the pastoralist Kitan. The type site for late-Liao-period *haner* tombs is at Xuanhua, about seventy-five miles northwest of modern Beijing, where a large cemetery belonging to the Zhang and Hann families has been found in a town still called Zhangjiakou. Both were distinguished *haner* families whose members had served in the Southern Administration. These tombs all feature Kitan pastoralist paintings representing horses, camel carts, and men in Kitan dress in the corridor and antechambers and representations of *haner* culture in the inner chambers. It is as if politically correct decoration had been required for the outer areas but personal taste allowed in the interior. These interiors display typical wooden-frame house architecture with columns or brackets and painted interior scenes. The inner chambers present a different picture of *haner* daily life inside homes, where women often predominated.

A number of tombs from the late Liao period speak eloquently of women's daily lives. A typical example is the tomb of Hann Shixun, who died in the early twelfth century. By this date *haner* had lived under Liao domination for two hundred years and had made many adjustments. Paintings in the antechamber show the Kitan pastoralist lifestyle, including a clansman with a saddled riding horse, a camel pulling a Kitan two-wheeled cart, and door guards in Kitan costume.[42] Paintings in the inner chamber focus on life inside the home. (See figures 2.10 and 2.11.)

Women of the family wear Chinese-style silks, warm capes, and mobcaps. The scene in figure 2.10 shows four elegantly dressed younger women gathered around a table chatting and preparing drinks, probably tea. Their clothing is notable for its Chinese style and silk material, falling in many folds, contrasting with the heavier wool or felt garments of tribesmen in the wall paintings of the antechamber. Pale-green cups and bowls suggest celadon porcelain. A small spotted lapdog accompanies the ladies. The main theme in the burial chamber of this tomb resembles nothing so much as "Grandma's Birthday Party," or perhaps more likely "Grandma's Funeral," with the deceased presiding over the ceremonies (fig. 2.11). An elderly lady clad in silks, clearly "Grandma," sits on a hassock behind a large red table on which dishes are laid out. Two male servants in Kitan clothing attend her; another is playing an *erhu* (two-stringed, guitarlike instrument often associated with "barbarians") and a smaller figure is dancing. Wine or koumiss jugs sit on a low table in the foreground. A pet animal similar to the first appears under the table. In an adjacent scene two women and a man in a Chinese-style hat are preparing boxes that look like sutra containers and imply a Buddhist context. Tea, too, may have a Buddhist ritual significance. Below the table in this scene, however, is

Fig. 2.10. Wall painting of women preparing food and drink from the tomb of Hann Shixun, panel 1. *Wenwu*, 1992, no. 6, color plate. Permission of Cultural Relics Press, Beijing.

a tray containing bones and tusks, hinting at shamanistic rituals. Sutra boxes with Sanskrit writing were found in adjacent tombs.[43]

The tomb of Hann Shixun, in which women figure so prominently in the wall paintings, included one, possibly two, female corpses and one male corpse. Artifacts from these Xuanhua tombs mirror those in the wall paintings and include draperies, tables, beds, and chairs, indicating that the *haner* used more household furniture than did the Kitan.[44] Pottery, porcelain, and kitchen utensils were also found in the Hann and Zhang tombs at this site. The existence of *ding* ware and *qingbai* porcelain discovered in these tombs indicates a Han taste in tableware, even if northern kilns produced it.

A second tomb nearby, belonging to Zhang Wenzao, displays another aspect of the lifestyle of *haner* living near the Southern Capital.[45] As in others, typical pastoralist figures are featured in the antechamber, where tribesmen in Kitan dress are shown standing beside a saddled horse. These figures may

Fig. 2.11. Wall painting of celebration with elderly lady and entertainers from the tomb of Hann Shixun, panel 2. *Wenwu*, 1992, no. 6, color plate. Permission of Cultural Relics Press, Beijing.

represent *haner* males in a Kitan context. The scene in figure 2.12, from the interior of this tomb, takes place inside a house, where household activities include servants preparing food, children hiding behind a chest of drawers, and an upper-class woman in Han-style dress presiding from behind a red table.[46] A woman servant is shown standing on the shoulders of a kneeling man to reach fruit in a high basket. A small spotted dog is running around at the feet of children and servants, who in this painting display Kitan hairstyles and dress, but the tall woman with elaborately arranged hair wears a Chinese-style silk gown. Distinctions between Kitan and Chinese dress are clearly based on gender, class, age, or a combination of these factors. Altogether, the scene presents commonplace aspects of daily life. The tea preparation may have a Buddhist connotation, although the scene appears to be more secular than religious.

Fig. 2.12. Wall painting of interior genre scene from the tomb of Zhang Wenzao. *Wenwu*, 1996, no. 9, color plate. Permission of Cultural Relics Press, Beijing.

A similar mural from Zhang Shiqing's nearby tomb shows a woman in Chinese dress standing on the left while servants in Kitan dress prepare food and drink, fan a brazier, and go about daily life. Here too are children with braids; one child, fanning the brazier, has conspicuously crossed eyes, suggesting that an actual person might have been the model.[47] One aspect of Kitan daily life on which we have little information, apart from these murals, is children. Surely Kitan society included many children, who played around the yurts and perhaps took their first riding lessons on the backs of sheep, as observers recorded for Mongol children. The names of sons and sometimes daughters are listed in the biographies of their fathers, and a few children appear in wall paintings. Beyond this, however, we do not know how Kitan children were raised.

Class distinctions are more clearly evident in *haner* representations than in purely Kitan wall paintings. Lower-class servants and herders are dressed in Kitan style, while *haner* men typically exhibit mixed Kitan and Han styles, sometimes with official-style hats but always with Kitan boots. Entertainers, who were clearly lower-class, also wear Kitan-style clothing. Children, like the ones in figure 2.12, generally wear Kitan-style clothing and little braids, making it difficult to know whether they are servants, *haner*, or Kitan children. Upper-class women, however, are clearly distinguished from their inferiors by their Han Chinese–style silk dresses and piled hairstyles. No one could mistake "Grandma" for anyone but an aristocratic matron! Her posture, dress, and the respect shown her by the other figures all proclaim her status. Nor could the women in figure 2.10 be other than her daughters and daughters-in-law, who were surely part of the household. If *haner* men habitually wore Kitan or mixed-style clothing, perhaps by regulation, while women wore Han style, we can postulate that the cultural heritage of *haner* rested with the women as preservers of the culture that had existed prior to the Liao. Articles of daily life illustrated in the paintings include high and low tables, trays, draperies, hassocks, dishes, pottery, and porcelain. The role reversal by which *haner* had Kitan servants may reflect class distinctions.

The contrast between the wall paintings in the antechambers of these tombs, featuring outdoor, masculine Kitan pastoralist activities, and the interior scenes, which feature feminine themes, is striking. The Hann and Zhang family tombs aptly illustrate the dualism in *haner* existence. Such families appear to have maintained a *haner* culture evolved from Tang and Five Dynasties' precedents distinct from the culture suggested by Kitan tombs and from the Han culture of the Song Chinese. In their design and structural components, these tombs resemble Northern Song tombs more than the tombs of the imperial Kitan. The *haner* as represented in the paintings used such household furniture as tables and chairs, chests of drawers, hanging baskets, braziers, pots, bowls, pitchers, cups, and dishes of all sizes and descriptions. The same utensils of daily use painted on tomb walls have been found inside the tombs. Household pets were also common, notably cats and small spotted dogs. *Haner* tombs exhibit a much wider and more varied vocabulary of household objects than do Kitan tombs, and the scenes on interior walls clearly depict solidly structured houses. Women acted as culture conservators in preserving Han culture in the home. They were part of the cultural interface that saw some women, like Chen *shi* and Lady Zhen, as culture bearers and others—equally important—as cultural conservators. In this respect too these women echo Wenji, who preserved her Han culture under demanding circumstances. In depicting servants and others of lower class in Kitan dress, the *haner* exercised a curious kind of role reversal. Since these are tombs of the most elite Han families, the occupants may well have had lower-class Kitan as servants. Or the use of Kitan styles for children and servants may have been a kind of subtle statement on the subordinate status held by *haner* in general. Dress might also correlate to language if, as Kane maintains, the Liao elite spoke Chinese while the lower classes spoke only Kitan-Chinese or Kitan.

One theme common to both Kitan and *haner* tombs is the depiction of celebrations. From the wedding of a princess to Grandma's birthday or funeral, many celebrations are illustrated on tomb walls. That drinking was an integral part of such parties is demonstrated by the ever-present tall brown jugs and heated teapots (for wine or koumiss?) in nearly every scene in Kitan tombs and in many *haner* tombs. A number of pivotal events in Liao and Jin history—including Jin emperor Aguda's rebellion against the Liao emperor—took place at parties when the principal players were strikingly drunk.[48] Depictions of tea preparation in *haner* tombs reinforces cultural links with China, since tea was imported from south of the Yangtze River. Tea is often associated with Buddhism, and depictions of tea or tea drinking are common in *haner* tombs where Buddhist inscriptions or funeral artifacts have been found. More evidence of Buddhism can be seen in the decoration and artifacts and in burial customs such as cremation common to *haner* tombs. One must assume that these celebrations, if not otherwise indicated, were connected to the funeral of the deceased.

Horse culture, an essential component of pastoral life, is much less evident in *haner* tombs and, when present, is confined to the outer chambers. Small household pets were popular in *haner* households but are not seen in Kitan depictions. Thus, the daily lives of *haner* under Liao domination may have conformed outwardly to pastoralist customs of Kitan daily life, whereas internally distinctions between Kitan and Han culture were maintained, most notably by women inside the home. *Haner* women played a much more significant part in conserving Chinese culture than did *haner* males. Women preserved, served, and passed on Han culture in many forms in a setting of a largely pastoralist society. One form of acting as a culture bearer was to be a cultural conservator.

Buddhism seems to have been more prominent in *haner* life, as indicated by their tombs, than among the Kitan elite, as seen in other tombs from Xuanhua. Zhang Shiyou and his wife were cremated; their ashes were placed in cedar boxes inscribed in Sanskrit. Hann Shixun's tomb features Buddhist door guardians.[49] The tombs of Zhang Shiqing and Zhang Wenzao and his wife have Buddhist decorative motifs, though the bodies were not cremated. Zhang Wenzao and his wife were laid side by side in a simple wooden coffin placed in the tomb's inner chamber, possibly a concession to Kitan custom. Dishes with food were placed in a wooden box next to the coffin, on which are Buddhist inscriptions in Sanskrit. The wall decoration of the inner chamber features images of cranes, bamboo, and flowers, usually interpreted as Daoist but often found in Buddhist contexts. The domed ceiling has a circular star chart but no zodiac figures. Several tombs feature representations of the Chinese zodiac on burial chamber domes, and several also have Western zodiac figures. One such configuration showing concentric circles around a central lotus was found in the otherwise strongly Buddhist tomb of a single woman occupant identified as Zhang *shi*. The first circle features a set of Western zodiac symbols. The second shows star constellations. The outside ring consists of twelve robed Han-style figures with small animals on their hats, representing the Chinese zodiac (fig. 2.13).[50] Stars and constellations are common on the ceilings of Kitan tombs and may refer either to pastoralist customs or to Daoist images, but archaeologists suggest that the zodiac figures such as Taurus, Cancer, Sagittarius, and so on must be chance intrusions, probably Zoroastrian imports. The central lotus, damaged in this representation, connotes Buddhism. Taken together, the presence of zodiacs and other intrusions in a predominantly Buddhist context continues a religiously eclectic trend seen in these tombs.[51]

The tomb of Zhang *shi* is unusual, for few *haner* tombs feature single women occupants, in comparison with Kitan tombs, in which women are notable in single burials. Burial of couples was much more common among the Chinese. *Haner* women in Liao society seem to have spent more of their time in domestic occupation, as opposed to Kitan women, who were engaged in pastoralist activities such as riding and herding. They probably possessed less independent agency than did Kitan women, a suggestion that finds reinforce-

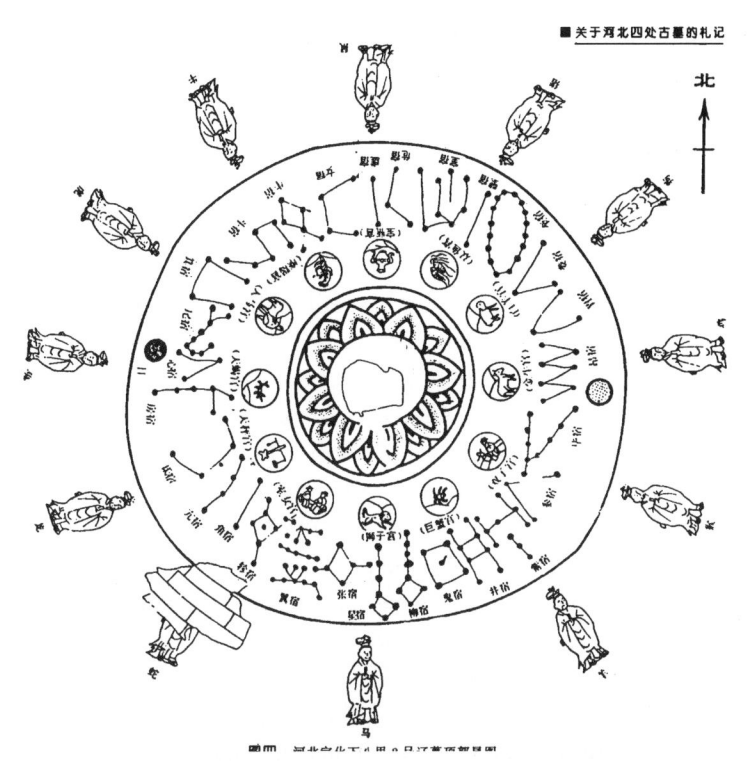

Fig. 2.13. Zodiac in four circles, from the tomb of Zhang *shi*. *Wenwu*, 1996, no. 9:61. Permission of Cultural Relics Press, Beijing.

ment in the burial of couples together. Han Chinese women living under Liao rule had, judging from their tombs, complicated identities. On the one hand they were dedicated to preserving Chinese cultural attributes, including Buddhism, but on the other, many aspects of Liao life intruded. The degree of intrusion seems to have varied by gender, with males adopting more pastoralist aspects and women preserving more Han culture.

Conclusion

One major assumption in this chapter has been that pictorial and archaeological evidence accurately reflect Liao daily life. The *Fan ma* painting is consistent with Kitan tomb art to such an extent that the authenticity of the painting is confirmed by murals in Kitan tombs and the painting reciprocally supports the accuracy of tomb art in depicting daily life. In contrast, Song-dynasty paintings of "barbarian" scenes show generic tribesmen all dressed alike without the variations in dress and hairstyle seen in the *Fan ma* painting and in tomb murals. These works, many of which have been surveyed by Irene Leung, were done with the intent of showing exotic grassland life to sedentary Chinese. Leung points out that many of the aspects shown in Song-dynasty depictions of "barbarians" are "a pastiche of familiar tropes" and may be stereotypical in some respects.[52] The most authentic of the corpus of such works is believed to be four album leaves in the Boston Museum of Fine Arts depicting "Lady Wen-chi's Return to China."[53] Tomb wall paintings, however, are far more vivid depictions of life on the frontier without reference to Chinese literary creations. Their authenticity is unquestionable. They seem intended to represent the world of the deceased as an extension of pastoralist daily life. For all these reasons, I am confident in presenting them as accurate representations. Artifacts of daily use such as vases, pots, sutra boxes, tables, and so on included in the tombs speak for themselves.

Literary, pictorial, and archaeological evidence suggest Kitan life was centered on traditional pastoralist customs. The pastoralist lifestyle revolved around herding and was shared by both men and women. Pastoralists lived in easily transported yurts, many of which—in various shapes and sizes—are illustrated in scroll paintings and reflected in tomb architecture.[54] Furniture was limited to a few wooden tables but included rugs, cushions, pillows, and hassocks. Kitan women were important in Liao society; they enjoyed high status and, judging from their tombs, respect. Men and women alike rode and hunted game. Celebrations were a prominent part of Kitan culture and included—according to the paintings and tomb artifacts as well as literary sources—a considerable quantity of alcoholic drink. Daily activities included herding, moving with the flocks and herds, and living in yurts. Liao cities, such as Shangjing and Zhongjing, were populated with mainly yurts rather than permanent constructions. The Kitan deliberately tried to limit the extent of Chinese cultural intrusions.

Although the Chinese in Liao and Jin territories became "barbarized," they maintained selected aspects of preconquest Han culture and, as their tomb walls show, lived in urban settings in constructed homes.[55] Men among the *haner* adopted aspects of Kitan dress and hairstyles, but women tended to preserve Han culture and preconquest dress.

The Kitan chose to memorialize themselves in their tombs with the accoutrements and reminders of the pastoralist Kitan lifestyle that reflected traditional values and the culture of steppe pastoralists: riding, hunting, and herding. Literary sources show that the Kitan were highly class-conscious, but this aspect is hard to confirm in tomb murals. Even in the tomb paintings showing the wedding of an imperial princess, discussed in chapter 4, class distinctions are not readily visible. Male Kitan shaved their foreheads and wore short braids in different patterns, which may have connoted class status to those who recognized them.

The great Liao tombs belonged exclusively to the Yelü and Xiao clans; smaller tombs are associated with elite *haner* families. Among the *haner*, however, Kitan dress and hairstyles signified servants and others of lower class. Gender distinctions are also indicated by dress. Elite women wore Chinese-style silks and put up their hair according to Chinese customs. Men, however, wore mostly Kitan dress, but their hats differed and it is difficult to ascertain male hairstyles. Whether male Chinese wore a queue, as seems to have been true in the Jin period, is unclear.

In terms of religion, great Buddhist temples and pagodas dominated above-ground architecture, some of which are still standing. Liao tombs demonstrate a much more varied set of beliefs. Buddhism, Daoism, animism, and even aspects such as a zodiac symbols and patterns borrowed from Zoroastrian iconography are seen in Liao tombs. The *haner* population appears to have lived bifurcated lives, partly preserving Chinese culture—in which women played an important part—and partly subject to "barbarian" influences. How their lives were changed and the ways in which they adapted to alien rule will be taken up in the subsequent chapters of this book.

THREE

Jin Women's Daily Lives

From the examination of Jin *lienü* in chapter 1 we know that Jurchen women were praised for martial acts, and eyewitness reports of Jurchen society describe how Jurchen girls were free to walk the streets singing of their accomplishments. They participated in raucous parties and drank with men, rode astride, and hunted, and they took part in abduction or elopement marriages—willingly or otherwise. Betrothals and marriages were serious commitments, in which most wives became—in effect—the property of the groom and his family. Dowries, which in other contexts provided married women with a certain degree of security, were not part of Kitan and Jurchen culture. Jurchen women resembled Kitan women in many of the ways described in the preceding chapters, but they also displayed particular customs, the focus of this chapter.

Most of our information about Jin society comes from histories and other written sources.[1] Archaeological excavations, which have offered much on Liao women, are not a rich source of information about Jurchen women's lives, with one exception, the burial of the Prince of Qi, which is described later in this chapter. Apart from the *Wenji* painting, also examined in more detail below, most extant works of art also reveal very little that is specific. However, histories and other documents, ranging from the *Jinshi* and *Da Jin guozhi* (History of the Great Jin State) to reports by contemporary observers such as Hong Hao, who was held hostage by the Jin for fifteen years, and incidental information from collections of Jin literature, plus various sources of information on material culture in the Jin period, can be used to establish the historical context in which Jurchen women lived their lives.[2] This chapter first discusses what can be known about the lives of women in Jurchen culture and then turns to the lives of *haner* women (former residents of the Liao state) and former subjects of the Song dynasty who lived under Jin rule. Archaeological and written sources are much more abundant and informative regarding the lives of *haner* women.

Jurchen Culture

According to the *Jinshi*, the Jurchen followed the precedents of the Liao and worshipped heaven with ceremonies combining non-Chinese animistic and shamanist elements with Han Chinese traditions, but it must be remembered that the *Jinshi* was composed well after the dynasty had ended, and the Chinese elements may have been enhanced later. Literary sources tell that the predynastic Jurchen followed a simple lifestyle that included hunting, fishing, raising stock, and some agriculture. From early on, Jurchen tribes had been located in the Sungari (Songhua) River valley and surrounding regions. Unlike the pastoralist Kitan, who moved about following their flocks, the Jurchen were a primarily village-based people, who lived in villages or stockaded strongholds that left few traces on the landscape. They engaged in agriculture or pastoralism depending on the ecological nature of the region where they settled.

Information on the predynastic Jurchen comes largely from Xu Mengxin, who, citing a (lost?) work by Li Shanqing, asserts that the Jurchen clans originated in the region north of the Changbaishan, along the Heilong River valley, or even farther north. In the Sui-Tang period, Jurchen were recorded as having seventy-two or more different tribes. They raided Tang and Bohai settled areas. Xu describes Jurchen living in the Donghai area (east of the Liao River) as having yellow or brown hair and beards and yellow eyes, for which reason they were known as "yellow-headed Jurchen." They lived among fields and forests and raised horses, sheep, and pigs.[3] Pastoralists like the Kitan did not raise pigs, which were considered Chinese livestock; that the Jurchen did so suggests a more settled mode of existence. The text goes on to describe Jurchen burial customs as lacking in proper respect for the dead. The Jurchen were so brutal that in hard times they even killed their fathers and mothers, showing a lack of filial piety, and they were especially savage in warfare.[4] These references to exotic physical appearance, lack of filial piety, and other non-Chinese customs echo other writers as far back as Sima Qian, who said similar things about the Xiongnu, who "despise the weak and the aged. On the death of his father, a son will marry his stepmother, and when brothers die, the remaining brothers will take the widows as their wives."[5] Such comments about the Jurchen, therefore, repeated old shibboleths and were not necessarily based on empirical evidence.[6] Nonetheless, some of Sima Qian's observations coincide with features typical of steppe people over several millennia. His comment about brothers marrying their stepmothers and the wives of their deceased brothers describes the levirate tradition that persisted in the Liao, Jin, and later periods. What rings true about the description of the early Jurchen quoted in Xu is the locale where they originated, their villages, and their agricultural and livestock practices—if not the color of their hair. Paintings of Jurchen warriors feature dark-colored beards.

Modern historians agree on Jurchen geography and probable origin. The Jurchen emerged from earlier Mohe tribes south and west of the Changbaishan and north of the Bohai kingdom. By the Liao period, Chinese records divided the Jurchen into two groups. The first consisted of *sheng* (wild, literally "raw") Jurchen, who followed the relatively primitive lifestyles of their ancestors based on hunting and herding. The second group was more sedentary, raised crops and livestock, and paid taxes or tribute to the Liao; they were known as *shu* (civilized, literally "cooked") Jurchen.[7] Some groups had affiliated with the Bohai state prior to its assimilation by the Liao. The Jurchen were restless, and Liao history is punctuated with Jurchen revolts, sometimes in alliance with dissident Bohai. The final revolt, 1115–1123, overthrew the Liao state and established the new Jin Empire.[8] The two first Jin emperors, Aguda (r. 1115–1123) and his brother, Wuchimai (r. 1123–1138), made their principal capital at Shangjing, also called Huining, in the Songhua River valley homeland.

The subsequent two emperors moved the main capital to the former Liao southern capital of Yanjing, renamed Zhongjing, on the site of modern Beijing. Jin-dynasty Nanjing was on the site of the former Song capital at Kaifeng, which was conquered in 1127. While the dynastic Jurchen rapidly adopted Han culture, other *sheng* Jurchen tribes remained outside the cultural nexus and retained the indigenous customs of their ancestors.[9] By the twelfth century, these tribal Jurchen had become so marginalized from the Jin state that they were regarded as outsiders, even sometimes as enemies. Led by Wanyan

Aguda, Jin armies were noted for their ferocity and military effectiveness. The Jurchen elite abandoned their *sheng* origins soon after founding the dynasty, influenced first by acculturated Bohai and subsequently by the incorporation of much of northern China and its large former Song population.

The Liao had distinguished between Kitan, Xi, Bohai, and *haner*. The Jin followed a similar but more explicit policy, ranking Jurchen first, Bohai second, and Kitan, Xi, and other allies third. The *haner* ranked fourth. After the conquest of the Northern Song, *nanren* (southern Chinese), meaning those from the former Northern Song state, were ranked fifth.[10] This Jin social hierarchy followed Liao precedent and predates the better-known Yuan ethnic division of society.[11]

Jurchen tribal culture is best represented in the painting *Wenji gui Han*, discussed briefly in the introduction and in more detail below.[12] Although there is no groundline or background in the painting and the space is defined by only the figures themselves, a landscape is implied and a strong wind seems to be blowing from the right. Most of the figures shield their faces from the wind, either with their sleeves or by hunching down in their saddles. One rider, who appears to be a Chinese-style official, uses a fan to deflect the wind. In this painting, clansmen sport mustaches and beards; their long, unkempt hair and their horsemanship are emphasized. These details match physical descriptions of *sheng* Jurchen reported by Xu Mengxin, as noted above.[13] The riders wear leggings, boots, and short jerkins with woven medallions on the back. Medallions seem to have been a Jurchen hallmark and are seen in several other paintings featuring Jurchen tribesmen.[14] Physiognomy, hairstyles, and clothing identify these horsemen as *sheng* Jurchen. Their long faces and noses bear a striking resemblance to the physical appearance of seventeenth- and eighteenth-century Qing emperors Kangxi (r. 1661–1722) and of Qianlong (r. 1736–1796), who were in fact direct descendants of the twelfth-century Jurchen.[15] But their cringing positions show that they were not intended to represent the heroic early Jurchen that Emperor Shizong (r. 1161–1190) so admired. To members of the sophisticated Jin court, these figures would have seemed bizarre, an aberration from the past. These physical details coincide with those found in the burial of the Prince of Qi and are surely typical of the Jin imperial elite at a specific point in the late twelfth century.

Six women are shown in the painting: Wenji herself at the center of the composition, two servants running beside her horse, a woman on the lead mare holding a flag, and two women among the group on horseback. The three tribeswomen are dressed in customary Jurchen costumes, with leggings, skirts, aprons made of some kind of animal hide, jackets, scarves, and cloth or fur hats. The two women on horseback, whose faces are visible behind other riders, wear round fur hats. Since they are mounted, they are probably of elite rank. The rest of their figures are obscured by the other riders, so it is impossible to say whether they are dressed as tribeswomen or are wearing Han-style clothing. Both turn their faces away from the wind. Wenji herself is dressed in Jurchen-style clothing. Her jacket is ochre-yellow, with a silver-colored "cloud collar," a symbol of high rank. She also wears boots and a fur hat with earflaps. Ribbons and scarves stream out behind her. (See figures 3.1 and 3.2.)

With the exception of the Han Chinese official, the male figures wear typical *sheng* Jurchen clothing, as with the costumes associated with the burial of the Prince of Qi. The last rider is accompanied by an emaciated-looking dog and carries a hawk. Only Wenji among the figures in the painting faces

Fig. 3.1. *Wenji gui Han*, section 1, "Tribesmen." Permission of the Jilin Provincial Museum, Changchun.

Fig. 3.2. *Wenji gui Han*, section 2, "Wenji and Women." Permission of the Jilin Provincial Museum, Changchun.

the wind unflinchingly. The famous Chinese historian of the Communist era, Guo Moruo, described this wind as the harsh north wind of the steppes.[16] But if Wenji is returning home, as the title of the work indicates, the wind in her face must have come from the south. It is the strong wind of civilization that causes the tribesmen to flinch and hide their faces. Wenji is, therefore, a heroine of the civilized south, even though she is shown in a Jurchen context. To the Jin court of the early thirteenth century, the civilized south was Jin China and the *sheng* Jurchen have become stand-ins for the "barbarians" who abducted Wenji. At the time of this depiction, they are returning her to the southern, civilized Jin court.

Qing-dynasty emperor Qianlong wrote an inscription on the *Wenji* painting, then in the imperial collection, in which he identifies it as an heirloom from the Jin dynasty, noting that Wenji was "a shining example" whose "heart could not wait, but looking [back] at her two sons, she wept."[17] Qianlong did not mention the role of the Jin as predecessors of the Manchus, a topic that was much in play earlier in the dynasty, but instead interpreted Wenji's story in the context of contemporary Qing political culture, which embraced Confucianism and the kind of filial piety embodied in his comment.[18] However, the Wenji of this painting is not weeping. She does not seem dismayed over the prospect of returning to Han civilization despite leaving her sons behind. Her appearance is forceful and stalwart. The authenticity of the depiction of Jurchen *sheng* warriors in the *Wenji* painting is supported by details from several Jin burials, most notably the well-preserved burial of the Prince of Qi and his wife, discussed below.

Jin Material Culture

Much of our information about Liao daily life comes from the elaborate multichambered Kitan tombs and wall paintings depicting various aspects of pastoral life. Nearly all extant Jurchen tombs, however, are simple rock-lined rectangular sepulchers with no wall decoration and few artifacts. The Jurchen did not share the Liao funeral customs of embalming the body or covering it in gilt wire and gold mask. The meager Jurchen interments have typically attracted little archaeological attention and only a few reports on them have been published. Three examples are examined in the following section: an early thirteenth-century burial of an unknown person, the burial of the Prince of Qi and his wife near the old capital of Huining from the late twelfth-century, and the Jin imperial tombs near Beijing.

A typical tomb located near Beijing and dated approximately to the early thirteenth-century is representative of many Jurchen burials.[19] Constructed during the High Jin period near the principal capital, it consists of only a small stone coffin, just large enough to hold the body of the deceased, and a few grave goods. Name, class status, and even the gender of the occupant are all unknown. Porcelain objects suggest a certain degree of sophistication, but its extent cannot be determined.[20] Other Jurchen tombs of similar construction have been discovered, either identified by archaeologists as Jurchen or found in areas of Heilongjiang and Jilin that make a Jurchen identification probable. These sites have yielded only a few pottery items and jade or gold jewelry, in one case several earrings and necklaces that might have been worn by either men or women.[21] The fact that so few Jurchen burials have been excavated or studied suggests that the extreme simplicity of such burials that have been found militates against further archaeological research. The scant archaeological evidence is consistent with translations of documents describing funerary practices to the effect that the Jurchen either did not use coffins or used only simple wood coffins, which were buried "in the mountains or forests, without building a tomb or planting a tree."[22]

The recent discovery of the burial of the Prince of Qi and his wife has confirmed the Jurchen identity of the figures in the *Wenji* painting and corroborates the details of dress and comportment seen there. In 1988, a burial was found near the old Jin capital Shangjing (Huining), at Acheng in Heilongjiang province. It was intact and had not been robbed. The simple wooden coffin contained the bodies of Wanyan Yan, Prince of Qi, and his wife, with an inscription dated ca. 1162.[23] The coffin was in a rectangular grave without a tomb. Only a few grave goods were included. However, the couple's clothing and associated artifacts were exceptionally well preserved.[24] The prince and his wife were fully dressed in numerous layers of clothing, which in style duplicate the attire of Lady Wenji and the warriors accompanying her. That members of the Jin imperial family would be dressed in such an archaic style is puzzling, since, by the late twelfth century, Han Chinese cultural attire was standard throughout Jin society, especially for elites. However, in the case of the Qi burial, the mode of dress can be explained by the location of the tomb and its date during the reign of Emperor Shizong (r. 1161–1190)

Shizong rejected the kind of indiscriminate Han acculturation that had occurred under the previous two emperors, which had resulted in loss of military prowess. He emphasized the archaic values of the old *sheng* Jurchen in an effort to revive the former Jurchen militarism, culture, society, and language. Shizong ceremonially restored the capital at Huining and spent several months there each year. This effort even extended to having Chinese works such as the *Classic of Filial Piety* rewritten in Jurchen script. Although Shizong's Jurchen revival was an unsuccessful attempt to stem the sinicization of the Jin realm and did not survive him, the Prince of Qi's burial appears to have been part of this movement. The couple was dressed in the style of the old Jurchen nobility, whose ethics and ideals the emperor was trying to resurrect.[25]

The prince, like the *sheng* Jurchen warriors, had a beard, mustache, long hair, and earrings. He wore drawers, padded leggings, a jerkin, and boots. Over these was a padded jacket with woven medallion designs back and front, and over all was a silk wrapper. He had on socks and soft shoes and a small hat. His wife was dressed similarly in a short apron, a padded wrapper, trousers, and leggings, over which she wore a padded silk skirt and robe with gold motifs. She had silk shoes with soft soles and turned-up toes. Gold, jade, and other jewelry, including earrings for both, were recovered from the burial site.[26]

Although the style of the clothing is archaic, the materials used were not the rough-woven wool, felt, and animal-skin leather of *sheng* Jurchen wear but rather fine silk in a variety of weaves, some decorated with gold thread. Class distinctions are marked by the elegance of the materials found in the Qi burial and implied in the attire of Lady Wenji versus the rougher materials of the lower-class women in the painting. The contrast between the old style of dress and its rendition in luxurious fabrics parallels the inherent paradoxes of Shizong's movement.[27] The couple's mode of dress exhibits self-consciously luxurious taste in a deliberately primitive style. Like the *Wenji* horsemen, the Prince of Qi was equipped to set off across the countryside, and Lady Qi, dressed much like Wenji in the painting, might also have been expected to be a horsewoman, although neither husband nor wife wore boots. Judging by this burial, the society of late twelfth century Huining was not an unsophisticated tribal remnant of earlier Jurchen society. However, Jurchen attire in the late twelfth century was fraught with different and conflicting meanings. On the one hand, according to Emperor Shizong's program, it signified military prowess; on the other, it was worn mainly by *sheng* Jurchen, who had by this time become marginalized. Ordinary Jurchen dress could also signify lower-class status, as seen when servants portrayed in Han tombs are dressed in modified Jurchen styles.

Until more Jurchen burials come to light, the *Wenji* painting and the burial of the Prince of Qi are virtually the only sources that can provide physical details of Jurchen lifestyles and customs to supplement literary sources.

A few examples of Jurchen customs can be found in the details from twelfth-century Han and *haner* tombs in Hebei, which are far more elaborate than the simple Jurchen burials. Like the tombs of *haner* elites in the Liao period, the Jin-period Han elite were buried in small mausoleums, consisting usually of a single domed chamber with a sloping corridor and sometimes including a small anteroom. Some tombs include painted Jurchen figures in subservient roles such as door guards, much like the Kitan servants in Liao tomb scenes. In wall paintings, lower-class women in servant roles wear a variant of *sheng* Jurchen dress, while upper-class women wear Han styles. In one example, a pair of guards painted at the doorway to a tomb at Xiabali, Xuanhua, are depicted in Jurchen hot-weather summer costume, wearing aprons and gaiters but no trousers. (See figure 3.3.) Both figures have mustaches. Another guard shown in the same tomb interior wears winter clothing, with a jerkin, clasped on the left, featuring a typical Jurchen medallion.[28] Judging from Liao examples, we might then ask whether dress also suggested linguistic differences, by which the Jurchen elite spoke Chinese and the lower classes still spoke Jurchen.

Fig. 3.3. Jurchen door guard, *Wenwu*, 1990, no. 10. Permission of Cultural Relics Press, Beijing.

The Nongtan tomb, near Beijing, sheds no light on women's issues since even the gender of the deceased is not known. In the Prince Qi burial, costume alone, however intriguing in its parallels with the *Wenji* painting, tells us little of women's daily lives. We are almost entirely ignorant of other aspects of Jurchen lifestyle such as dwelling units, domestic animals, kitchen utensils, and even warfare because archaeological information is so scant.

The Jin imperial tomb mausoleum, located southwest of Beijing, was begun during the reign of the fourth Jin emperor, known as Hailing *wang* (r. 1150–1161), and carried on by subsequent emperors until the end of the dynasty. Even Shizong, who revered the old capital at Huining, administered the empire mainly from Zhongjing and was buried, not at Huining as he might have preferred, but in the imperial tombs outside present-day Beijing.[29] These tombs present problems of archaeological interpretation because of the destruction of the original site in the Ming period and its attempted reconstruction in the Qing dynasty. Built in the twelfth century, the imperial mausoleum precinct contained the bodies of some nine emperors, excluding the last emperor, Modi (d. 1234), whose location at the time of death is unknown. The remains of some of Aguda's earlier ancestors were transported and reburied at the site. The site was preserved by the succeeding Yuan dynasty, but during the following Ming dynasty, the imperial Jin tombs were thoroughly razed and the bones scattered. Efforts to restore the tombs were made under the Qing emperor Qianlong.[30] Consequently, there is some difficulty in distinguishing the original constructions and artifacts from Qing reconstructions.

Although foundations provide evidence that above-ground structures once existed and the area had extensive landscaping, the Jin imperial burials were enclosed in simple stone sarcophagi inside tombs that were far simpler in structure than the monumental underground Liao imperial structures. One tomb, numbered F 4, whose foundations and lower walls have been uncovered, was reached by a vertical shaft lined with bricks. A flat barrel-vault tunnel led to the main chamber, but this corridor turned back on itself three times like a maze. A short extension of the tunnel led to a small, round burial chamber. In another example, M 6, the carved marble coffin was set in a small stone crypt, barely big enough to hold it, with a single stone slab as its cover.[31]

The coffins measure no more than six feet in length by less than three feet in width and height. The sarcophagus in tomb M 6-3 appeared to be intact. It featured elegantly carved phoenixes on both sides and ends, suggesting it had belonged to an empress. Inside were the remains of a gold wire headdress and jade ornaments, indicating the occupant was a woman. Tomb M 6-4 was similar but carved with dragons, suggesting the occupant was an emperor, but it had been broken into and looted.[32] Only a few jade ornaments and gold buttons remained. These two burials were probably an emperor and empress, whose identities remain unknown. Broken pieces of funerary steles provide tantalizing clues but no answers.

One tomb, designated M 9, has been tentatively identified as being related to Emperor Shizong, either the tomb of the emperor himself or that of a close relative. Two carved pillars with dragon motifs originally guarded the door to the tomb's interior. An elaborate funerary temple existed in the Jin period at that location and was reconstructed in the eighteenth century. As for the other tombs, only a few human bones and, in one case, cremated remains in a pottery jar remained for archaeologists to find. Artifacts included a single sword, a few pottery and porcelain jars, and a few Jin coins.[33] Jin emperors preserved the simplicity of the Jurchen burial tradition even in imperial tombs. Consequently, little can be gleaned regarding Jin imperial women from these tombs. The Jin archaeological record regarding women is thus limited and we must turn to the literary record for more information.

Literary Sources

As the Jin *lienü* exemplars discussed in chapter 1 attest, Jurchen women were praised for their military acts. They led troops and defended cities—but mainly when male leadership failed. Jin society was increasingly influenced over time by Confucian concepts and moved closer to Chinese cultural ideals. In spite of this trend, the *lienü* examples preserve great respect for female military activity. A different set of values is expressed in the *Jinshi* chapters on empresses and imperial concubines.

The first *Jinshi* biography of a woman describes the conduct of the wife of Jingzu, an ancestor of the Jin imperial clan, who was posthumously ennobled as Empress Dowager Zhaosu. In this apocryphal account, she is described as traveling with her husband and discussing all political and legal matters with him, thus they made decisions together. She does not reprimand him for his excessive drinking but serves their guests graciously. But the next day, she embarrasses them—and her husband—by quoting their drunken conversation. After Jingzu dies, his sons and brothers depend on Zhaosu's direction.[34] While this story is undoubtedly a later interpolation, it shows the agency attributed to Jin women and sets forth an idealized standard of conduct. We see a *sheng* Jurchen woman behaving like a Confucian paragon in this tale.

Disregarding for the moment the Confucian aspects of this tale, the story illustrates how women could party freely with men. The Jurchen, like the Kitan, were renowned for their drinking, and the rowdy behavior attributed to the emperor and his friends is probably culturally accurate. Song Chinese visitors to the Jin state also remarked on the participation of women in Jin banquets. Zhao Liangsi, a Song envoy to the Jin court in 1119, was astonished that Emperor Aguda's wife sat beside him on a kang (a heated brick seat or bed) to receive guests. The second wife rolled up her sleeves and served food.[35] Zhao's description may have been intended to denigrate the Jurchen but tells us as much about Song cultural expectations as it does about Jin practices. At the Song court, an empress would never have appeared casually in public, nor would an imperial wife or concubine have acted as a servant. But this account accords with the story of Zhaosu. Both, clearly, were written after the fact, and while they each contain some information about Jurchen culture, both tales also include implied Confucian-based criticism.

Unlike the exclusive marriage pattern of the Yelü and Xiao clans practiced by the Liao imperial line, the first Jin emperor, Aguda, set the standard for the Jin nobility by marrying strategically with Bohai elite women and among selected Jurchen tribes. The Jin state issued a number of edicts forbidding marriage between Jurchen and others, such as Kitan, *haner*, or Han Chinese from the south. These edicts also prohibited marriage across social classes, rules that were ignored by members of the imperial family.[36] Chinese cultural influence spread quickly among the Jurchen elite, in large part because of Bohai influence. The Bohai were accounted the second-ranking group in Jin society. Bohai women had a special role as culture bearers in transmitting Confucian culture to Jurchen elites. As a result, acculturation was especially rapid, and Jurchen women also accepted Confucian norms of feminine comportment. Their values are reflected in the following accounts of imperial women.

Li *shi*, a concubine of Prince Ruizong, Aguda's eldest son, and the mother of the esteemed emperor Shizong, came from the Bohai nobility. She "enjoyed reading the classics, had good manners, proper behavior, and maintained good relations with her husband's concubines." When her son became emperor, she corrected him sternly whenever she saw anything improper in his behavior.[37] Thus, she exhibited good Confucian virtues: caring for others first, reading the classics, and admonishing her son. Liu *shi*, whom Emperor Shizong sought as a bride for his son, the heir apparent Xianzong, was also from an elite Bohai family. However, the emperor first asked his mother's opinion, and only when Empress Dowage Li approved of the girl was she accepted. According to the official history, "[she] was very intelligent; when she read something, she never forgot it. She could finish reading the *Classic of Filial Piety* in only ten days and was very fond of Buddhist books." Although Xianzong died before attaining the throne, Liu *shi*'s son became Emperor Xuanzong (r. 1213–1224).[38]

Xuanzong's empress corrected her son in the Confucian virtue of filial behavior. The mother of future emperor Aizong (r. 1224–1234) was very strict with her children and even beat the future emperor for misbehaving—right up until he became emperor. When Aizong learned that his brother, Prince Jing, was plotting a coup, he wanted to kill the prince. The empress dowager dissuaded him, citing filial piety between brothers and describing the plight of Emperor Zhangzong (r. 1190–1209), who had set a bad example when he killed his brothers and consequently suffered bad luck afterward. The abashed emperor followed his mother's advice.[39]

Sometimes Confucian virtues are illustrated through negative examples. Ironically, the more salacious tales in biographies of imperial women concern the emperor known as Hailing *wang*, who had been one of the most expansive promoters of Han acculturation. He was considered so evil that shortly after his death his successor, Emperor Shizong, demoted him and gave him the lesser title of prince (*wang*). Hailing routinely stole wives or concubines from his officials. Some of the women to whom he was attracted, including Pucha Alihu, a thrice-married concubine, were supposedly as evil as Hailing himself.[40]

Before becoming emperor, Hailing had sought to marry Alihu, who was the concubine of a court official, but was refused. When he ascended the throne, Hailing issued a divorce and made her his concubine. But she was fond of alcohol, so "his love for her diminished." He then seduced her daughter. After Alihu killed a maidservant in a drunken rage, Hailing put her to death.[41] The story discredits Hailing, who was notorious for forcing women to leave their husbands, but also reveals another side of female behavior. While women often participated in parties, excessive drinking was discreditable. This entry demonstrates ways in which certain Jurchen actions conflicted with Chinese morality.

Confucian ethics are prominent in other accounts. Many of the brief biographic sketches of Jin imperial women sound more like candidates of *lienü* status than representatives of Jurchen cultural values. Clearly, in their daily lives, women negotiated between the traditional forest customs of the Jurchen and the Confucian virtues. Jurchen women, following the Confucian model, shaped their own identities increasingly in Chinese cultural terms, but not without exceptions.

Han and *Haner* Women

In 1127, Jin armies occupied the former Northern Song capital and captured both the retired emperor, Huizong (r. 1100–1126), and the new emperor, Qinzong (r. 1126–1127), along with the rest of the Song court who were present at the time. When the Jin took over the territory of the former Northern Song, the *nan* (southern) residents of the area became the majority in the Jin state and continued practicing their traditional Han culture. The Jurchen promptly followed suit. Even Emperor Shizong's efforts to revitalize the old Jurchen culture in the 1160s could not stem the overwhelming tide of *nan* influence. By the mid-twelfth century, sinicized Jurchen of the court and capital differed little in dress, literacy, and social customs from the *nan* Chinese of the former Song, so much so that the Jurchen population of the Jin Empire might have appeared indistinguishable from the *hanren* to a foreign observer.

The Han people living under Liao culture continued earlier *haner* styles in both tomb construction and the burial of couples together, a practice that has led scholars to associate marriage and burial as a linked metaphor in middle-period tombs.[42] However, in contrast with Liao burials, few single female Jin burials have been discovered. Han tombs, unlike the simple burials of the Jurchen, reveal many details of life under Jin rule, and they maintained the dualism characteristic of late Liao *haner* burials. Tombs were typically constructed of brick, with a domed burial chamber, sometimes a small anteroom, and an entrance corridor. In terms of construction, little distinguishes the tombs of the Han living under the Jin from those of the *haner* elite under the Liao.

Pastoralist aspects appear in the outer chambers of the tombs of Han families from the early Jin period, while domestic scenes decorate the inner chambers. As with *haner* under Liao rule, class distinctions seem to be clearly defined. Tomb paintings record increasingly secular attitudes, with portraits of the deceased inside their comfortable homes and even depictions of attendance at theatrical dramas (possibly funeral entertainments). Han tombs are also more consistently Buddhist in character. But the main impression of these tombs is an appreciation for a comfortable home life, complete with curtains at the windows and couples seated at a table laden as if for dinner, with small pets scampering about.

A tomb from Pingding in Shanxi offers a typical example. Pastoralist subjects occur in the corridor wall paintings, including a camel laden with goods led by a groom (fig. 3.4).⁴³ The camel is a quintessential creature of the steppes and Silk Road. The groom has a queue of braided hair down his back. The Jin, like their Manchu descendants, required Han men to shave their foreheads and wear a queue as a symbol of subservience.⁴⁴ The tomb's construction and its location in Shanxi suggest that the unnamed occupant was probably Han. No tombs of this type have been associated with Jurchen named personages.

Class distinctions between servants in Jurchen dress (fig. 3.5) and elite women in Chinese styles (fig. 3.6) are evident in a tomb from Jiaozuo in Henan.⁴⁵ The burial chamber is lined with panels of life-size men and women. Two figures in figure 3.5 are servants, in Jurchen costume, carrying a vase and a tray, respectively. While more refined than the *sheng* Jurchen in the *Wenji* painting, their dress is clearly distinguishable from the Han Chinese dress in figure 3.6 Notable is the split skirt or long apron over leggings worn by both

Fig. 3.4. Leading a camel, *Wenwu*, 1996, no. 5, color plate 1 facing p. 16. Permission of Cultural Relics Press, Beijing.

men and women. Both also wear simple, long-sleeved jerkins seamed down the front with a round collar and a belt.

The two elegantly dressed women, in contrast, wear long, V-necked gowns with many folds, suggesting thin silk material. They wear mobcaps, shoulder shawls, and high cummerbunds. Their demeanor is also quite different from that of the servants with downcast eyes. One carries a net or whisk and the other holds writing brushes.

Fig. 3.5. Servants in Jurchen costume, from a tomb at Jiaozuo, Henan. *Wenwu*, 1979, no. 8, plate 1 facing p. 16. Permission of Cultural Relics Press, Beijing.

Jin Women's Daily Lives

Fig. 3.6. Women in Han dress, from a tomb at Jiaozuo, Henan. *Wenwu*, 1979, no. 8, plate 2 facing p. 16. Permission of Cultural Relics Press, Beijing.

In this example, the art reveals other aspects of Han acculturation. For example, the lines in the painting seem to have been rendered with brush and ink and modulated with many details. The painting has more in common with Song-dynasty artistic conventions than with Liao styles. The rendering is notably more fluid, similar to paintings in the Yanshan temple (discussed below). But while influenced by Song China, Jin culture was never identical to it, as literary sources attest.

Travelers' reports by Song visitors to the former Song territories bewail the destruction wrought by the Jin conquest and comment on how these areas have changed. Fan Chengda (1126–1193), who visited the Jin on a diplomatic mission in 1170, more than forty years after the conquest, sadly noted the ruined state of many of the towns through which he passed. Kaifeng, the former Song capital, was woefully neglected and former suburbs had turned into plowed fields. He remarked that

> the people have long been exercised in barbarian customs. Their attitudes and judgments, their likes and fondnesses, have all mutated in accordance with [the Jin]. This is most apparent in their varieties of dress and guise, the style of which are now completely barbarized. . . . The only thing that has not changed very much is the women's mode of dress.[46]

This comment reveals that men had adopted items of Jurchen dress, whereas women's styles were still similar to those in the south, although outdated. Fan remarked on the more strident colors in women's dress and commented that few women wore hats, preferring instead to "enfilade their hair into a chignon. . . . Members of honorable families use beads that tinkle and jingle to cover [the chignons]."[47] At a time when respectable Song women in the south were increasingly sequestered inside the home, the sight of women on the streets would have attracted attention—another example of Fan's "barbarization."

Daily life in Jin China is further illustrated in the large murals at the Yanshan temple in the Fanzhi district of Shanxi province, created around 1167 under the direction of Jin master artist Wang Kui, who may have learned his craft at the Northern Song capital.[48] (See figure 3.7.) The paintings were completed some twelve years prior to Fan's visit but display numerous similar details. As temple decoration, the paintings were intended to illustrate cycles in the life of the Buddha and other Buddhist tales. Some of the most elegant parts feature architectural renderings of mythic palaces. However, genrelike scenes at points in the composition also depict aspects of daily life, including a water-powered mill, agricultural work, milking cows, and other ordinary activities. The street-market scene described below is part of an illustration of the life of a Buddhist figure known as Little Blue Robe. She is seen in the lower-right corner, an otherwise insignificant figure were it not for the cartouche over her identifying her. She is shown leaning over the balustrade, apparently gazing into the water rather than collecting golden lotuses.[49]

This scene features a temple market square. On the left is the temple's portico, several bays wide, and on the right is a river frontage where an elegant pavilion is set on the bank. Various vendors have small stands in the area between the temple and the pavilion. Several men walk about the square or shop at the stands, and five or six women, both old and young, some with children in tow, are shopping. Three Buddhist monks are shown gathering around a horse led by its rider. Indistinct Buddhist deities appear in clouds above the pavilion. Various actions in the mural may be examples of Buddhist benevolence, for example, giving alms, or the focus of Buddhist critique, such as the revelers in the pavilion. The casual appearance of women on the street seems to support Fan's observations, and the scene features nearly as many women as men, although the gender is indistinct in some cases.[50]

The pavilion, observable in figure 3.7, is skillfully rendered with curved eaves set on intricate brackets and a finely drawn balustrade that projects out over the water. Its flag proclaims fragrant wine and "wildflowers."[51] Several young women are seen inside the open-air pavilion; one is holding or playing a pipa (lutelike stringed instrument), and another may have a pipa, set on a table. Their hair is worn piled on top of their heads—just as Fan noted. They are accompanied by five or six gentlemen. One man is bantering with figures in the street below.[52] The scene of female entertainers together with males in a casual setting might have been shocking to the Song or Buddhist sense of morality, and certainly it contrasts with the sedate temple facing the square on the left. But the ease with which women walk freely on the streets, shop, and mingle with men is striking. This vignette provides a glimpse of daily life in a Jin town in the mid-twelfth century. The strict separation of sexes that marked Southern Song gender relations is not apparent either in Fan's report or in the temple murals.

Susan Bush has noted the unusual prominence of women in the Yanshan murals. She points out that women are depicted as protagonists both in the genre scenes and in the Buddhist dramas. She also suggests that this aspect of the murals may have been designed to appeal to female worshippers on the pilgrimage route where the temple is located in Shanxi province.[53]

Besides the Yanshan murals, Han tombs contain evidence of women's customs. The religious character of the mid-Jin tombs seems to be Buddhist, but less evidence of religion appears over time, suggesting that the culture may have become more secular. The well-preserved wall paintings in the tomb of

Fig. 3.7. Street scene from Yanshan temple (based on Chai Zejun and Zhang Chouliang, *Fanzhi Yanshan si*, 128). Drawing by author.

Chen Qing, a Jin official, and his wife, Li *shi*, buried in 1159 near Datong, are typical.[54] Women wear elegant Han-style flowing gowns with high cummerbunds and have elaborately arranged hairstyles. Men wear Han-style gowns and caps. Chen and Li, judging from their names, were Han or *haner* and thus identified with Chinese culture, but the life of a minor military official in the Jin government was probably not significantly different from that of an acculturated Jurchen of the same period.

Lavish draperies appear in later Jin illustrations and tomb furnishings. So much silk is in evidence in women's dresses and wall hangings that one may speculate that northern China must have had an active sericulture industry at this time or that silk was imported in quantity from the Song—or both.

In both the Liao and Jin dynasties, daily life in the early days was frugal but proceeded, as the dynasties wore on, to become increasingly luxurious. This observation also accords with the findings of Patricia Ebrey, who noted increased commercialization of textiles with reference to women's culture in the Song period.[55]

Other Jin tombs in southern Shanxi exhibit scenes of couples seated at a table together enjoying domestic life. In one example, the wall paintings include a couple in Han-style clothing seated at a small table laid with dishes and an oversized bowl and ladle. Under the table are two wine pots. A female servant or child waits behind each chair. A little pet animal (dog or cat) can be seen under the wife's chair. The wife wears a long gown with a jacket, and the husband is dressed in a long, light-colored robe and wears a small black hat.[56] This scene, with small variations, is repeated in numerous Jin and Song tombs.[57]

Just such a domestic atmosphere also dominates a set of tombs in Houma, Jishan, in Shanxi. The interior decoration features elaborately carved architectural friezes and molded brackets in high relief, much like domestic interiors.[58] The theme of husband and wife seated at a table set for a meal or with a flower vase occurs with increasing frequency. Often the couple is seated on chairs facing each other across the table or side by side facing the viewer in rigidly frontal poses like Victorian spouses in nineteenth-century photographs. Smaller figures stand on either side and often a pet is included. These domestic scenes seem to be entirely secular. One can imagine these couples as prosperous urban dwellers.

Jin tombs with elaborate interior brick carving and decorative features imitating wooden architecture have been found in the Houma region, dating to the latter part of the Jin period. Two tombs in particular merit attention.[59] The occupants were probably former Song Chinese, judging from the geographical location of the tombs. Architectural details and decorative features absent in Kitan tombs and limited to painted doorways, windows, and roof brackets in *haner* tombs become increasingly important in the latter part of the Jin period. At first architectural details were merely painted, but as the dynasty progressed, such elements were constructed in relief to define the tomb space and reproduce the interior features of a home. In such scenes, the couples at table assume more relaxed poses. Often wine jars are shown under the table. The brown jugs, similar to those seen earlier in Liao tomb paintings, are perhaps the only reference to "barbarization." Apparently the Kitan and Jurchen consumption of liquor was adopted by the Han people as well.

The trend involving couples seated together at a table in a domestic setting, common to both Jin and Song tombs in the general region of Shanxi, may well correlate to the Song-dynasty trend toward companionate marriages, exemplified most famously by Li Qingzhan and Zhao Mingcheng and paralleled by the increasing numbers of couples buried together, as noted by Christian de Pee.[60] Such emotional attachment between husbands and wives is apparent in poems by Southern Song authors as well.[61] However, surprisingly, certain late Jin tombs introduce an entirely new theme, showing not only a couple at the dinner table but also one seated together at what appear to be theatrical performances.

Theatrical Representations

Parties, a wedding, funerals, or other celebrations were important themes in Liao, *haner*, and earlier Jin tomb decoration. The theatrical scenes show couples seated side by side behind a balustrade as if in a theater, as seen in tomb M 4, in Jishan. (See figure 3.8.)[62]

The couple in this example is seated as if spectators in a private box marked off by pilasters projecting into the tomb in three-dimensional relief. Scenes from dramatic tableaux line the walls in carved and painted relief, showing military encounters with flags flying above combatants and horsemen galloping about.[63] In this tomb and others like it from the Pingyuan region, the theme of theatricals takes a prime position.[64] These theatrical portrayals can be seen as a culmination of the long history of celebrations in Liao and Jin tomb decoration, extending at this point to include a couple—probably the deceased—in a theater setting. Chinese theatricals were often part of a religious ceremonial event, and the scene in the illustration may represent the funeral entertainments. Nancy Steinhardt has identified the dramas portrayed on the walls of Pingyuan-region tombs as typical *zaju* drama, assorted dramatic scenes that may or may not have had religious significance.[65] *Zaju* performances most probably took place in temple settings, as was the case with the theatrical scenes identified by Anning Jing in association with the Daoist Water God's temple of the Guangsheng monastery, dated in the

Jin Women's Daily Lives

Fig. 3.8. Theatrical scene from the tomb at Jishan, number 4 (based on Su Bai, *Zhonghua renmin gongheguo zhongda kaogu faxian*, 509). Drawing by author.

Yuan period.[66] These scenes point the way to further development of theatrical themes in Yuan-dynasty art. They also show women as participants and observers—in Bush's terms, as protagonists.

Conclusion

The daily lives of Jin women varied according to whether they embraced Han, *haner*, or Jurchen culture. Preconquest Jurchen are known from equivocal and probably mythic descriptions by Chinese authors. Accuracy improves in accounts by authors who actually observed Jurchen in the early Jin period. The *sheng* Jurchen lived a much more frugal lifestyle than did later, acculturated inhabitants of the Jin state, who enjoyed a comfortable, even lavish, lifestyle. Although Jurchen tombs and even the Jin imperial tombs offer scant evidence of material culture, the burial of the Prince of Qi and the extant *Wenji* painting provide a somewhat fuller—if still limited—picture of Jurchen life. More information on the daily lives of Jurchen and Bohai women in the latter part of the Jin period comes from literary and pictorial sources than from material remains.

The *haner*, who during the Liao dynasty had lived a divided existence, conforming outwardly to Kitan codes of dress and hairstyle while preserving aspects of Han culture at home, continued these practices under Jin rule. Tombs belonging to the former *haner* families at the beginning of the Jin period are very similar to their Liao counterparts. With the conquest of northern China and the large numbers of the former Song population, the *haner* melded into the Han and *nan* Chinese, so that it becomes increasingly difficult to distinguish between *haner*, Han, and *nan*. According to Fan Chengda, everyone had, by his time, become "barbarized." Judging from pictures and artifacts in their tombs, *haner* and Han, whether living in the Beijing area or in the former Song territories north of the Haui River, dwelt in houses with carved and decorated doors and windows, used quantities of fabrics for wall hangings, swags, and bed clothes. Elite women continued to wear Chinese styles and silk dresses, even if the styles were out of date by Southern Song standards, while men wore mixed *han* and Jurchen clothing in wool or silk robes and official-style hats. Class distinctions were portrayed through dress and activities; the lower classes were distinguished by Jurchen dress. Whether a woman wore a Jurchen costume or Han-style silks depended also on her class status as much as on her cultural identity.

The most interesting trends reflected in Jin tombs are the domestic settings featuring married couples and the interest emerging late in the dynastic period in theatrical performances. The increasing number of couples in burials and tomb paintings suggests a rise in companionate marriages, similar to that in Song China. Despite the appearance of women as protagonists in the Yanshan murals and women's freedom to appear in public, both the style of burial and depictions of women in tomb art suggest that Jin women may have had less independent agency than women under Liao rule.[67]

However, two aspects of women's daily lives emerge from this investigation: First, Han Chinese women living under Liao or Jin rule became the keepers of tradition, preserving in their homes Han customs from preconquest days. Second, class status came to be demonstrated through attire and possibly also language. Meanwhile the nonacculturated *sheng* Jurchen became increasingly peripheralized in Jin society, which resulted, in the *Wenji* painting, in tribal Jurchen being depicted as "barbarians." But the meaning of the Jin *Wenji* painting to the palace women of the early thirteenth century would surely have emphasized Wenji's loyalty—a loyalty they could easily transpose into Jin terms, *guojia*—our nation—a concept that would take on additional urgency when the Mongols began to attack the Jin borders in the next decades. Under Jin rule, the *haner* and Han population of northern China became more affluent, followed Buddhism, drank tea, had household furnishings and draperies, kept small pets, may have enjoyed more companionship with their spouses, and developed an interest in theater.

Acculturation went both ways, as Fan Chengda tells us: the former inhabitants of Song China under Jin control became "barbarized," especially with regard to bright colors and jewelry. The evidence suggests that although Jin women might have engaged in military efforts in emergencies, in general they had less agency and power than Liao women and fewer opportunities to shape their own identities. On the other hand, they were much freer than contemporary Song Chinese women in terms of access to public venues, premarital sexuality, and in independent voice. One Jin woman of presumably Han descent, Yang Miaozhen, who is discussed in more detail in chapter 6, shaped her own identity by adhering to the marital customs of Liao and Jin women and leading her own bandit army.

FOUR

Sexuality and Marriage

Sometime during the Tonghe period (983–1012), the Liao emperor Shengzong married off his daughter, Princess Yueguo, to the nobleman Xiao Xiaozhong (983–1012). We do not know the exact date of the wedding, but since the emperor was twelve when he began his reign, a daughter born to him could not have attained marriageable age much before the year 1000, and the marriage must have taken place before 1012, when Xiaozhong died. Very little is known of Princess Yueguo, but she might have been as young as thirteen or fourteen at the time of her marriage. According to Xiao Xiaozhong's biography, he received the fief of Yueguo at the time of the marriage. He was promoted to a high military rank and became a minister in the Northern Administration. According to the *Liaoshi*,

> He gave the emperor sage advice. He suggested that the division of the empire into two, the Northern Court and Southern Circuit, was dividing the people and recommended that the two systems be united into one so that all the people under heaven would benefit.[1]

Xiaozhong died at age twenty-nine, before his recommendations could be accomplished. The emperor himself attended the funeral, grieved over his death, granted amnesties in his name, and sent his own guards to protect Xiaozhong's grave. The princess died at about eighteen and was buried with him, but she was clearly the more important of the two, reflecting once again the prominence of women in Liao society.[2]

The marriage of an imperial princess was an important event in the Liao calendar. The emperor and empress hosted banquets for the two clans, where the bride was toasted in many glasses of wine and liquor. Her husband doubtless brought many head of prime livestock for his imperial father-in-law and may have ritually observed three years' service to the emperor. The marriage ceremonies for an empress and for an imperial princess are described in detail in the *Liaoshi*.[3]

Scenes of just such a wedding ceremony were painted on the walls of a tomb that had originally belonged to the Xiao noble family near the town of Kulunqi, discovered by archaeologists in 1972. This site, which contains other Xiao tombs, was not far from the Liao primary capital of Shangjing. Tomb number 1 is the most elaborate and probably one of the latest, dated to the 1080s.[4] Although the tomb contents had been stolen, the wall paintings and some artifacts remained. The frescoes along the corridor in this tomb feature scenes of pastoralist life, while the interior chamber features predominantly Buddhist scenes. I have identified, in a previous article, the scenes on the corridor walls as depicting the marriage of an emperor's daughter.[5]

The wedding scenes appear on the north and south corridor walls and show clansmen and -women engaged in various activities. The scene on the north wall displays numerous male figures, dressed much like the Kitan examples discussed previously, in long jackets, boots, and with hairstyles featuring short braids. The composition's main focus is a large, two-wheeled cart with two camels resting behind it. As described in the section of the *Liaoshi* on the "Wedding of a Princess," the cart in which a princess came to her wedding was "a covered camel cart with wide axles and high red wheels; wide behind and counterbalanced in front like a boat . . . , unsuitable for mountain travel but designed for covering vast distances and shallow streams."[6] (See figure 4.1.) Nearby, several women wearing long gowns of some heavy material such as wool are seen carrying bundles. In dress and in demeanor, they seem to be identical with women depicted on the south wall. However, two women on the south wall can be identified as the bride and an older aristocratic lady. (See figure 4.2.) Whether these women carrying bundles represent servants or are members of the wedding party is unclear. As noted in the previous chapter, class distinctions are not readily visible in painted depictions of the Kitan.

The wedding carriage differed from the type for daily use in that, according to the *Liaoshi*, it was drawn by two camels, not one, and equipped with

Fig. 4.1. Kulunqi tomb number 1, north wall, depicting the wedding of a Liao princess. *Wenwu*, 1973, no. 8:32. Permission of Cultural Relics Press, Beijing.

blue curtains and had finials capped with bronze or silver heads of immature dragons, with no horns or beards. Exactly such a vehicle with finials in the shape of immature dragon heads is depicted on the north wall.

On the south wall, a number of men are shown gathered around a tripod of flags and drums. The presence of flags and drums is frequently mentioned

Fig. 4.2. Kulunqi tomb number 1, south wall, depicting the wedding of a Liao princess. *Wenwu*, 1973, no. 8:32. Permission of Cultural Relics Press, Beijing.

in the texts, but the specific nature of the assemblage is unclear. It may mark a special encampment or the presence of high nobility.[7] A small decorated cart and an antlered deer held by two men can be seen to the left of center. Alongside are two women, one holding a mirror. (See figure 4.3.) On the lower left behind the women is a saddled horse, perhaps the groom's mount.

The *Liaoshi* describes a ceremony in which the bride walks forward while seeing her face in a mirror held by an older woman walking backward, just as visible in figures 4.3 and 4.4. Both women wear long gowns of heavy material, belted at the waist, and small hats. The older and taller woman is holding a mirror in which the younger woman, wearing a black cap, sees her reflection (fig. 4.3).[8]

The bride was required to bring to her wedding a second vehicle, described as a small two-wheeled cart with curtains and a canopy, which was to include a sheep or other sacrificial animal.[9] Beside the women in the mirror scene is a small two-wheeled cart with a canopy matching the description and an antlered deer that may have been intended as a sacrificial offering. (See figure

Fig. 4.3. Kulunqi tomb number 1, south wall, depicting two women with a mirror. *Wenwu*, 1973, no. 8:32. Permission of Cultural Relics Press, Beijing.

4.4.) The groom was to provide his funeral bier, probably the canopied litter seen being lifted by four men in the scene on the north wall.

One unique feature of imperial Liao wedding ceremonies was the presence of an *ao* woman. According to the *Liaoshi*, "when an emperor [or empress or princess] marries, one of the highest-ranking noblewomen from the imperial clan was selected to be in charge of the ceremony. The ceremony was called *baiaoli* [bowing before the *ao*]." The *ao* tradition probably recalled predynastic Kitan rituals of some antiquity, when a shamaness presided over important ceremonial functions.[10] Animal sacrifices were found in niches in the tomb, and the prone skeleton of a fully grown male, which archaeologists believe was a sacrificial victim, was discovered under the entry to the tomb. Human sacrifice too had been part of the traditional Kitan funeral ceremonies, and bodies of sacrificial victims have been found in imperial tombs.[11] All these elements clearly indicate a shamanistic or animistic context for both the wedding depicted on the walls and for burial ceremonies. A human victim appears to have been sacrificed at this tomb as well; the skeleton of a full-grown man, facedown, was discovered under the tomb's doorway. However, the main burial chamber shows a markedly Buddhist context. Thus, the Liao elite in their funeral ceremonies combined predynastic animism with Buddhism. The wedding ceremony, in contrast, seems to be entirely pastoralist in nature, especially with regard to the *ao* woman, the sacrificial animals, and the human victim.

These paintings add to our knowledge of daily life insofar as they present the typical dress, livestock—camels and horses—and vehicles of the Kitan pastoralist life. Documentary sources present evidence of strong class divisions in Liao society, but in this set of paintings class differentiation is puzzlingly unapparent.

The presence of the bride with a mirror, the camel carriage, the funeral cart with a sacrificial animal, and the groom's funeral bier in the wall paintings may be regarded as evidence that these wall paintings portray the marriage of an imperial princess, likely commemorating the wedding of Princess Yueguo to Xiao Xiaozhong. The tomb, taken as a whole, provides a unique window into the lives of noblewomen in the tenth century, especially with regard to marriage and death.

Including funeral equipment in a wedding ceremony was probably unique to the Kitan. Christian de Pee has recently explored the connections between

Fig. 4.4. Kulunqi tomb number 1, north wall, depicting a small carriage with deer. *Wenwu*, 1973, no. 9:32. Permission of Cultural Relics Press, Beijing.

weddings and funerals in later Chinese society.[12] Although his investigation does not address the Liao period, the origin of funeral connections with weddings may well lie in this unusual Kitan practice.

Premarital Sexuality

Prior to marriage, young women in the Liao and Jin states often enjoyed a period of relative sexual latitude by which they could mingle with men in social settings. Marriage alliances among the elite were usually contracted by the parents and celebrated with elaborate betrothal parties, but the parents of poor girls sent their daughters out to sing of their beauty and household accomplishments on the street corners. Abduction was a common preliminary to marriage, and virginity was not a requirement. After marriage, however, women became the property of their marital establishments. Ancient custom called for a widow to follow her husband in death. Alternatively, a widow could remarry within the family to a younger brother or cousin of her deceased husband's, a practice known as levirate.[13]

Sources for evidence on women's sexuality, marriage, and chastity are varied. Principal sources include the Liao, Jin, and Song dynastic histories, where information on sexuality is embedded in biographies and in the *lienü zhuan* sections. Unofficial histories like the *Kitan guozhi*, *Da Jin guozhi*, and collections of literary works, including the modern collection *Quan Liao wen*, offer varied and sometimes conflicting accounts. Travelers' reports are often more informative but may also be less reliable. Because Liao and Jin standards governing a woman's sexuality prior to marriage were very different from those of the Song Chinese, they attracted the attention of Chinese visitors, who emphasize what to them were shocking or exotic practices. Some of these accounts are as objective as anthropological reports, others contain some disparaging remarks but are generally reliable, while still others are openly salacious and derogatory, but even these may contain valuable information.[14] Jennifer Holmgren has attributed the lack of emphasis among the Mongols on a bride's virginity to the frequency of abduction marriage and the practice of levirate.[15] However, Liao and Jin sources indicate that premarital permissiveness was a widespread and well-entrenched social custom, one predating Mongol practices.

Women in Liao and Jin society were not sequestered from contact with men. Girls were allowed to stroll freely in public spaces, ride horseback, and go hunting in the company of men. Nothing offers a greater contrast to the care the Chinese lavished on their daughters and their carefully arranged dowries and marriages than these tales of wild and unchaste barbarian women. As reported by Hong Hao (*jinshi* 1116), a Song envoy who was captured and lived at the Jin court for fifteen years,

> Daughters from poor families parade in the streets.... Among the richer families, men drink and have dinner parties at night with wine; women of the same rank join them at these parties. At first the women just watch, but the men invite them to join in.... Women drink and dance for the men and sing songs. If one of the men wants [a] woman, he will ask her to run off with him on horseback. But if the women do not want to "play," they will run away; then the men ride after them and chase them.

Sexuality and Marriage

If both parties agree to the relationship, the man will take the woman away. Only later will they go together to inform the woman's parents. This is called *baimen* [visiting at the gate].[16]

Hong was a meticulous observer. He also noted that among poorer families, a Kitan or Jurchen girl's sexuality was advertised as if for sale. "At the time when girls put in hairpins [ceremony of coming of age at around fifteen], parents allow their daughters to go out on the street and sing songs." The songs recounted a girl's family background and domestic skills. In that way, girls demonstrated their attainments in order to attract mates. "Anyone who liked the singer could take her away. The couple would return later to the girl's family to inform the parents of this marriage."[17] Observers like Hong disapproved of the ribaldry in the north and clearly found the easy promiscuity of the "barbarians," who disregarded proper rites, scandalous.

At the Lantern Festival, on the fifteenth day of the first month, men and women mixed together openly on the streets to view the lanterns in the Jin capital.[18] Even on nonfestival occasions, Jin women were seen in public places and did not seem embarrassed in the company of men.

Fan Chengda, who accompanied a diplomatic mission to the Jin in 1170, remarked on the sexuality of northern women. Not far from Anyang, Fan and his company had an unusual encounter with a woman from the south, who had, in Fan's words, become "barbarized." She was wearing a "large-sleeved gown of teal and cinnamon with gold filament and a purple gird cord [also] with gold filament. Lifting up the drapes [of a window] she said that she was the scion of the [Song] ancestral house and [a member of] the family of the former commander-protector." She spoke the Wu dialect of Fan's home.[19] What the woman may have wanted from Fan's company is not clear, but her boldness was remarkable enough for Fan to have included it in his account. He seems to have pitied her. Fan leaves the exact circumstances unclear, but the woman was likely soliciting him for news of home if not for sex.

In the set of Jin-dynasty Buddhist murals at the Yanshan temple, discussed in chapter 3, a temple market vignette shows young women entertaining men in the pavilion. The flag outside the pavilion advertises, "Wildflowers [girls] from throughout the land bloom here; full jars of local fragrant wine."[20] "Wildflowers" often referred to young women whose sexuality was for sale,

87

and indeed one woman in the pavilion seems to be in the arms of one of the men. Obviously Jin society did not sequester its women in the home. Other scenes from the temple walls show men and women freely mixing in a variety of palace scenes not limited to the inner quarters.[21]

Song attitudes with which Fan Chengda was familiar are reflected in the celebrated late Northern Song painting *Qingming shanghe tu*, now in the Palace Museum, Beijing. Although executed some sixty years earlier, this painting, with its many genre scenes, offers a contrast with the murals at the Yanshan temple. Over nine hundred figures appear across the fifteen-plus-foot length of the Qingming scroll, but of these, fewer than twelve are women, who mostly peer from windows or sedan chairs. A few young women gathered on the street in front of a restaurant are likely "wildflowers" from the establishment. Otherwise, two elderly women are seen on donkey back in the countryside and three old women gather at a well on a city street. Judging from the very limited number of female figures depicted in the scroll, women generally did not move freely about the streets and by the early twelfth century were already keeping largely within the household. The temple scene of the street market and pavilion arguably reflects contemporary Jin social life just as the Qingming painting reflects that of the Song capital sixty years earlier, where respectable women did not appear in public.[22] Eventually the practice of binding the feet of young girls became widespread in Song and Ming China. Foot binding had the effect of limiting their mobility and thus increasing the likelihood that girls remained obediently at home and chaste until marriage.[23] Not so their northern sisters, who freely mingled with men on the streets and in social settings and where foot binding was apparently unknown.

Abduction and Wife Stealing

Abduction of women and wife stealing were common practices in the conquest states. Although some abductions—often with the girl's willing permission—resulted in marriage, many ended in rape. Abducting women and wife stealing were common practices among nobles and tribesmen alike, probably reflecting predynastic customs ensuring exogamy, according to which members did not marry within the tribe.[24] Under these circumstances, the chastity of the bride was not an issue.

The most notable case of abduction by a member of the high Liao nobility is that of Lady Zhen, the daughter of a well-known Latter Tang scholar, who was "obtained" by the future emperor Shizong while he was accompanying Deguang, Emperor Taizong, on a raid. Her biography states that she was a palace woman of the Latter Tang. The verb used in the text is *de*, which has several meanings, including "obtain," "take," and "seize." Shizong may have kidnapped his bride, or she might have been part of a diplomatic exchange. The future emperor married Lady Zhen. The chapter on empresses and imperial concubines in the *Liaoshi* lists her as a concubine but notes that Shizong raised her to empress. But this source also lists Empress Huaijie, surnamed Xiao, so Shizong had two empresses, perhaps concurrently.[25] When Shizong's son, Emperor Jingzong, came to the throne, he held ceremonies honoring two empresses. If the *Kitan guozhi* is accurate on this point, as seems likely, she was probably the birth mother of Emperor Jingzong (r. 969–982).[26] Lady Zhen's story resonates with the Wenji legend in many of its details, including abduction, the preservation of Han culture, marriage to a northern ruler, and the bearing of sons.

The Kitan abducted women in Chinese territory and raided in the Sixteen Prefectures. According to one inscription, "every year the Kitan go out looking for Han women and girls to abduct. Han parents are afraid, so whenever the Kitan are out hunting girls, parents hide their daughters. If a woman has to go out, she disguises herself and wears no makeup."[27] The imperial prince Yelü Longqing (973–1017) was especially criticized for such escapades. According to one text, "he hunted for girls among the Han and Kitan, and chose the best ones for his concubines and wives."[28] Abducting girls may have been a Kitan habit, but Longqing's behavior was clearly considered excessive.

The Jurchen also practiced abduction marriage. In 1147, Emperor Xizong (r. 1138–1153) "sent officials to scour the land to select from among the common people girls between the ages of thirteen and twenty. Altogether more than forty girls were gathered in [a single] year."[29] These imperial hunts provide a precedent for the well-known Manchu custom of *xiunü* (literally, "presentation of daughters") five hundred years later. The *xiunü* required that all girls between thirteen and sixteen from various Manchu, Mongol, and Chinese banners be presented to the Qing court in a ceremony held every three years.[30]

This absence of emphasis on virginity for marriageable Kitan and Jurchen women is striking in contrast to the Song custom, according to which parents closely guarded young women's premarital sexuality. Women who married late, as many Kitan and Jurchen women did, would have enjoyed considerable freedom during their teen years. Premarital sexual license and the widespread customs of levirate marriage among the Kitan and Jurchen also militated against virginity being a primary consideration in marriage. Freedom of choice was emphasized by Hong Hao, who remarked, "as to their custom, it is said that a marriage determined upon by a man and a woman themselves is superior to one that is fixed by the presentation of gifts."[31] But the obverse side of the freedoms accorded to Kitan and Jurchen women, whether entertaining men or walking the streets unprotected, meant that they were also subject to the dangers of kidnapping and rape. On the other hand, premarital sexual activity, which undoubtedly often resulted in pregnancy, would have been a guarantee of fertility and may have made such women more valued in marriage, especially in early times.

Betrothals

The birth of a daughter among the Kitan and Jurchen was not a cause for disappointment but rather for joy because of the goods and services she would bring upon her betrothal and marriage. Betrothals were serious affairs among the Liao and Jin peoples. Since the lower classes usually did not have the resources for formal betrothals, the custom, at least as described in existing sources, was practiced mainly by elite families.

According to Hong Hao, "The man's family pays a 'bride-price' to the woman's family. . . ." The arrangement was sealed with a party, for which the groom's family provided the food and drinks. "Richer households offer tea, poorer households serve koumiss."[32] Liao and Jin betrothal practices appear to have been very similar. Betrothal and marriage parties to which the guests rode on horseback and were offered cups of liquor belonged to the steppe tradition. Men and women sat together, but the groom's family knelt on the floor in a ceremony described by the phrase "men assume a lower position than women," signifying the groom's obligation to work for the bride's father for three years after the marriage. Gifts included clothing and livestock, espe-

Sexuality and Marriage

cially horses.³³ Only after completing his term of service could the groom take his wife to his own home, a pastoralist practice seen among the Mongols as well.³⁴ Once sealed by the banqueting and gifts, betrothals were as serious a commitment as marriage—possibly more so—and could be broken only with great difficulty and feelings of betrayal on both sides. The prospective husband and his family effectively purchased a bride with extravagant gifts and services and thereafter the woman's body belonged exclusively to them. The marital family controlled sexual access, reproduction, and remarriage. Sexual relations may or may not have been condoned during the betrothal period, but once a woman was betrothed, she was no longer allowed to have relations with others. Betrothal vows were taken very seriously, sometimes replacing the marriage ceremony itself.

Among the more unusual Jurchen customs—one apparently not shared by the Kitan—was a tradition known as "pointing at the belly," in which "betrothals are made [prior to the birth of the children] . . . when the mothers are still pregnant. When the children grow up, such a betrothal can never be cancelled, [not even] if family circumstances change."³⁵ The method of betrothal was the only novel part of this practice, however, since the other formalities took place just as they would have in any arrangement and a bride-price was still paid.

Jin rulers were attentive to marriage customs from an early date. In 1120, the first emperor, Aguda (r. 1115–1123), decreed after a battle in which Jin forces had conquered new territory, "These people, after surrendering, can no longer marry within the same kinship group but must marry outside."³⁶ And in 1123, another decree ordered that "stepbrothers and stepsisters cannot marry."³⁷ In 1125, a new decree forbade marriages between commoners and slaves.³⁸ The idea behind these edicts was to bring local practices into conformity with the wider Jin customs related to marriage.

Among *haner* living under Liao control, betrothal and marriage practices varied. Some followed Kitan customs. Others, however, continued the Chinese practice of giving daughters dowries, a crucial component of Chinese marriages and a major distinction between "barbarian" and Han marriage practices. The goods and property included in a woman's dowry were hers throughout the marriage. If widowed, she would be allowed to keep anything remaining from the dowry. She could then leave the deceased husband's family and make a new marriage. Bettine Birge has noted, "During the Sung dynasty, a widow could easily contract a remarriage and her right to do so was protected by law."³⁹ These laws also protected a woman's right to her dowry. No such laws existed in the northern states.

Marriage in Liao and Jin Society

Marriage and control of women's sexuality were crucial issues. For Liao and Jin males, marriage was a stage in the course of their lives, an event that brought a bride into the home who would produce heirs and continue inheritance patterns. Although a man was obliged to serve his wife's father temporarily, he neither moved to a new place nor changed his lifestyle or identity. For a woman, however, marriage meant leaving her natal home, entering an entirely new environment, and constructing a new identity. Marriage was the central event of most women's lives and took place under a variety of circumstances. Usually a bride severed ties with her own family and clan when she moved to her new husband's home. She brought no dowry with her, becoming essentially the property of her marital family, as were any children born to her. But at the same time—as wives, mothers, and sometimes warriors—women played a conspicuous part in negotiations involving cultural identity, class, and power relations.⁴⁰ As regents, imperial women often influenced or controlled certain aspects of the state, especially matters concerning succession. Certain laws and customs had a profound effect on marriage patterns. One of the most significant was that the imperial Yelü clan intermarried with only members of the Xiao clan.⁴¹ These two clans made up the high nobility of the Liao state and were the only Kitan to have surnames.

The first Liao emperor, Abaoji, married a woman from the Shulü clan, who later became Empress Yingtian and who, it is noted in the *Liaoshi*, descended from the Huihu and was born in Kitan territory.⁴² Liu Pujiang believes that the Shulü may have been a Xi clan rather than originally Kitan, thus the emphasis on the first empress having been born in Kitan territory.⁴³ The second emperor, Taizong (Deguang), married Empress Yingtian's niece. He had other wives after she died, but no further empress. The Xiao clan name was created at some point in the second or third reign, after which the pattern of Yelü-Xiao intermarriage was retroactively applied to all imperial spouses. However, Daniel Kane points out that no Kitan-language equivalent for the Chinese character corresponding to the name "Xiao" has been found in inscriptions. Instead, the names of individual clans appear, including Shulü, Bali, and Yishiji, which were "apparently merged during the course of the dynasty" to create the Xiao-surname clan.[44] The only other exception is Lady Zhen from the Latter Tang state, who was married to the third emperor, Shizong.[45] The empress of the fourth emperor, Muzong, is listed in the chapter on empresses as "Xiao *shi*," daughter of Zhifan, but this may have been a later interpolation. The Yelü-Xiao intermarriage pattern was firmly institutionalized with the marriage of the fifth emperor, Jingzong, to Xiao Chuo (called Yanyan), who was the granddaughter of Yingtian's paternal uncle. She became Empress Ruizhi (later Empress Dowager Chengtian).[46] Thereafter, the Yelü and Xiao pattern of intermarriage continued unabated until the end of the dynasty, resulting in intricate interlocking patterns, which have been extensively studied by Karl Wittfogel and Feng Chia-sheng and by Jennifer Holmgren.[47]

The Xiao had a little more flexibility and occasionally married outside the imperial clan. Also, certain especially favored *haner* individuals, such as members of the Hann and Zhang families, were honored with a bride from the Yelü or Xiao clans.

Edicts promulgated in 921, 994, and 1070 distinguished between the Kitan, Xi, Bohai, and Han and prohibited intermarriage among these groups. Judging from the frequency with which edicts against intermarriage were reinforced and the special exceptions that were occasionally awarded, Liao subjects were expected if not required to marry within their own classifications, although, according to Wittfogel and Feng, these restrictions became somewhat more relaxed over time, especially with regard to Kitan officials stationed in the Southern Circuit, who were frequently permitted to marry Han women.[48] Intermarriages probably occurred even more frequently without permission and would have been a major factor in acculturation.

Early Kitan and Jurchen tribes practiced polygamy, by which a man might have multiple wives and all wives were equally legitimate, instead of distinguishing between a primary wife and concubines as in Chinese practice. Abaoji had only one empress, the formidable Yingtian, and his son, Deguang, Emperor Taizong, also had one empress, Yingtian's niece. Concubines make an appearance in the historical chronicles beginning with the third emperor, Shizong, who had two empresses and one or more concubines. Jingzong had one empress but multiple concubines, and Shengzong had one empress but married a second after her death, and he also kept concubines. Thus, over time, the Liao adopted the Chinese pattern, in which an emperor had only one empress but could acquire multiple concubines. The third emperor had two empresses but whether at the same time or sequentially is unclear. The dynastic history, written much later, tends to conflate earlier practices with later traditions of imperial marriage, in which the emperor had only one formal wife. Holmgren dates this standardization of monogamy with concubinage to the reign of the sixth emperor, Shengzong.[49] However, the practice clearly predates the fifth emperor.

Weddings

Both the Kitan and the Jurchen practiced exogamy in marriage; women married outside their immediate kin group or clan. Originally males in the Liao and Jin cultures could have several wives of roughly equal status, but over time, as the Kitan and Jurchen became familiar with Chinese practices, primary marriage became limited to a single wife, while concubinage became more common. Marriage was not necessarily universal for Liao and Jin women. Girls could remain in the natal household and avoid marriage altogether, as did (Yelü) Changge, praised in the *lienü zhuan* section of the *Liaoshi*.[50] Whether remaining single meant that she was a virgin, however, is debatable given Liao customs regarding sexuality. For a woman to remain single was at variance with established Chinese cultural practice, according to which all girls were expected to be married out of the natal household.

Like betrothals, weddings were celebrated with much partying and many rituals, lasting up to three days. Marriage among imperial clan members was enormously important. The *Liaoshi* contains two descriptions of imperial weddings, one of an empress and the other of an emperor's daughter.[51] An idea of the nature of such weddings may have been gained from the description of the wedding of an imperial princess at the beginning of this chapter. Although such ceremonies were designed for the highest nobility of the realm, they shared certain elements with more-ordinary Kitan celebrations, such as the offering of gifts and livestock and the ceremonial consumption of wine or koumiss and probably a number of the rituals such as the one in which the bride saw her face in a mirror and another in which the bride jumped over a saddle. First, however, an auspicious day was selected for the ceremony—probably with the assistance of a shaman—and for imperial weddings, a special hall was prepared in the imperial compound.

As recounted in the *Liaoshi*'s description of the wedding for an empress, the future empress rose early on the first day of the wedding ceremony and together with her entire clan awaited the imperial messengers, who came to the gates of her family compound bearing wine, food, and sacrificial animals. When these formalities were concluded, the future empress stepped into her wedding cart. Wine was served all around. As she left her home, the road filled with relatives and well-wishers, to whom the empress distributed gifts as she passed. Upon her arrival at the emperor's compound, she was invited by an older woman to descend from the cart. Carrying a silver jar and a weaving instrument, she walked along a specially prepared yellow carpet. Before her an older woman walked backward, facing her and holding a mirror, just as in a princess's wedding. The bride beheld her future in the woman facing her while viewing her past through the mirror. The bride then stepped over a saddle, a reference to the pastoralist lifestyle.

As the bride entered the wedding hall, she bowed to the emperor's ancestral tablets, probably a Chinese addition to the ceremony. The empress's sisters accompanied her. After honoring the imperial spirits, the bride and her sisters received gifts of clothing, pearls, jade, and other jewelry. The presence of the empress's sisters in the ceremony may have been a remnant of the sororate, when sisters were required to replace the empress in the marriage if she died or was unsatisfactory, for example, failing to produce a son. This custom emphasizes the practice of regarding marriage as a contract between families, not individuals.

The presence of an *ao* woman, as mentioned in connection with the marriage of a princess, was also required for an empress's wedding. On the second day, the emperor hosted a banquet for the empress's clan. The entertainment ranged from dancing to horse races and wrestling contests, and much ceremonial drinking ensued. On the third day, the emperor presented gifts to the bride's family and clan members, wine was again served, and the empress's family took their departure.[52] When the wedding ceremonies had concluded, the bride—whether an empress or an ordinary commoner—was separated from her natal family without right of return. In practice, however, imperial women seem to have kept up ties with their natal families, and the same may have been true for commoners.

To a culture counting wealth in terms of possessions and flocks rather than land, the gifts daughters brought to the family at their weddings, consisting of portable material goods and livestock, meant that the birth of a girl was greeted with joy and not viewed as a future burden on her family otherwise obliged to prepare a dowry for her. Girls were well treated in their natal families and enjoyed higher status and more perquisites than did their sisters in China. Payment of a bride-price, in kind or in labor—often both—was common among pastoralist peoples. The high status of girls was reflected in the willingness of these families to invest in education for their daughters, a matter examined in more detail in chapter 7. Formal, primary marriage, as described above, was only one of the forms of marriage available to the Kitan and Jurchen. Other recognized forms of marriage included levirate, sororate, and secondary marriage to concubines.

Marriage Diplomacy

Marriage alliances have sealed peace treaties and cemented diplomatic relations in many times and places. Marriages were arranged between daughters of Chinese noble families and high-ranking pastoralist chieftains (known as khans or kaghans) as far back as the Eastern Zhou state (771–256 BCE). Archaeological data from the Altai Mountains at the well-known Pazyryk site in Siberia shows that at least one Chinese bride was entombed with an Altaic tribal chieftain sometime in the fifth or sixth century BCE.[53] The first Han emperor formalized these exchanges, known as *heqin*, or "peace between relatives" treaties. After being defeated by the Xiongnu in 198 BCE, the emperor sent an imperial princess to Xiongnu chieftain Mao Dun.[54] Mao Dun even had the audacity to ask for Empress Lü's hand shortly after the first emperor's death. In 33 BCE a famous beauty and lady-in-waiting was sent in lieu of an imperial princess, ending the use of immediate members of the Liu family but continuing to exchange women in cross-cultural marriage alliances.[55] The purpose of such exchanges was to create brotherly relations between the two states and slowly seduce the barbarians into adopting peaceful Chinese customs and ceasing their warfare. And of course the abduction of Lady Wenji and her marriage to a Xianbei chieftain was also a form of diplomacy.

The use of women in diplomacy resumed during the Sui and Tang dynasties. For example, women and livestock were given to the Sui as prizes after their armies defeated Kitan forces in 605.[56] After the Kitan and the Xi had sworn allegiance to the Tang in 714, marriages with Tang princesses sealed the pact and maintained the peace. In 745, Tang princesses were again given to the Kitan and Xi leaders, only to be murdered at the end of that same year when the Kitan and Xi rebelled against the Tang.[57] Tang rulers also received Kitan women as gifts, although little is said about the reciprocal nature of such bargains in Chinese sources.

Song emperors, alert to the mistakes of the Tang, did not engage in marriage diplomacy, neither sending women to the "barbarians" nor receiving brides from the Kitan, Jurchen, or Xi Xia. Their refusal cut off one avenue of diplomacy between the Song and their adversaries to the north. In contrast, the Liao court sent a princess to marry a ruler of the Xia in 989, and in 1031 another Liao princess was married to the powerful Xia ruler Li Yuanhao.[58] A third princess was sent in 1105 as an effort to placate the Xia and convince them to join the Liao in a war against the Song.[59] Jurchen rulers also utilized marriage alliances to reinforce political and diplomatic ties. Clearly, marriage and politics were related issues.

The first Liao emperor, Abaoji, used his marriage with Empress Yingtian to obtain the support of her relatives, whose support was crucial to Abaoji's success in establishing an imperial institution in which sons succeed their fathers, as opposed to the traditional Kitan practice by which a kaghan selected by a council of elders served a three-year term, after which a new kaghan would be selected, an office to which Abaoji's brothers felt entitled.[60] To offset the ambitions of Abaoji's male relatives, the empress's relations, including her brothers and uncles, were integrated into the Liao state and given important offices and powers and later named as the Xiao clan.[61]

Aguda, the first Jin emperor, used marriage ties to secure support within Jurchen tribal affiliations, negotiate with the Bohai, and strengthen his claims to the imperial throne. The Jurchen, however, did not repeat the pattern of exclusive marriage clans. The imperial Wanyan clan members married widely among the Jurchen and Bohai and Kitan elite for political advantage. Aguda married several wives from other leading Jurchen clans and Bohai nobility and at least one Kitan woman from the Xiao clan.[62] Other noble Bohai were later incorporated into the Jurchen imperial house. In these ways, the Kitan and Jurchen leadership wove a complex web of marriage relationships that excluded their enemies and rewarded their supporters, thus building a multiethnic state. As was the case with the Xiao in the Liao state, the Bohai nobility in the Jin continued to rise in status, whereas the less-civilized Xi and the *sheng* Jurchen clans were marginalized and rejected by their own countrymen.

Generation-Gap Marriage

Another unique aspect of many Kitan and some Jurchen marriage arrangements was a deliberate generation gap. Males, especially among the elite, customarily married up into an ascending generation, while women married down to younger men. We do not know the relative ages of Abaoji and Empress Yingtian, but since she lived some thirty years beyond his death, she may well have been younger. However, the second emperor, Taizong, married a Xiao woman of an older generation.[63] Shizong's empress, Lady Zhen, was said to have been forty at the time of her marriage, thus making her older, but since the same passage says she bore him six sons, forty hardly seems likely.[64] The generation-gap pattern was followed in many, although not all, subsequent pairings.[65]

A senior in generation did not always mean older in years. It is possible, for example, in the case of two brothers that a child of the younger brother might be the same age as a grandchild of the elder brother, but the child of the younger brother would be senior in generational terms to the elder brother's grandchild. However, in general, Yelü women were older than their Xiao husbands and Xiao women were older than their Yelü spouses.[66] Noblewomen knew their husbands would be but boys when the marriages were solemnized.[67] The ages recorded for Yelü males at marriage are often surprisingly young, averaging only sixteen for prospective emperors. The prince who became Emperor Daozong (r. 1055–1101) was married at twelve. Although some imperial Yelü women married as young as twelve, most were between sixteen and twenty-two.[68] In several Liao tombs, archaeological excavations have revealed double burials where the woman is sometimes visibly more mature than the male, supporting the contention that Yelü and Xiao women married down. For example, two adjacent tombs (dated around 926) discovered at Baoshan, Chifeng, Inner Mongolia, near the Liao main capital, contained bodies of a married couple, of which the male, (Yelü) Qinde, was fourteen at the time of his death, while his wife (name unknown) was an adult.[69]

Generation-gap marriage was not absolute. Princess Chenguo, for example, was eighteen at the time of her death in 1018, whereas her husband, Xiao Shaoju, was sixteen years her senior.[70] The fifth Liao emperor, Jingzong, married Xiao (Chuo) Yanyan when she was fifteen, but he was in his late twenties. However, this is a case in which although younger in age, Yanyan may have been senior in generation, a point taken up in more detail in chapter 7. Princess Yueguo, whose marriage was discussed earlier, was younger than her husband, Xiao Xiaozhong, and apparently died much later than he, for the tomb at Kulunqi was dated somewhere in the 1080s. Jennifer Holmgren and Karl Wittfogel and Feng Chia-sheng have traced the marriage lines between the Yelü and Xiao clans but do not speculate on the actual ages of the persons involved in the marriage arrangements.[71]

Although Yelü-Xiao intermarriage was exclusive in theory, certain *haner* officials were permitted to marry Xiao or even Yelü daughters as a special mark of favor. Exceptional individuals like Hann Derang, discussed in more detail in chapters 6 and 7, were awarded honorary surname status as Yelü or Xiao.[72] Thus the high nobility of the Liao state became over time less a family of kin and more an extended status symbol.

In spite of these imperial exceptions, the primary marriage pattern in which younger males married somewhat older women was common among both upper- and lower-class Kitan. Although Jin sources are less explicit, the Jurchen also evidently followed the generation-gap pattern in arranging marriages, and the practice can also be seen among the later Manchus.

Secondary Marriage Practices: Sororate and Concubinage

Sororate was a steppe custom in which a man married two or more sisters at the same time or sequentially. The practice had echoes in China, for the legendary sage-king Shun was said to have married two sisters.[73] An epitaph for

Xiao Yulu recorded in the *Quan Liao wen* notes that he "married three women from the Yelü clan; the last two were sisters."[74] Several Liao inscriptions suggest sororate as well, since successive wives had the same surname. Customary behavior is notoriously difficult to eradicate. A Liao law in 939 lifted the requirement for sororate, but it continued in common practice, as repeated laws subsequently passed against it demonstrate.[75]

In another example, Emperor Daozong's empress, from the Xiao clan, who married the emperor in 1076, "came from a [younger] generation. . . . The emperor promoted her to the rank of empress but she did not conceive a child. . . . She said to the emperor, 'I have a younger sister who conceives easily, but she is now the wife of [Yelü] Yixin's son.' " The emperor forced the younger sister to divorce her husband and become his concubine.[76] Sororate was adopted by the *haner* under Liao rule as well. According to his epitaph (991), Hann Yu had two wives, both from the Xiao clan. The Hann clan was especially privileged because of the service of Hann Yanhui to the first emperor and Empress Yingtian, and his sons and grandsons had exceptional careers as government officials. After his first wife died, Hann Yu married a third Xiao daughter.[77] From the relatively frequent references in various sources, including funerary inscriptions, to marrying sisters, this practice appears to have been well entrenched in Liao and Jin society.

Both Liao and Jin practices came increasingly to follow those of the Chinese, with one wife and one or more concubines. Concubines were subordinate to a wife and had lower rank and fewer privileges. Women abducted or captured from rival states often became concubines. Imperial concubines were members of the inner court and were ranked much as in the Tang practice, beginning with Huifei (Gracious Concubine), Defei (Virtuous Concubine), Guifei (Valued Concubine), and so on.[78] Concubines who had won the emperor's favor could be raised above the others and were sometimes elevated to empress. Empress Qinai, for example, was praised because before her death she instructed Xiao *shi*, a concubine, on proper comportment when she should become empress.[79] An otherwise unremarkable concubine might be promoted to empress dowager when her son came to the throne, but in general concubines constituted a distinctly inferior category. An epitaph of 1075 praises Emperor Xingzong's empress, Renyi, for maintaining good relations with all the imperial relatives. She was also "in charge of all of the imperial concubines."[80]

Virginity was not a requirement for concubines. For example, the favorite concubine of Emperor Tianzuo (r. 1101–1125?), Xiao Wen *fei*, the daughter of the emperor's mother's brother, was a concubine of the emperor's kinsman, Yelü Tage, when Tianzuo first encountered her.[81] The emperor arranged a divorce and named her as his own concubine. She bore the emperor two children, after which she was even more favored by the emperor.[82] According to her epitaph, Wen *fei* had received an excellent education that included classical literature and history and was praised for her literary studies and love of reading.[83]

"Concubine" is often taken to be synonymous with palace intrigue. Concubines were not infrequently blamed for distracting an emperor. However, Wen *fei*, concubine to the notoriously lazy last emperor, Tianzuo, admonished the emperor and warned him against arrogant officials. In the poem below, she uses incidents from the Qin dynasty over a thousand years before, comparing Tianzuo to the second Qin emperor, who lost the state because he had depended on venal officials.

Using the Past to Instruct the Present

The prime minister's sword and ornaments jingle jangle in the court
The hundred officials resent him in their hearts but keep silent.
Disasters take place on the frontier, but what do our sighs accomplish?
Loyal officials are persecuted because [you/emperor] have no way of distinguishing good from bad.
The imperial in-laws have their own factions and domains.
Ministers and military men have their private armies.
We see from history that in such times the second emperor [of Qin] hoped for a peaceful reign in vain.[84]

Concubine Wen's warning fell on deaf ears. Emperor Tianzuo, like the Qin emperor, lost the state. We cannot of course be certain that a woman actually wrote this poem. The parallel with the Qin, which would only have made sense after the dynasty had been lost, suggests that it was written later and not by Wen *fei*. Male writers could use women's voices. The parallel between Tianzuo and the Qin emperor suggests that the poem was actually written sometime after the dynasty's fall as part of a cautionary story about neglectful emperors. But the story illustrates a significant point regarding women's literacy: Wen *fei* had to have been literate for the poem to be attributed to her.

Jin emperors Aguda, Wuqimai (r. 1123–1138), and others acquired concubines as a matter of course. Fan Chengda, who visited the Jin court, reported that the Jin palace housed many elegant favorites, including the ten consorts, among whom he named Prime Virtue, Chaste Beauty, and Gentle Reverence as outstanding. Fan goes on to note that government officials, even servitors and underlings, also took several wives, such that one could determine the official's rank from the number of wives he possessed. In contrast, Fan reports, "common people may take only one wife."[85] According to Hong Hao, ordinary Bohai women were exceptionally jealous and strong willed. Hong recounts a story of Da *shi*, who created a group of ten "sisters" from among her friends with the intention of detecting one another's husbands in indiscretions. "They did not allow the husbands to have concubines . . . [and] would kill [concubines] by poison." If one of their number was unaware of her husband's infidelities, the other nine "sisters" would tease her until she came to her senses and took action. "[These] women are very proud of their jealousy."[86] Therefore, though Kitan and Jurchen men could have relations with concubines, servants, and prostitutes, Bohai males were restricted by their women.

Nevertheless, commoners as well as the nobility had concubines, as clearly demonstrated by a passage in the *Jinshi* praising Yilayuliye, a Kitan commoner living under the Jin who had one wife and one concubine. His wife had six sons; the concubine had four, making an enviable total of ten sons:

> When his wife died, her sons moved to live near her grave and rotated staying by the grave overnight. The concubine's sons said, 'Although [she] was not our own mother, we still take part with our brothers.' So they rotated the duties over ten days, each taking one day, for three years. Not one day was missed. When the emperor learned of their story, he was moved and gave 500,000 in cash to reward this good behavior. These ten sons were truly an example to the whole country.[87]

Two points in this story are notable: first, that a Kitan commoner possessed concubines shows how widely the Chinese custom of taking concubines had spread in spite of claims to the contrary. Second, the reference to filial sons reflects the influence of Confucian ethics even among commoners.

Light is shed on *haner* marriage practices by tomb inscriptions and epitaphs. One inscription commemorates the family of a *haner* official, Zhang Jianli.[88] His tomb, constructed in 968 after the death of his first wife and one of his sons, housed Zhang's two wives, a son, and one of his two *niangzi* (young women). According to the inscription, Zhang had two wives simultaneously. His first wife, Yue *shi*, who came from a noble family, had three sons. Zhang's second wife, Fan *shi*, bore one son. Zhang also had two *niangzi*, who were twenty years his junior: Du *shi*, who "was very pretty ... and did all the work of the household," and Cao *shi*, who became a Buddhist nun after Zhang's death. She and Zhang's daughter built the tomb and reburied all the family members together.[89] Whether a *niangzi* had sexual relations with her husband is unclear. These *niangzi* were full members of Zhang's family, but neither seems to have had children. Their status seems to have been somewhere between concubine and adopted daughter.

Concubines were conspicuous in the Jin state at the imperial level as mothers of emperors. Raised by their sons to the status of empress dowager, these women were praised for their knowledge and sage advice. Aguda, Prince Ruizong, Hailing *wang*, and Shizong all had Bohai concubines. The mothers of Hailing and Shizong also came from Bohai nobility.

One story of a conniving concubine involves Chen *fei* and the Jin emperor Zhangzong. As the pampered grandson of Emperor Shizong, Zhangzong had been spoiled and was easily distracted by flattering ministers and devious women. His favorite minister, Jiang Yuan, always spoke "with a sweet tongue." Jiang recommended Chen *fei*, a beautiful dancing girl, who was "exceedingly charming and cunning." The emperor fell in love with her, "visiting her morning and evening." More than once after drinking with her into the night, he missed his morning audience, leaving authority in the hands of Jiang Yuan. Sometimes the concubine sat on his lap while he gave her the vermilion brush (to sign imperial documents).

Chen *fei* consoled the emperor when he was saddened over battle losses, holding his wine cup and singing. "Defeat," she said, "is not uncommon. . . . Don't pay it any attention." The emperor continued to drink from morning to evening and so neglected his duties and spoiled Chen *fei*. Even military reports came first to Chen *fei*, who concealed any bad news. Thus the emperor was unaware of disastrous defeats until one day two generals reported to him in person. Shocked to hear the truth, he asked those around him, "Why didn't you tell me? Did you not know?" The general replied, "Throughout history, disasters have been caused by women with long tongues."[90]

On the basis of this tale, Chen *fei* joins a select number of concubines, led by the celebrated Yang *guifei*, consort of the star-crossed Tang emperor Ming Huang, who brought down empires by so distracting the sovereign that he neglected his duties. The simplistic rhetoric of the story marks it as a moral cautionary tale. However, the Jin state did not fall during the reign of Zhangzong. Only with his successors, Weishao *wang* and Xuanzong, did the Mongols first gain a foothold, conquering the Jin state in 1234.

The historical sources and literary accounts view concubines in a mixed light. On the one hand, concubines were a well-entrenched institution at the Liao and Jin imperial palaces. Some were sincere in attempting to correct an emperor's failings, but others—more so than empresses—could be blamed for seducing an emperor from his duties.

The Status of Women in Liao and Jin Society

The Chinese had long observed a division between male and female in all social activities. Women's sexual behavior depended to a large degree on their cultural identity. In Liao and Jin society, virginity was not a prerequisite, and girls enjoyed sexual freedom prior to marriage. Abduction marriage was common among high and low alike. Betrothal and marriage traditions had a profound effect on women's status since daughters were viewed as assets who would bring betrothal and marriage gifts into the family rather than as nuisances who had to be provided with dowries by their natal families. However, the absence of dowries meant that Liao and Jin women had no resources of their own to fall back on if widowed or divorced. Their possessions, their children, and their bodies belonged to their husbands' families.

Apparently contradictory values are reflected in the *Liaoshi*'s *lienü zhuan* chapter in which the Liao princess Changge is praised for lecturing the emperor on Confucian ethics while three other women are honored for following their husbands in death.[91] Women living under Liao and Jin rule combined steppe and Han practices in a wide variation of interpretations. Practices such as following in death, levirate marriage, and Buddhist seclusion had lasting effects on Chinese concepts of chastity and widow purity.[92]

Sexuality and Marriage

The high value initially placed on the birth of a girl in the Liao and Jin states gradually eroded as Chinese norms of female education, sexuality, and chastity were introduced. *Haner* women appear to have been more constrained socially. Families who adopted the customs of their rulers also gave women high status. Kitan and Jurchen women experienced increasing exposure to Chinese influences during the course of the conquest dynasties and adopted Chinese customs and values selectively. Women's education in the Confucian classics was lauded in Liao and Jin society. As soon as families began viewing female children in terms of a dowry rather than as an asset, the status of women entered a decline.

FIVE

Widowhood and Chastity

EMPEROR TAIZU, the first emperor of the Liao dynasty, died in the late summer of 926 and was laid to rest after a long period of mourning.[1] One can imagine the scene of the concluding ceremony, held on a bleak afternoon of a bitterly cold day in the last month in the second year of Taizong's reign. The sky was dark with low, scudding clouds and stinging snow was blown horizontal by the wind—then suddenly red blood stained the white ground! According to the *Liaoshi*, when the emperor died, his wife, Empress Chunqin, took the title of Yingtian as empress dowager, *taihou*, and "assumed the reins of government." She had made known her wish to conform to steppe custom and follow the emperor in death. Thus she lulled the suspicions of the emperor's relatives, who plotted to seize the throne. But when the time came to bury the emperor, she stepped forward at the last moment and—in a dramatic gesture—seized a sword and "cut off her right hand at the wrist and threw it into the grave." Thereafter, according to the account in the *Liaoshi*, "the empress ruled the country in both civil and military matters."[2]

The *Kitan guozhi*, composed in the twelfth century, which is an earlier account than the fourteenth-century *Liaoshi* and one of its sources, tells the story as given above much as it was repeated in the *Liaoshi*. But the *Kitan guozhi* also includes a second biography of Empress Yingtian. In this telling, Yingtian "used her wisdom and power to make [her second son] Deguang emperor." However, before his death Abaoji (Taizu) had named his eldest son, Bei, to succeed him. When some of the Kitan nobles protested the choice of the second son, Yingtian ordered them to submit their protests to Taizu him-

106

self. When they arrived at the imperial grave site, they found Yingtian had prepared a surprise. She had more than a hundred dissident officials killed. However, one official, Zhao Siwen, either had not been present at the time or had refused the invitation to commit suicide with the other officials and nobles. He went to the emperor's tomb later, alone with the empress. "Yingtian said to him, 'You were very intimate with Taizu, so why do you refuse to follow [him in death]?' Siwen replied, 'No one was closer than your majesty; if you go, I will follow you.' She said, 'It is not my decision not to follow Taizu in death, but my sons are young and weak. The country lacks an emperor. So I cannot follow Taizu.' Therefore, she cut off her hand to accompany him."[3] This second account has the ring of truth. Instead of a dramatic gesture at the imperial funeral, the empress made her sacrifice alone with only Zhao Siwen accompanying her. Like the Xiao family heroines in the *lienü zhuan*, the deed was done privately sometime after the funeral ceremonies. The *Kitan guozhi* makes no effort to reconcile the two accounts or clarify the differences. But one implication of the story as told in the *Kitan guozhi* is an exoneration of the empress in the deaths of the court officials and an implication that they committed suicide voluntarily.

Thereafter, Yingtian enjoyed, as a widow, her period of greatest power. In the crucial months after the emperor's death, the empress persuaded her eldest son, Prince Bei, whom the late emperor had chosen as his successor, to stand aside and allow Deguang to assume the throne. She monitored government affairs during her son's reign and, after Deguang's death, led an imperial revolt in an attempt to put her third son, Lihu, on the throne. At her death she was buried with full military honors and an *ordo* (battalion) was set to guard her grave. Empress Dowager Yingtian's refusal to follow her husband in death highlights the problems widows faced in the Liao and Jin periods.

The Widow Problem

Widowhood presented a special challenge for women. Remarriage of widows was a sensitive issue in Kitan and Jurchen societies, where wives became the property of their husbands' families. Chastity was not expected of unmarried girls but was required after marriage. As related in chapter 4, a husband and his family had, in effect, purchased the bride's sexual services and any children she bore. Many epitaphs praise women's purity and loyalty after marriage. Once widowed, however, women could not return to their natal homes, where their parents might arrange a new marriage, as frequently happened in Song China.[4] According to steppe tradition, a Liao widow had only two alternatives, suicide or levirate. As time went on and more Chinese influence was accepted in Liao society, some widows sought release from these alternatives by becoming Buddhist nuns and, increasingly over the three hundred years of the Liao and Jin dynasties, by remaining as chaste widows in their own homes. The Jin state legislated—ineffectively—against widow suicide but continued to support levirate.

Many scholars regard practices involving dowries and widowhood as touchstones of cultural attitudes.[5] As Mark Elliott has pointed out, widows were economically vulnerable, ritually superfluous, potentially socially destabilizing, and sexually threatening.[6] Whether a woman was purchased with a bride-price or brought a dowry into her marriage influenced her position and conduct within marriage and her opportunities both inside marriage and if widowed. With no dowries to support them, Liao and Jin widows had few alternatives. The death of a husband was the ultimate calamity in steppe society—as everywhere in preindustrial society—since life in any household headed by a woman on her own would be extremely precarious.[7] The customs of bride purchase and levirate ensured that the deceased husband's family would take care of a widow and her children. Levirate reinforced the idea that marriage was a contract between families, and women were regarded as property and could be inherited like any chattel. The *levir*, brother, stepson, or nephew, who married the widow was required to be younger than the former husband. Marriage with a male relative older than the late husband was a serious transgression in Liao, Jin, and Mongol society.[8]

Elliott and others identify following in death as a widespread Altaic custom,[9] and Karl Wittfogel and Feng Chia-sheng believe that it was required of the widow of a ruler prior to Empress Yingtian's famous refusal.[10] Women, as many archaeological reports have confirmed, were often buried together with their husbands, although suicide probably cannot be confirmed. If a widow outlived her husband, his tomb was usually reopened for a later burial. Even after Yingtian's sacrifice, following in death remained honored throughout the dynasty, as illustrated by the stories of virtuous Xiao women in the *lienü zhuan* chapter of the *Liaoshi*, discussed in chapter 1.[11] Elliott shows that following in death continued to be practiced among the Manchus and to a lesser extent among other banner minorities as late as the Qing period.[12] Following in death should not be confused with the Confucian cult of widow chastity that emerged in subsequent dynasties, which, in its most extreme expression, took the form of suicide—usually by drowning or hanging.[13]

Levirate remained a common custom during the Liao and Jin periods and was still prominent among the Mongols, which Holmgren characterizes as a strategy "for the preservation of the social and economic integrity of the family."[14] The rule proscribing a widow's marriage to her late husband's elder brother or uncle was strictly observed in both Liao and Jin society. Hong Hao reported on one specific instance where this rule was broken, but only with imperial permission. The first Jin emperor, Aguda, had eight sons, the eldest of whom, Gulun, was the son of a concubine. When the empress's eldest son, Shenguo, died, Gulun took his brother's wife in a levirate marriage. Gulun was older than Shenguo and should not therefore have been allowed to marry her. But "since the younger brother had a higher status, it was allowed."[15] According to the *Da Jin guozhi*, "When the father dies, the son will marry the mother; when the older brother dies, the younger brother will marry the elder's wife. When the uncle dies, the nephew will marry his wife. Everyone has more than one wife, no matter how rich or poor."[16] The *Da Jin guozhi* was written by a Song scholar, Yuwen Maozhao and therefore must be taken with caution since Chinese authors tended to exaggerate the more exotic or "barbaric" aspects of Liao and Jin society. Levirate was deeply shocking to Song Chinese observers, who found it equivalent to incest, one of the strictest of Chinese taboos.[17] Thus Yuwen's inclusion of sons marrying mothers was probably designed to shock his audience and in any case was not true, although a stepson might marry his deceased father's wife, who was not his birth mother. Chinese sources often cite levirate as proof of the uncivilized behavior of "barbarians" and castigated practices like levirate and sororate as "fornicating like dogs or pigs."[18]

Levirate had an obvious appeal to spousal families wishing to keep the economic resources of a widow and ensure inheritance and succession of heirs.[19] Even *haner* and Bohai peoples adopted the custom. Jin emperor Shizong first issued a prohibition in 1169 against cultural groups other than Kitan and Jurchen practicing levirate, effectively banning the practice among Bohai and Chinese. Han and Bohai widows, according to this edict, could return to their natal homes and remarry.[20] But popular custom—and greedy in-laws—demanded levirate be continued, so in 1170 Shizong reversed himself and issued a second decree allowing *hanren* and Bohai to continue the practice of levirate marriages.[21] However, the Jin law code known as the *Taihe* code again outlawed the practice among Chinese in 1201.[22] If these successive decrees seem contradictory and confusing, it would not be the first time that legal regulations differed from common practice. The new regulation required only that such marriages must follow the rites, although what those rites were was not specified.[23]

Although Emperor Shizong stoutly maintained that common Jurchen had only one wife, all classes of society practiced levirate and therefore many, if not most, men had more than one wife. The apparent opposition between levirate as practiced and the emperor's claim that his subjects were monogamous can be explained in one of two ways: either the Jin did not consider a wife acquired by levirate as contrary to monogamy, or Jin practices changed over time. Older women married to much younger men in levirate unions may have been treated as merely family dependents or honored aunts.

Violations also occurred. Hailing *wang* was guilty of several transgressions involving the rules of levirate and reportedly killed his uncle so he could marry his wife.[24] This story ought to be taken with caution, however, since both Jin and Chinese sources delight in attributing all kinds of sexual transgressions to Hailing *wang*. Another such instance is reported in the *Jinshi*. In 1138, Prince Changsheng, brother of Emperor Xizong, died, leaving a widow. Xizong married the widow, but he later killed his empress and several concubines, intending to make his brother's widow the new empress.[25] Xizong as the younger brother was within his rights in marrying the widow but not in murdering his empress and concubines.

Remarriage of widows other than in levirate was prohibited. The strength of rules against remarriage is illustrated by one of the few exceptions, when, early in the Liao period, a group of men who had lost their wives during warfare petitioned to be allowed to marry widows. Because they came from clans that had supported Abaoji's claim to the throne, the second emperor granted their request.[26] Regulations against remarriage of widows applied especially to wives of deceased officials, who presumably might be role models for others.[27] Many were *haner* officials, and thus the prohibition extended to the Chinese population under Liao control. Strictures against the remarriage of widows in any form other than levirate continued to be a problem well into the Jin period. Critics were especially vocal on issues of remarriage and levirate after the Jin conquest of northern China; statutes forbidding levirate for the Han population began to appear toward the end of the dynasty, suggesting levirate became less common as the dynasty progressed.

Widows and Chastity

The frontier zone was a place of cultural contact and exchange; as a result, both pastoralist and Chinese customs flourished there. As the Liao dynasty wore on, more Chinese customs were selectively adopted, including some involving widows. The custom of following in death was certainly a compelling reason for widows who did not wish to die to seek alternatives, and levirate may have been distasteful to many women. Thus, widow chastity and Buddhist retreat became attractive alternatives. Women who chose these options, according to their epitaphs, were almost always *haner* or Han. Such choices may have been influenced by the desires of women themselves or by the contempt the Chinese generally held for levirate.

Increasingly, widows could remain unmarried and stay in their homes to raise their children. After the passage of a number of years, these women seem to have been left in peace even after their children were grown, as neither following in death nor levirate seemed appropriate at that point. Although social customs did not extol or honor widows who remained chaste for many years after their husbands' deaths, widow chastity became more popular as each of the northern states adopted ethical practices that were more Confucian in character.

Inscriptions preserved from the Liao period praise women who had remained faithful to their betrothed spouses, even if the marriage had not yet taken place. As seen in chapter 4, betrothals were taken seriously in Liao society. Women, either betrothed or married, undertook an enduring obligation to their husbands and spousal families. Living as a chaste widow had precedents in the lives of women who either had been widowed during the betrothal period or did not marry at all. Yelü Changge, discussed in chapter 1, did not marry but "remained pure." The numbers of Liao tombs in which women are the sole occupants also suggest that other women may never have married. The later age at which women married under the generation-gap custom also suggests that having waited until perhaps the age of twenty-eight or thirty, some women failed to marry at all. The alternative, therefore, was for an unmarried woman to live chastely within her natal family and earn praise and respect as a single woman—a choice not available to women in China proper, where all girls were expected to marry out of the natal household.

Funeral steles of women with *haner* names do not mention following in death or levirate. They do, however, frequently mention widows who remained chaste or sought asylum in Buddhism. Maintaining chastity either through self-restraint or by retiring into a Buddhist institution was becoming an option for Liao women toward the end of the dynasty and was much more common during the Jin period. This trend suggests that Confucian values may have influenced such women. Some remained in the family household, and others chose to enter Buddhist nunneries, as shown in the epitaph below:

> Wang Ze dedicated this stone for his stepmother, Qiu *shi*, in 1051. His own mother died when he was small and his father married Qiu *shi*. After the death of his father, she became a nun. Wang Ze was so filial that he [still] paid respects to his stepmother . . . and supported her financially.[28]

In another example, an inscription on a pagoda, dated 1101, tells of Li *shi*, who married a prime minister of the Liao state [name omitted]. When widowed at the age of thirty-six, "she refused to remarry but stayed in the home to care for her children. Then, after they were grown, she cut her hair and became a nun."[29] Thus, raising children may have been a valid excuse for a widow to remain single, avoiding levirate.

As Buddhism became increasingly significant in Liao and Jin society, more women found convents a convenient refuge from the restrictions placed on widows. There they could live out their lives without fearing they might be forced to follow in death or marry in-laws. Buddhism's popularity among women and the support they offered to the Buddhist establishment are discussed in more detail in chapter 6.

Bettine Birge has linked the tradition of levirate and women's desire to avoid it to the development of a cult of widow chastity in the Yuan period.[30] However, avoidance of suicide or levirate was not the same thing as a woman's dedication to Confucian ethics. Jennifer Holmgren underscores this point in noting that "it is . . . incorrect to speak of 'widow chastity' within the tribal elite of the Yuan era as examples of acculturation or sinicization."[31] Further exploration of the widow problem with regard to sexuality can be found in chapter 6, in the story of the Jin warrior woman Yang Miaozhen, and in chapter 7 in the story of the romance of Empress Dowager Chengtian and her high minister of state, Hann Derang, and whether or not it might have been considered adultery.

Adultery

The sight of women in social situations together with men both in public and in private was commonplace in the Liao and Jin states. The general ease with which men and women mingled in public places and at the Liao and Jin courts impressed Song observers like Fan Chengda, who no doubt took the presence of women on the streets as another sign of "barbarism."

Because the Liao and Jin, unlike the Song, did not practice separation of the sexes, men were not prohibited from the inner quarters of homes and palaces, nor were these areas reserved exclusively for women. But women who were seen in the frequent company of men other than their husbands in the inner quarters might be vulnerable to accusations of adultery. An example of the way in which the presence of a man in the inner quarters could lead to tragedy is demonstrated by the story of Liao empress Yide, wife of Emperor Daozong (r. 1055–1101).

As recounted in an inscription from the *Quan Liao wen* collection, the Liao minister Yelü Yixin submitted a memorial to Daozong in 1070. Yixin began by asserting that he had come into possession of the testimony of a palace maid named Deng who recounted the empress's behavior with a singer named Zhao Weiyi. Zhao had originally been invited to the palace to entertain the emperor, but the empress was so taken with his performance that she persuaded the emperor to give him special permission to play for her in the rear palace (women's quarters). While the emperor was away, Empress Yide invited the singer to entertain her. The maid Deng reported that

> [the empress] played a musical instrument and sang songs to his accompaniment. As darkness fell, she asked the maid to light the lamps and then to

leave them alone. But, thinking this strange, the maid stayed outside the room to eavesdrop.... The empress then asked the singer to remove his outer official clothing so that he might be more at ease [and] did the same herself. They played music and drank wine until midnight. After midnight, the music stopped but the maid still heard their voices and laughter, and according to the noises she heard, the maid became excited and her heart moved within her, so she crept closer.

She heard the empress promise the singer a high rank. The singer replied that he was just a small snake and could not compare with the emperor, a real dragon. The empress said that he was indeed "a very active small snake, which was much better than a big lazy dragon." After that, there was silence, but certain noises continued.[32]

Before dawn, the empress called the maid to come in and awake the singer and help him dress. Before he left, the empress gave him gold and silks.

When the emperor returned several days later, he asked for Zhao Weiyi, but the singer was afraid to appear. The empress, who deeply missed the singer, wrote a poem expressing her regret. The singer unwisely showed this poem to a friend, who seized it and gave it to Yelü Yixin.

Upon receiving Yixin's memorial, the emperor apparently found the story plausible. Yixin declared furthermore that the maid's report was supported by a second, unnamed, palace attendant. The conversation that supposedly took place between the empress and the singer was calculated to enrage the emperor. The conditions that made this tale credible included the custom of permitting males access to the inner palace quarters, a privilege extended usually only to family members. But the entire story was in fact false—part of a plot to remove the empress and the crown prince, who stood in the way of Yixin's ambitions, so that a woman of Yixin's choice could be installed in the emperor's harem and might then become empress. Daozong was deceived and ordered the empress to commit suicide. Although Empress Yide was later exonerated, both she and the prince had already been put to death.

But while Yixin's tale deceived the emperor, other officials suspected treachery. Wang Ding, an official serving in the Liao government, maintained that the empress had been wrongly accused. Wang blamed Yixin for the crime, noting, "officials ... all want to report strange and exciting news in order to bring attention to themselves." He observed that, "from ancient times, all disasters of state are caused by the small things [*xiaoshi*]." The first mistake according to Wang had been allowing the singer to enter the women's quarters. Moreover, the maid acted improperly by "wrongly listening to what went on behind the screens." Further, Wang noted, "[if] the empress had not been accused and put to death, her son, the crown prince, would also not have died, [for] he was the heir. If the crown prince had not died, the emperor would not [have reason for] regret." But the empress herself was not free from blame. Wang enumerated the reasons for this tragedy. First, the empress was too fond of music and too adept at playing, and second, "if the empress had not been so well educated, she could not have written the incriminating poem."[33]

Wang's remarks reveal a deeply Confucian sense of ethics. He implicitly believed in separation of the sexes and argued that women should not be allowed to invite men into their quarters. He condemned education for women, since, as he noted, "teaching them to play music and have beautiful calligraphy invites dangers."[34] However, Kitan society did not necessarily share Wang's opinion. A surprising number of elite women in the Liao state were well educated, as is discussed in greater detail in chapter 7.

The denouement of this tale is told in Yixin's biography in the *Liaoshi*, contained in the chapter on "Treacherous Officials." Yixin, "a handsome man," became a low-ranking government official during the reign of Emperor Xingzong (r. 1031–1055). One of his duties was to care for the imperial seal, so he had an opportunity to enter the inner quarters. The empress appreciated him for his fine manners and so she recommended him for promotion. The chronicle notes, "The higher he rose, the more corrupt he became."[35]

When Emperor Daozong came to the throne, Yixin became envious of the crown prince, and so he conceived a plot against the empress in which he accused her of adultery with the court singer. After her death, he replaced her with his own protégée, whom the emperor married and made empress. Yixin rose to an even higher position in the government, but he still harbored envy of the crown prince, so he accused the prince of plotting to depose the emperor and take over the government. Once again, the emperor believed Yixin and imprisoned the crown prince, who was then murdered by Yixin's henchmen. Only when he found that his son had been killed did the emperor realize the depth of Yixin's treachery. Yixin was exiled but apparently died a natural death. But when Emperor Tianzuo (1101–1125) came to the throne, he had Yixin's body exhumed and torn into "a thousand pieces."[36]

This story is not only intriguing for its drama and pathos but also reveals some of the customs and ethical standards of the period. Clearly, sexual relations outside marriage were prohibited for elite women and also for commoners. However, while a part of the palace grounds were marked off as inner quarters, visiting males were not necessarily excluded from them. Male family members and guests were permitted in the women's private spaces.[37] The empress's supposed transgression was not so much in entertaining the singer in her private quarters as in engaging in sexual relations with him.

Adultery was punishable under both Liao and Jin statutes. But the definition of adultery was somewhat slippery, and the documents show that the Jin, in particular, wrestled with the problem. In 1123, the Jin emperor Taizong ruled that "men and women who are related by marriage [stepbrothers and stepsisters] cannot marry."[38] Such conduct would constitute adultery except, of course, in cases of levirate. According to an imperial Jin mandate of 1170, officials' wives who had committed adultery were prohibited from enjoying their husbands' ranks, but women who had attained a certain rank because of a father's or son's position were not so affected, even if guilty. Herbert Franke suggests that passage of this law means that the Jin did not fully define nor prohibit adultery prior to that date, except in specific cases.[39]

Normally the charge of adultery applied only to women since men were polygamous. However, under some circumstances a man could be guilty of adultery. In 1137, Qu Renzhi, the son of a high minister of the Jin state, committed adultery with one of the concubines of the emperor known as Yuan *fei*. Both were sentenced to death.[40] In this case, the man suffered equally because he had seduced an imperial concubine. And when Emperor Shizong's son's concubine committed adultery in 1177, she was executed and her father was demoted and his titles were removed.[41]

Both the Liao and Jin punished a wife's adultery outside the household. But whether sexual relations within the spousal family constituted adultery is questionable. Relations within the family might have been tolerated so long as the wife had relations with only younger males in the family, since if widowed she would be expected to marry one of them. Shuo Wang has recently examined cases of murder in the early Qing period, in which a Manchu male killed his Manchu wife. These cases reveal that Manchu women in the seventeenth and eighteenth centuries could be accused of adultery if they allowed male family members into the inner quarters. The women defended themselves on the basis that Manchu customs were permissive on these matters and even having sexual relations with younger male family members was defensible according to the old customs. The husbands, however, who had become acculturated to stricter Chinese standards of morality, not infrequently flew into a rage and killed the offending woman. According to Wang's analysis, these women lived by the old Manchu rules, while their husbands, who were accustomed to moving about in Qing society, had adopted more sinicized standards and expectations for womanly behavior.[42] Inasmuch as the Manchus were the direct descendants of the thirteenth-century Jurchen, it is not surprising that these old customs stretch back to the Jin period.

Divorce

The Liao and Jin were as lenient on questions of divorce and remarriage after divorce as they were strict about the remarriage of widows. Many cases of divorce and remarriage are cited in the annals and inscriptions of both states. For example, in the reign of Shengzong, a Kitan princess and her husband obtained a divorce in 983 on the grounds of incompatibility. The princess had the higher rank, so her husband, a capital official, was blamed for their differences and exiled to a minor post in the hinterland.[43] In another example:

> Empress Qin'ai bore two daughters, the first of whom, Yenmujin, married Xiao Chuobu. Yenmujin [later] married again to Xiao Haili, but as they were not compatible, she divorced him and married Xiao Hudu. Again there was incompatibility. She divorced Hudu and married the prince of Han, Xiao Hui.[44]

Yelü women married males only of the Xiao clan, no matter how many divorces or remarriages might be involved.

Divorce could be initiated by women, and no barriers to remarriage existed in cases of divorce. Emperors could arrange divorces for women whom they wished to add to their harem, as in the case of the Liao emperor Tianzuo, cited earlier.[45] Divorce could even be part of a punishment: in the 1032–1055 reign period, a member of the imperial clan, Yelü Shucheng, was convicted of a crime that had actually been committed by his wife. When the case came up for judgment, it was ruled that they should divorce.[46] Jin laws emphasized that women were their husbands' property, but a new law established in 1145 allowed most regulations to follow the Song legal code. However, a few items differed from the Song code. For example, beating a wife to death carried no punishment unless a knife was used. Women apparently took exception to this law as unduly harsh, since the Song law had forbidden wife beating altogether.[47] Jin attitudes on divorce and remarriage were permissive in the early part of the dynasty, but they later changed. Because of Hailing *wang*'s exploitation of divorce—he did not hesitate to kill husbands who demurred—divorce became less popular and marital fidelity more honored under his successor, Emperor Shizong, and subsequent rulers. The critical moment of transition may have taken place when Wulinda *shi*, wife of the future Emperor Shizong, refused to comply with Hailing's orders to leave her husband:

> [Shizong's] wife was from the Wulinda clan and was noted for her beauty. Summoned by Hailing *wang*, she was ordered to divorce her husband and become Hailing's concubine. She said to Shizong, "If I do not go, it will mean certain death for you. I must go to protect us from Hailing's retribution." When she reached Liangxiang, a place halfway along the road, she took her own life. Thereafter Shizong honored her, and during his lifetime he raised no other woman to the position of empress.[48]

By obeying Hailing *wang*'s command, she shielded her husband from his wrath. By taking her own life, she refused to prostitute herself and thus preserved her chastity. In so doing, she met both Jurchen and Chinese standards as a virtuous woman. Consequently, chastity was more frequently praised during and after Shizong's reign. The ease of divorce and the lack of strictures against remarriage in such cases represent additional pastoralist customs practiced by the Liao and Jin that shocked Chinese to the south.

Conclusion

Widowhood, divorce, widow chastity, adultery, and remarriage are complex issues. From following in death and levirate as the only options for widows, customs on widowhood expanded and changed. Buddhist retreat became more common and, as time went on, women, especially Han or *haner* women, could remain as chaste widows in their own homes—although not in the homes of their husbands' families, where they would have been subject to levirate. But Liao and Jin strictures were consistent on one major point: other than in levirate, a widowed woman could not remarry. State laws and customs varied as to the degree to which pastoralist practices affected the Han and *haner* populations under their control—at one point denying levirate to Bohai and Chinese and yet at another allowing both Bohai and Chinese to enforce levirate on widows. Remaining chaste as an unmarried woman, as a betrothed woman whose intended spouse has died, or as a widow became an option for Liao and Jin women. Divorce, on the other hand, was available to women, and remarriage after divorce carried no stigma.

One curious point, and one that will come up again in chapters 6 and 7, is whether widows could engage in sexual relations, which may have been tacitly permitted. For those who chose chaste widowhood, this may not have been an issue. Obviously chastity was not expected of widows who made a levirate remarriage. But, as in the case of adultery, sources are unclear on this point. As we shall see in chapter 6, Yang Miaozhen, a Jin warrior woman, seduced a rival general at a time when she believed herself to have been widowed. Song sources castigate her for this lapse, but Jin sources omit any mention of the incident.[49] Even more problematic is the behavior of the Liao empress dowager Chengtian *taihou*, who was widowed at the age of thirty. She is reputed to have taken as her lover her chief minister, Hann Derang, with whom she enjoyed a nearly thirty-year relationship that lasted until her death. The same sources that relate this tale also point out that prior to her marriage to the emperor she had been betrothed to Derang. Did a prior betrothal justify sexual relations at a later date? Were prohibitions on a widow's remarriage flexible as to her later relationships? The Song sources relating this story are clearly critical of the empress's behavior, but this incident is examined in more detail in the context of Liao society in chapter 7.

The reader should also beware lest one's twenty-first-century notions intrude upon an understanding of how women in the tenth through twelfth centuries may have regarded widow-related alternatives. We perhaps find repugnant women's following in death or undergoing a levirate remarriage. But the Liao and Jin *lienü* chapters describe women's embracing following in death voluntarily, even joyfully. Jin heroines sought death in different contexts: to shame a husband into fighting, to preserve their husbands' reputations, or to avoid rape or remarriage. Women who chose to preserve their lives for the ostensible reason of caring for their children sometimes found it necessary to justify their decision or apologize for it. Nor were such customs unique to the Kitan and Jurchen. Widow suicide was also practiced since early times in China, as attested by female skeletons buried with the king as early as the Shang dynasty, and in other cultures. One well-known example of widow suicide is the Hindu custom of sati, in which a wife immolates herself on her deceased husband's funeral pyre. Following in death for widows and others close to the deceased was a widespread Altaic custom. One alternative that was preferred in Chinese culture, a widow's joining the household of a son, does not seem to be mentioned in Liao and Jin references, possibly because it was common and therefore did not merit special attention. Certainly, joining a son or daughter's family was a common practice in China and elsewhere, for example in Europe.[50] The practices of Kitan and Jurchen widows outlined here that seem to have had the most long-lasting effects, however—levirate and its alternatives, Buddhist retreat, and widow chastity, which became hallmarks of various later conquest and Chinese societies—developed only slowly.

The extent to which women were able to make their own decisions in these matters is not always clear. Empress Yingtian exercised her own agency and power when she refused to follow the emperor in death and instead sacrificed her hand. The Xiao women in the *Liaoshi*'s *lienü* chapter made and carried out their decisions to follow their dead husbands in secret. Even Yingtian, in the more plausible version of her story, went sometime after the funeral with only one person accompanying her to the emperor's grave site. But many women were unable to avoid levirate unless they had children to raise or the opportunity for Buddhist retreat. Urbanization may also have been a factor in successfully pursuing an alternative. A widow in the pastoralist culture on the steppes was clearly vulnerable. Thus, for her, a levirate remarriage may have been a blessing, or she might have voluntarily embraced following in death. A widow in an urban setting, however, may well have had greater access to alternatives since she lived in a more protective environment where it might have been possible, given financial means or support from relatives, to remain as a chaste widow or to join a Buddhist institution. Since many more Han Chinese women lived in cities during the Liao and Jin periods, they may have had more opportunities to become chaste widows or Buddhist nuns.

SIX

Warrior Women

As the *Liaoshi* reports, Liao women, including empresses and imperial concubines, were skilled in military affairs, shooting, and riding. Many were well educated, and some proved to be skilled and capable administrators as well. Considered fully in their time and place, the warrior women of the Liao were truly unprecedented. Among the most remarkable were three women discussed in this chapter. The first is Empress Yingtian, wife of the first Liao emperor, Abaoji, who assisted the emperor on numerous occasions in military affairs and commanded her own military division. The second is the Liao empress dowager Chengtian, who ran the state as regent for her son, Emperor Shengzong, for nearly thirty years and led Liao armies to victory over the Song at the Battle of Chanyuan.

The third exceptional martial figure is Yang Miaozhen, a warrior woman at the end of the Jin dynasty who led her troops variously for and against the Song and Mongol forces and is celebrated as a Jin heroine. Dynastic histories stick to established conventions when presenting officially sanctioned sketches of virtuous women, portraits of imperial women, or, in the case of Yang Miaozhen, tales of dastardly women associated with evil officials. They emphasize the qualities that society esteemed or conventional traits denoting undesirable aspects. The sources used for this chapter include the Liao, Jin, and Song dynastic histories and unofficial histories, including the *Kitan guozhi*, and inscriptions collected in the *Quan Liao wen*, as well as a variety of secondary accounts. I argue in this chapter that women's martial actions can best be understood in the historical context of the Liao and Jin periods, but the activities of neither female regents nor martial women were unique, since other examples dot the histories of the Song, Yuan, and Xixia states as well.

Empress Yingtian

Empress Yingtian (878–953) was arguably the most famous woman of the northern conquest dynasties. The story of the dramatic sacrifice of her hand to avoid following the emperor in death has been told in chapter 5. Let us here explore her activities as a warrior woman.

Yingtian's official biography in the *Liaoshi* states,

> [She] was a daughter of the Shulü clan; her childhood name was Mingle. Her ancestors were Huihu dating back to [an ancestor named] Nuosi.... Her father was Pogu Yuewan, who was an official of the Yaonian tribe, who married the daughter of the Yundejia king. She was born in Kitan territory.[1]

Immediately clear from this entry is that Yingtian, and probably many women like her, came from a mixed background. Inasmuch as her line, later given the surname Xiao, became the exclusive marriage clan to the imperial Yelü line and its members took their place among the highest Kitan nobility, the identity of the empress's clan is of some interest but is also a source of some confusion. This clan was descended through several generations from the Huihu, usually understood as Uygur. Taizong's genealogy complicates the issue by making a point that the empress's mother had been a member of the Yaonian clan, a Kitan clan.[2] Intermarriage for political and security reasons was a common practice among the steppe pastoralists. However, the text here mentions a specific clan, Yaonian, and then provides a generalized reference to the Uygur but not to a specific branch or clan. Putting these two statements together, a possible assumption is that the Shulü had Uygur ancestors. The biography of Abaoji's mother also lists her as a member of the Yaonian clan.[3] Even if this reference borders on the mythic, it indicates a high regard for the Yaonian clan, though it separates them from the Kitan. What then was the relationship between the Yaonian and the Shulü, the empress's natal clan?

Chinese historian Liu Pujiang, who has studied this problem, believes that the reference to Uygur is misleading and that the Shulü was a Xi tribe. The Xi shared an ancient origin with the Kitan and had been their frequent allies.[4] The *Kitan guozhi* (1125), written earlier than the formal dynastic history, states that she was "originally from the Shulü clan, which was of the same country as the Kitan."[5] This statement implies that the Shulü were not Kitan, although the point is made that the future empress was born in Kitan territory. The Xi and Kitan had frequently intermarried, and Liu's contention, based on a notation in the *Jinshi*, that the Shulü were one of the five clans of the Xi makes sense.[6] It is certainly possible that the Shulü clan included both Xi and Kitan and that being born in Kitan territory gave her some degree of Kitan identity. If so, the Xiao noble clan that was the Yelü marriage partner was originally Xi as well, although it was most probably of mixed origin, like the empress herself. Identifying the first empress as Xi would also help explain why Xi nobles were given high status in the early Liao period. The Xi state was established as a semi-independent kingdom with its own capital—where the Liao Central Capital, Zhongjing, was later built.[7] The Xi were also designated the second-ranking people in Liao society in the early part of the dynasty. The Kitan ranked first.[8]

The date of Abaoji's marriage to Yingtian is not known, but it must have taken place prior to his rise to the position of kaghan of the Kitan in 907. Yingtian's brothers and uncles provided crucial support for his successful establishment of an imperial paternal line in which sons succeed their fathers—as opposed to the traditional Kitan practice, under which a kaghan was normally selected by a council of elders to serve a three-year term.[9] Abaoji served three consecutive terms. Under traditional arrangement, Abaoji's brothers or younger kin would have expected to succeed him when he stepped down. Not surprisingly, they opposed his imperial ambitions and plans for direct patrilineal inheritance of the throne by his own sons. In return for support from Yingtian's relations, Abaoji appointed her brother to the important post of prime minister of the Northern Administration.[10] Her family was then integrated into the Liao state and later ennobled with the surname Xiao to become the exclusive marriage clan to the Yelü imperial line.

Yingtian's career as a warrior woman began with her protection of Abaoji during this time of transition. According to a Chinese account in the *Xin Wu-*

daishi, Yingtian devised a plan to defeat her husband's opponents. The future emperor, following her advice, set a trap for his enemies, inviting them to a conference at a salt lake to discuss salt revenues. First, Abaoji entertained his guests at a banquet, and "when the wine began to take effect, hidden soldiers came forth and killed all the tribal chieftains. Then he set himself up and was not replaced again."[11] According to the account in the *Liaoshi*, the Xi king and Yingtian's relations aided him in this ambush.[12]

Yingtian appears to have been a woman of unusual initiative and agency, who collaborated closely with her husband. Not only did she come up with the plan to eliminate the opposition and secure Abaoji's hold on the throne when his brothers threatened him with rebellion, but she also "selected well-trained and valiant barbarians, called *fan* ["frontiersmen," a more neutral term than "foreigners" or "barbarians"; probably Xi] in the *Liaoshi*, and Chinese to form the Shushan army," which she commanded. Later, when the emperor was away, she discovered plans by two clans to revolt, and, as recounted in the *Liaoshi*, "she therefore held back a part of the army, and when the rebellion took place, she led out the troops against these rebels and put down the rebellion."[13] This story illustrates the lingering opposition Abaoji encountered, largely from within his own family, and shows how Yingtian used her connections and military command to secure her husband's claim to the throne.

Having thus secured the throne with the support of his wife and her relations, Abaoji relied on her advice in military affairs as well. As recounted in the *Liaoshi*, "Whenever the emperor was making ready to lead the army into battle, the empress always planned together with him in preparation." She also accompanied him on military campaigns.[14] The empress was attuned to cultural aspects of administration. In 924, a Uygur mission visited the Liao, but no one could speak their language.[15] Yingtian advised the emperor to place a man who was clever at languages among members of the mission for twenty days, after which he became their translator.[16] She was also instrumental in organizing scholars to invent a written form of the Kitan language.[17] Thus, the first empress set precedents not only in military affairs but also in literary efforts.

Her most spectacular moment came after Abaoji died in the twentieth year of his reign, when, as described in chapter 5, she sacrificed her hand. She went on to enjoy another thirty years of active political and military engagement. She manipulated the succession so that her second son, Deguang, became the second emperor, Taizong. The heir apparent, Prince Bei, was compensated with the appanage of the former kingdom of Bohai.[18] In this way, the Yelü-Shulü line was secured in the succession and the principle of direct inheritance by sons established.

Taizong, in an apparent understanding with his elder brother, in turn named Bei's oldest son, Yelü Ruan, to succeed him. But when the second emperor died in 947, the empress dowager opposed the succession, despite the fact that Ruan had already been enthroned as Emperor Shizong. Yingtian backed her third son, Lihu, saying that had been the wish of Abaoji. Now in her sixties, the empress dowager named Lihu as the Zhangsu emperor and sent him with an army to attack Shizong. But when Shizong's troops defeated Lihu, the empress was confounded. One can envision the scene: the two armies drawn up on either bank of the Shira Muren with the black river between them. The elderly empress, still astride her horse, is seething with rage while her unsuccessful son, mortified with shame, sits by her side. Clearly, she could not succeed in her wish to make Lihu emperor. Yelü Wuzhi, the emperor's kinsman and trusted by all, crosses the river to mediate between the empress and her nephew. Yingtian announces her reason for raising the army, and Shizong in turn, as a gesture of conciliation, explains his rationale. Finally, glancing at her son in exasperation, she nods to Wuzhi, who raises flags to inform the emperor of her capitulation. A peaceful settlement is reached; the emperor promises that there will be no retribution on either the dowager or her son. The empress leads her forces across the river and, together with her humiliated son, they join the new emperor, Shizong, her grandson, on the long road back to Shangjing.[19]

When Yingtian died in 953, at the age of seventy-four, she had lived long enough to see the grandson she had opposed, Shizong, murdered and Deguang's son come to the throne as Emperor Muzong (951–969). One cannot know whether these events mollified the old lady. She was given a military funeral and buried near the tomb of her husband. Her mausoleum was called the Changning Palace and was guarded by an *ordo* (battalion). The land supporting Yingtian's *ordo* covered four prefectures and included thirteen thousand households, made up of Kitan, *fan* (Xi?), and transferred Chinese units; these households supported five thousand mounted soldiers,[20] no doubt drawn from units she had commanded in life. The military skills that the first empress exhibited were passed on to future imperial wives. Deguang's empress, Jing'an, Yingtian's niece, was also a warrior woman. She accompanied the emperor in battle, hunting, and wherever else he went.[21]

Yingtian's assertive courage and military leadership made her the premier model for warrior women during the entire conquest period. Other notable women especially during the Liao period were warriors as well. Empress Chengtian, her sister, Xiao Hunjan, and the last empress, Xiao *taihou*, who led the defense against the Song in 1122, all took her as their model. Yingtian's influence stretched into the Jin, to the martial heroine of the Liao-Jin period Yang Miaozhen, whose story brings this chapter to a close.

Empress Dowager Chengtian

Empress Ruizhi, better known as Empress Dowager Chengtian, came from the same extraordinary tradition as Yingtian. She was Yingtian's grandniece and was appointed first concubine, then empress to the fifth Liao emperor, Jingzong (r. 969–982). She may technically have been of an earlier generation than the emperor, Abaoji's great-grandson, even though she was fifteen years his junior, since her great-grandfather was Yingtian's elder brother or uncle. Her formal biography in the *Liaoshi* presents the following account:

> Xiao *shi*, Empress Ruizhi of Emperor Jingzong . . . called Yanyan in childhood, was the daughter of the northern prime minister, [Xiao] Siwen. She exhibited intelligence from a young age. When Jingzong became emperor, she was chosen as *guifei*, the title for a first-ranking concubine. Her first child was a daughter. But she was elevated to empress when her son [Longxu] Emperor Shengzong was born.[22]

The *Liaoshi* biography provides a thoroughly conventional account, including early signs of later prominence. The future empress's father, Xiao Siwen (d. 970), was promoted to the rank of northern military commissioner and northern prime minister, a position he held only briefly before his death, after his daughter became empress.[23] This source also notes Empress Ruizhi's increasingly important role in managing affairs of state during the emperor's illnesses. High-ranking ministers Yelü Xiezhen, an imperial kinsman, and

Hann Derang (941–1011), who came from a distinguished *haner* family that had risen to prominence under Yingtian, were her principal advisers.

According to the *Kitan guozhi*, Jingzong had a kind nature, was not forceful, and he enjoyed the company of women.[24] During Jingzong's reign, Ruizhi aided the emperor in managing government affairs, accompanied him to the front on occasion, and handled affairs of state during his many absences. The *Kitan guozhi* adds that his officials and generals all went to Ruizhi to discuss important matters, and once a decision had been reached, they informed Jingzong so that it could be promulgated in his name. The emperor was often ill and sometimes unable to direct the sporadic warfare along the border in which the Liao were often engaged. Even in matters concerning wars with the Song, Ruizhi was "the actual ruler of the Kitan and decided all matters." When the Kitan made war in "Yi, Ding, You, and Yan prefectures, it was the empress who made the decisions and sent out the signals."[25]

Ruizhi also gave birth to three sons and three daughters during the fifteen years of Jingzong's reign. Longxu, the oldest son, became Emperor Shengzong, and his younger brother, Longqing (973–1017), titled Prince of Qin-Jin, was well known at court. The annals also note a third son, named Longyu, whose title is given elsewhere as the Prince of Qin.[26] According to the *Kitan guozhi*, however, there were two more sons, one known as the Prince of Chu and another called Diange, who did not survive to adulthood.[27]

Here Chengtian's biography briefly notes the governmental crisis that ensued when Emperor Jingzong died suddenly at age forty-five while on a hunting trip.[28] The heir apparent was only twelve (eleven by Western count), and his succession was by no means secure. The empress dowager turned to her husband's two most-trusted ministers, Yelü Xiezhen and Hann Derang, for help. The *Liaoshi* continues,

> After Jingzong died, Ruizhi became empress dowager and regent, taking care of national affairs. She protested, "I am a widow and my son is young. Our relatives and subordinates are powerful, and neighboring countries threaten us with war. What am I to do?" But ministers Yelü Xiezhen and Hann Derang said, "Trust in [us], your officials; how then could you be anxious!" Then the empress dowager discussed national affairs with them and appointed [General] Yuexingge to lead the armies on the southern

border. In the first year of Tonghe [983] she received the title of empress dowager, Chengtian *taihou*.²⁹

Here again, the *Kitan guozhi* provides more detail than the official history. During Jingzong's illness, when Yanyan (this source uses Empress Ruizhi's personal name) managed state affairs, she relied greatly on Hann Derang. Meanwhile, Hann was active in military efforts and, aware of the emperor's ill health, had already been arranging support for the empress and her sons behind the scenes prior to Jingzong's death.³⁰

> Later, when the emperor's illness became worse, [Hann] realized that some members of the imperial clan and certain local lords posed a threat to the throne and the empress might be in danger. Instead of waiting for her order, he secretly sent his people to guard [her residence in] the inner court. At that time, the government was subject to the control of the powerful members of the imperial clan and local lords who had their own military forces. As for the empress, although she had been in charge for some time, she did not have much support from her relatives. The princes were still very young. So the court was facing a serious crisis. With the empress's approval, [Hann] replaced several high-ranking officials and forced the local lords back to their own domains, where he forbade them from contacting one another.³¹

With these safeguards in place, no trouble occurred when Jingzong died. The empress was appointed regent. Early in her regency, she arranged several successive "rebirth" ceremonies for the young emperor and took part in one herself to ritually secure his position.³² With Shengzong's accession solidified, the empress then "discussed national affairs" with these two ministers and ran the state as regent for her son. She also commanded military affairs, dispatching General Yelü Yuexingge to secure the frontier against Song attacks. Shengzong's reign lasted forty-eight years, longer than that of any other conquest-dynasty ruler of the middle period except Khubilai Khan of the Yuan, and marked the apogee of the Liao dynasty in military, political, and cultural affairs.³³ The foundation laid by his father, Jingzong, together with a series of excellent advisers accounted for the success of his reign, even if he himself was largely a figurehead. But the prime mover and main source of power during his reign was his mother, Empress Dowager Chengtian. According to the *Liaoshi*,

> The empress was intelligent in governing and she always followed good advice; therefore all officials were loyal to her. She was familiar with military affairs and commanded the armies at the Battle of Chanyuan [December 1004–January 1005] and led three divisions in person. She gave rewards and punishments justly. Shengzong can be called a good leader of the Liao state because he learned so much from the empress.[34]

The empress dowager dominated Shengzong's reign until her death in 1009. Her treatment of her son was so autocratic that she berated him in public and even beat him after he was a grown man.[35] Nevertheless, by all accounts she was an exceptionally able ruler.

Chengtian excelled in administration, which required competency in both Chinese and the Kitan written language as well as organizational skills. As noted by modern scholars, "while Chengtian was alive, there was no question of who was ultimately in control; these great ministers of state were the empress dowager's men." Furthermore Chengtian "was no capricious tyrant, but a ruler who deeply understood the realities of power and the art of governance and who was always willing to listen to advice. She won the deep loyalty of Liao officials, Kitan and Chinese alike."[36] The *Liaoshi* chronicles for Shengzong's reign show that while the empress customarily handled the administration from Shangjing, Hann Derang ranged widely throughout the empire, putting down rebellions, leading tactical military expeditions, and keeping the peace.[37]

Her first exposure to military matters came no doubt when she accompanied Emperor Jingzong on campaign, but her first real test came in 986, when the Song launched an attack on the Liao borders, hoping to take advantage of Shengzong's youth and inexperience. The attack was handily repulsed by Liao armies. Most remarkable was her military leadership at the decisive Battle of Chanyuan. In the campaign against the Song, Chengtian personally commanded the battle for Yingzhou—one source states that she "beat the war drum herself."[38] Military historian David Wright has termed Chanyuan "the bloodiest battle of the entire war."[39] Song forces were led by Emperor Zhenzong. Liao emperor Shengzong, now in his thirties, was ostensibly the commander on these campaigns, but no one doubted that his mother was in charge. Although already over fifty, she led three divisions of the Liao army that vanquished the Song.[40] Although her name does not appear among those present when Shengzong, Hann Derang, and Liao generals "gathered around a makeshift table" with the Song envoys to draft the treaty in January 1005, she led the argument for increased territorial concessions. Members on the Song side of the negotiations were well aware of the empress dowager's significance.[41] The terms of the Treaty of Chanyuan were highly favorable to the Liao and sealed Liao superiority over the Song. As part of the final contract, Empress Chengtian was given personal ritual status as the Song emperor's "junior aunt."[42] A measure of Chengtian's prominence is that when the first Song birthday tribute mission to the Liao was undertaken in April–May 1006, its main purpose was to congratulate the empress dowager, not the emperor.[43] When Chengtian died in 1009, her son was left in charge of the empire to a greater extent than ever before, although he still had the advice of Hann Derang for two more years, until Hann's death in 1011.

After Chengtian's death, Emperor Shengzong came under the influence of his wife, Empress Rende, who seems to have picked up where the empress dowager had left off. In her epitaph, Rende is said to have been humane and kind, humble even to servants, accomplished in womanly virtues, and a devout Buddhist, but the reality was less flattering. She had a reputation as a sharp woman who dominated her husband. When she died, Shengzong raised a concubine to the position of empress. This woman, Empress Qinai, also exerted considerable sway over her husband. Her political influence reached a peak immediately after the emperor's death when, as Empress Dowager Yitian, she was prominent in the selection of the succeeding emperor, Xingzong (r. 1031–1055).[44] Meanwhile, Xingzong's mother, Empress Dowager Xunqin, echoing Empress Yingtian's failed efforts, attempted to place his younger brother on the throne but without success.[45]

Empress Ruizhi began her career as a warrior woman under the tutelage of Emperor Jingzong but as Empress Dowager Chengtian she became by all measures the most active and successful of all the Liao warrior empresses. However, her story does not end with her military achievements. After being widowed, she allegedly enjoyed a nearly thirty-year-long affair with her chief minister, Hann Derang. This more private aspect of her life is examined in chapter 7.

Chengtian's sister, Xiao Hunjan, continued the martial tradition. She was married to (Yelü) Yansage, and after he died, she took over as head of his army. She was commander in chief of an expeditionary force against border tribes in the west in 994 and led her troops in a campaign against the Xi Xia in the west, where she was credited with the establishment of the northwestern city of Kodun. However, she was accused of an ambitious intrigue to overthrow the empress dowager in 1006 and died in 1007.[46]

The *Kitan guozhi* gives a more-detailed but confusing account. According to this source, Chengtian had two sisters, but neither is named. The older sister married the Prince of Qiguo. After his death, she commanded his army of thirty thousand troops near the Western Capital. She was a fine horsewoman herself and admired horsemanship. However, she became infatuated with a certain clansman, Talanabo, who was reputed to be very handsome. The empress, when she heard of this attachment, sent Talanabo away. But the following year, Princess Qiguo pleaded to be allowed to marry the clansman, and the empress permitted it—apparently an abrogation of widow conventions. Talanabo had great success and many victories on the western frontier, but he rebelled by attempting to set up his own kingdom. When the empress learned of this, she recalled the troops and exiled him.

The second sister married the Prince of Jiao. She plotted behind Chengtian's back to poison her, but the empress discovered the plot and made her sister drink the poison instead. According to this source, these problems with her sisters caused the empress a great deal of heartache.[47] If the *Kitan Guozhi* is correct, the first sister was Hunjan, who was a fine horsewoman and led armies on the western frontier. But it was the second sister, Princess Jiao, who intrigued against Chengtian and was imprisoned and so died.

In another display of military vigor, Empress Renyi, wife of Emperor Xingzong (r. 1031–1055), discovered a rebellious plot and informed the emperor. But he doubted the story. So, according to her biography, she said to him, "This is a crucial point for our county. So you must make a decision immediately." The emperor then took her advice, and when the rebellion broke out, the empress supervised the guards herself and successfully defeated the rebels.[48]

The last empress dowager of the Liao, known as Xiao *taihou*, was also a heroic and tragic figure. When the Liao state was collapsing and Emperor Tianzuo had fled, Prince Chun seized the throne as Emperor Tianxi (d. 1122) and declared the Jianfu reign.[49] He selected as his empress one of his concubines who had borne him a son. When Tianxi died suddenly after only three months on the throne, she became dowager empress. As regent for her son, she led the remaining Liao military against the Song forces in 1123. Her poem, written before the deciding battle, may be one of the few instances where we hear a woman's voice. In it, the empress expresses her military dedication and her love for her young son. Liao troops lost this battle. Empress Dowager Xiao held court to determine whether the Liao must surrender to the Jin state or the Song. She then wrote the surrender treaty to the Song herself.[50] But there is no further mention of her fate or that of her son.

Later, in the twelfth century, after the Jin had overthrown the Liao government, a Kitan general made himself king of the Western Liao. After his death in 1220, his wife inherited his position. In 1226, she traveled west to meet Chinggis Khan. The Mongol ruler exclaimed in surprise, "The strongest eagle cannot fly to this place, but you, a woman, were able to get here!"—a remarkable accolade from a man who himself was an unsurpassed warrior.[51]

Liao men and women both appear to have enjoyed hunting, where in addition to the sport they also exercised their military skills and trained for warfare. Princes and emperors were often accompanied by their empresses and concubines. When, in 1042, Emperor Xingzong's mother, Empress Dowager Xunqin, went hunting and killed a bear, the emperor gave a party to honor her achievement.[52] In 1066, Emperor Daozong's mother went hunting and killed a bear. The emperor distributed money among the officials to honor her feat. Later in that same year, she went hunting again, this time killing a tiger. The emperor threw a party to celebrate and asked the officials to write poems to praise the event.[53] In addition to hunting, and even when they did not lead armies, Liao empresses and concubines were often politically astute and participated in palace intrigues from behind the scene.

A question provoked both by the values embedded in these accounts and by those that are omitted concerns the bias of the sources. Whether the selection of virtues portrayed in the official sources was made by Liao historians, whose valuations were passed on to the Yuan historians who compiled the *Liaoshi*, or whether Yuan officials had some hand in the selections and thus possibly colored the accounts is not entirely clear. Do we hear a woman's authentic voice in the poem attributed to Wen *fei* and that to Xiao *taihou*, or were all such literary items ghostwritten by men of a later date to make a moral point?

Yang Miaozhen, Jin-Dynasty Warrior Woman

Liao women, as we have seen, were renowned for their courage, skill on horseback, and military attainments. Jin women are not conspicuously martial in the biographies and chronicles of the dynastic history, but the *Jinshi* chapter on *lienü zhuan* makes clear that women warriors who defended cities, carried on the leadership of fallen husbands or fathers, and acted assertively to defend their children or their chastity were greatly honored. That these women are so conspicuously praised for martial leadership and heroism demonstrates the respect that Jin society had for warrior women. Women in the chapter on imperial empresses and concubines, by contrast, display traits of a more subtle nature. Many were good wives who advised their imperial spouses well and caring mothers who brought up their sons to be good emperors. Powerful empress dowagers do not figure in Jin historical sources because Jin leaders were careful to ensure that only adult males came to the throne, with the result that there were no female regents. More than a few elite Jin women showed both agency and courage. This last example of a martial woman, at the very end of the Jin dynasty, drew censure from Song annals and praise from the Jin histories. Her story engages both martial leadership and the sexual mores of the time.

Yang Miaozhen was eulogized in the twentieth century as a Chinese heroine for rebelling against feudal oppression. Like Mulan (a mythic figure who is conspicuously absent in these histories), she lived on the periphery of Chinese culture. Miaozhen appears only briefly in the *Jinshi*, but a much more complete account of her exploits is recorded in the *Songshi*. The *Jinshi jishi benmo*, a later Ming-dynasty source, includes additional information.[54] Yang's husband, Li Quan, is featured as a villain in the section devoted to "Rebellious Officials" in the *Songshi*, where his biography occupies a full two *juan* (rolls, equivalent to chapters). In this source, Yang is regarded as a traitorous rebel whose promiscuous sexuality only enhanced her evil character. I argue that in her proper Jin-dynasty historical context, Yang Miaozhen (d. ca. 1234) emerges as the last of the warrior women of the Liao and Jin conquest dynasties.

Yang Miaozhen lived in a contested area of present-day Shandong province near Weizhou, which had been part of the Jin state since the Jurchen conquest of the Northern Song one hundred years previously. Born and raised in a village in northwestern Shandong, she was a member of the Yang family that included Yang Anguo, called Aner. Aner—variously described as Miaozhen's brother or uncle—was a leather worker who first rebelled against collapsing Jin rule early in the thirteenth century but was reconciled and rewarded with minor offices. In 1213–1214, the Mongols attacked the region, and, taking advantage of Jin weakness, Aner began to plunder the area around his strongholds. He even briefly proclaimed himself emperor in 1214 in Penglai, a town on the coast. The Mongols retaliated, and Yang, who had tried to flee by boat, was killed.[55]

Li Quan was another militia leader who had initially joined the Mongol invasion. But when the Mongols retreated and the Jin retook the region, he joined the Song side. In 1217 the Yellow River flooded in Shandong, and the Song, taking advantage of the situation that prevented Mongol or Jin cavalry action, offered official ranks to rebel leaders. Li Quan accepted Song support and was appointed as a general over the same troops that he had previously led. To secure this position, he handed over several Jin military commanders he had captured. But when Song rewards did not match his expectations, Li Quan defected again, and this time ran his own show as a minor warlord. As Jin government control eroded and the Song were unable to hold this area, Li became essentially independent.[56] He was one of several bandit-leaders who, in the midst of the turmoil, took advantage of the lapse of government control to assert their own powers.

At the same time, according to the account in the *Songshi*, Yang Miaozhen, who was herself "skilled with bow and arrow and excelled in riding," took over leadership of Aner's guerilla army and led more than ten thousand soldiers.[57] Pei-yi Wu adds that she was "crafty and assertive" and won out over other contenders, such as Yang Aner's nephew because of her merit and aggressiveness.[58] Li Quan admired Miaozhen and wanted to join forces, since she had the larger army. The *Songshi* reports that "Yang took the initiative; she first slept with him and then married him."[59] Song historians found these acts objectionable and considered her depraved. Wu echoes this attitude when he notes that she must have been "unusually charismatic" as a bandit-leader to have so overturned Confucian patriarchal standards in this manner.[60] In Jin society, however, where young women were permitted sexual discretion unknown in the south, as we have seen in previous chapters, it would not have been so unusual for a woman to initiate sexual relations, as Miaozhen is credited with having done. As seen in chapter 4, Liao and Jin women enjoyed a period of sexual freedom before marriage and often exercised agency in selecting marriage partners. Nor would it have been unusual to be skilled in horsemanship and archery, and even to have the charisma to lead armies.

Thereafter, Li and Yang together fought against the Mongols, Song, or the Jin, variously, as opportunities offered. Li was still nominally a Song vassal and hoped to profit thereby. Their main area of operations was around the town of Huaian, in Chu prefecture (modern Shandong province), which was claimed by the Song. While Li was on campaign, Yang rallied her troops to defend their home.[61] The Huaian region was ostensibly under the command of the Song official Xu Guo. When Xu arrived in 1224 at Huaian, Yang *shi* met him outside the town, but Xu Guo refused to greet her as an equal, a grave insult. Xu, however, was impressed by the size of the armies Li and Yang had assembled. Xu boasted in public and said, "Li Quan depends on my nourishment. As soon as I demonstrated a bit of my power, he made off in no time." When Li Quan returned, he decided to test Xu's sincerity and knelt down before him. When Xu did nothing to stop him from making this submissive gesture, Li became angry but hid his feelings and pretended to be polite. Xu in turn thought Li's compliance indicated submission. Li departed for Qingzhou while Yang meanwhile stayed with her troops. She feared Xu in her heart and secretly prepared her revenge. When Li Quan returned, together they rebelled against Xu Guo, who was killed in battle.[62]

Next, the Song sent Xu Xiji to be the new commander. Outwardly, he treated Li and Yang as equals but reported back to Song headquarters that affairs were "completely turned upside down" because women fought like men, a statement reflecting conventional Song attitudes.[63] Li, however, mistrusted Xiji. In 1225, Mongol armies returned to dominate the region. So Li turned against his former supporters and departed with his troops. Meanwhile a new rebel leader, Xia Quan, invaded the area around Chucheng, the prefectural capital. Hoping to stave off any further invasion, Yang sent envoys to bribe Xia Quan to halt his troops. While negotiations were under way, Yang heard that Li Quan had been killed.[64]

Needing allies, Miaozhen sent word to Xia Quan, who was on the point of joining the Song, telling him, "If the fox dies, should the rabbit cry? The Chinese have murdered my husband. If Li Quan died, how can you survive? How can you contemplate surrendering to them?" Xia Quan was impressed and came to visit her. According to the *Songshi*,

Miaozhen dressed herself in her best clothes and applied her makeup. She came out to greet Xia Quan. "My husband has died," she said to him. "I am nothing but a poor woman and cannot survive alone. All that I have, children, jade, silk, and weapons, are all yours. Please accept these gifts." Xia Quan's heart was moved, so he prepared a banquet. They ate and drank copiously and afterward he slept with Yang as if in his own home.[65]

Thus did Yang Miaozhen turn her former enemy into her ally and lover. Thereafter they fought against the Song. Xia Quan surrounded Chu prefecture and returned victorious, having driven out the Song troops. This time, however, Yang *shi* rejected Xia. Thinking Yang had betrayed him and intended to benefit only herself, he went to Xu Xiji to create chaos and discredit her, but there he was not successful. Consequently, Xia Quan surrendered to the Jin. Pei-yi Wu maintains that Yang seduced Xia only when she found herself in a crisis and thereafter abandoned him.[66] But, as we know, sexual assertiveness was one of the traits characteristic of Jin and Liao women and not necessarily to be condemned.

The Song appointed a new commander, Yao Chong, in 1227. Miaozhen was still collaborating with the Song, and this time received, from Yao, polite, deferential treatment. At first he conducted his business from a ship anchored in the harbor. Miaozhen, perhaps at the height of her powers, as de facto governor of the prefecture, permitted Yao to enter Chucheng, where he set up headquarters in a temple. "He tried hard to please her."[67]

The reports of Li Quan's death had been false. He had taken refuge in Yidu, where he was besieged for a year. Li Quan, in this desperate situation, wanted to surrender to the Mongols but feared that the local people would oppose it. He contemplated suicide. However, his comrades, Zheng Yande and Tian Si, saved him by saying, "[Today our situation] is like a robe, as long as the body is kept together, one doesn't worry about the sleeves." They urged him to surrender to the Mongols. Li Quan followed their advice and surrendered. Yuan troops occupied Qingzhou prefecture and appointed Li Quan governor of Shandong.[68]

Li's defection enraged the Song authorities, and Yao Chong turned against Yang *shi* and so offended the her supporters. Li Fu, Li Quan's second elder brother, discussed the matter with Miaozhen. They prepared a banquet for Yao. When Yao arrived, Miaozhen was absent. But Li proceeded with the banquet, and many people, including Yao's two concubines, were poisoned and died. Yao escaped with his life after great humiliation, but sometime later he died. However, all did not go well. Song loyalists Guo Anyong, Yan Tong, Zhang Lin, Xing De, and Wang Yishen revolted and planned to kill Li Fu and Yang *shi* and present their heads to the Song. Yan Tong mistakenly killed Li Quan's second wife, Liu *shi*, and sent her head to the capital, believing he had killed Miaozhen. The Song rejoiced and sent reinforcements, who took Chucheng and killed Li Fu and Miaozhen's remaining supporters. Miaozhen, however, had been warned and escaped.[69]

At that crucial juncture, Li Quan, now the Mongol governor pro tem of Shandong, returned to the south. He was furious over the destruction of his family and supporters and wanted revenge against the Song. Miaozhen and Li were reunited. Li was with the Mongol troops in 1231 when they penetrated deep into Jiangnan and attacked the city of Yangzhou. The *Jinshi* reports that Li was killed in this attack in February of that year.[70]

When Li's death was reported, his troops returned to Huai'an, the circuit that included Chu prefecture, to ask Yang *shi* to take over. But Miaozhen changed sides again, and this time she sought support from the Jin to revenge her husband's death at the hands of the Song. She constructed a floating bridge of boats at Chuzhou. Having crossed the river in this manner, she mounted an attack on Taoyuan city, which the Song had newly captured from the Jin. In this she was successful.[71] Subsequently, however, Miaozhen suffered a number of reverses as the Song army caught up with her. In the end, surrounded by Song troops, she spoke to her supporters, arguing,

> For twenty years I used my spear "Flowering Pear" and I found no opponents in the world. But now the situation is hopeless. The reason that you, my loyal supporters, refuse to surrender is because of me. You cannot bear to kill me and offer them [the Song] my head. If it were not because of me, who of you would not like to surrender? But without it [my head], how would you be accepted?

So she devised a strategy by which she could escape and her soldiers might also survive, saying,

> But now I want to retire to Lianshui. So, you can tell the Song that you intended [to take my head] but I discovered [the plot] and have already escaped across the Huai [River]. In this way you can surrender [without reprisals].[72]

Therefore, to spare her troops, she crossed the river and escaped into the marshes—the same marshes that had supported other bandits and were made famous in the Ming novel *Water Margin/Outlaws of the Marsh*. She apparently died several years later in unknown circumstances.

The *Songshi* biography considers Li Quan a traitorous Song official. From a Song standpoint, it is obvious that neither Li Quan nor Yang Miaozhen conducted themselves by Han Chinese standards. Miaozhen was a woman of Han extraction, and her story demonstrates that a Han woman born and brought up under Jin rule could plausibly behave in accordance with Jin standards of sexuality and military skills. In short, Yang Miaozhen behaves like a Liao-Jin conquest woman. Her aggressive sexuality in seducing Li Quan and marrying him only afterward is also typical of premarital sexuality in this period when women could select their own husbands. Her military skills and leadership compare with those of the heroines of the Jin-dynasty *lienü* chapters, who fought against bandits and Mongols.

The briefer mention in the *Jinshi* has quite a different tone. This account stresses Miaozhen's patriotic fervor in fighting against the Song and against the Mongols, and how she took revenge for Li's death by defeating the Song and capturing Taoyuan. The Jin account omits mention that she seduced Xia Quan.[73] When placed in her proper historical context, Yang Miaozhen emerges as one of the last of the militant women of the Liao and Jin—skilled in warfare and assertive in sexuality. She is a national heroine who fought against both the Song and the Mongols and ended up supporting the Jin cause. In a Jin context, her sexuality and her role as a military leader were entirely acceptable. Her military actions, agency, and sexuality all fit the pattern of warrior women. Pei-yi Wu is therefore quite mistaken in presenting her as an anomalous example of a Chinese woman warrior in the context of Han values. Yang Miaozhen was a conquest woman who operated in a Jin historical context in the tradition of empresses Yingtian and Chengtian, carrying forward the martial valor of *lienü* exemplars from the pages of the *Jinshi*.

Conclusion

Much about the lives of Liao and Jin warrior women and about the customs they maintained and those they selected to adopt can be learned from the exemplars discussed in this chapter. But the fact that, with the exception of Yang Miaozhen, the women under discussion are limited to the highest of the elite classes points up an intrinsic problem in this study. We know more about imperial women and women of the aristocracy than about lower-class women, or even the lesser elite of Liao and Jin nobility. The account of Miaozhen, a commoner, is a rare exception. We know even less about the *baner* and Han women under the Liao and Jin regimes, who are rarely mentioned in historical or literary sources. What is clear is that Jin and Liao women of the imperial court negotiated, often with consummate skill, between the martial values of the steppe and forest and the Confucian values of China, while a Han woman like Yang Miaozhen could adopt Jurchen martial standards of behavior.

The activities of noble Liao women, leading armies and becoming involved in palace intrigues, would hardly qualify them as paragons of virtue in any Confucian sense of the term. Military skills, martial arts, and horse riding were highly valued; so too was learning, clever retorts, and education in the Confucian classics. But Confucian concepts such as premarital purity, chastity, and filial care for in-laws are largely absent in Liao biographies, while on the other side of the border Chinese standards for virtuous behavior certainly do not condone military leadership, hunting, or sexual assertiveness. Liao imperial women exhibited both physical courage and a remarkable degree of independent agency. Empress dowagers Yingtian and Chengtian would be extraordinary in any setting and surely rival the better-known Empress Wu of the Tang dynasty. Taken together, these stories, biographies, and epitaphs tell of imperial women who outsmarted men, led armies to victory, and were active in state affairs.

Liao and Jin women may not have been as unusual as the *Liaoshi* claims. Liao, Mongol, and Jin women alike drew their strength from steppe traditions. To make a firmer case, however, we need to know more about women in steppe society beyond the frontiers of China. Meanwhile, we have the enduring image of Jin-dynasty Wenji on horseback in the pose of a martial heroine representing that most military of virtues, loyalty.

One might suppose that these warrior women epitomized Kitan and Jurchen culture, exercising power, independent agency, leadership, and exhibiting personal bravery. But, as the sources reveal, even as early as the first empress, these same women were already absorbing selected aspects of Han Chinese attitudes and attainments. Empress Yingtian refused to follow her husband in death so that she could continue to supervise her sons, a duty imposed on her by Abaoji's adoption of the Chinese government institution of direct patrilineal inheritance of the throne. Further, she engaged scholars to create a Kitan written language, showing she realized the usefulness of written language, an appreciation that could only have been modeled on Chinese. Empress Chengtian, another quintessentially Kitan woman both as a military and government leader, was undoubtedly literate in Chinese and Kitan and skilled in administration. Ironically, Yang Miaozhen, of Han Chinese background, is the only woman who seems to have wholly adopted the Jurchen warrior culture. Warrior women proved to be exceptionally skillful cultural mediators, and as the examples of Yingtian and Chengtian demonstrate, combined administrative and literary skills drawn from Han Chinese precedents with steppe culture and military leadership. They shaped their identities accordingly.

SEVEN

Private Affairs

THIS CHAPTER TAKES UP THREE AREAS of women's lives in the Liao and Jin periods that have been mentioned in passing in earlier chapters but that deserve more thorough treatment: first, the question of women's education; second, religion, with particular attention to Liao and Jin women's participation in Buddhism; and last an alleged romance between Empress Chengtian and Grand Councilor Hann Derang.

As discussed in the preceding chapters, many notable women had a love of learning, wrote poetry and prose, read the classics, and were skilled in argumentation based on Confucian texts. Women's education was clearly important in the Liao and Jin periods and deserves to be more thoroughly known. Education for women, insofar as we can tell, was a private matter. Religion also may be regarded as a private sphere in women's lives. Although the great Buddhist monuments, some still standing, were public and often heavily subsidized by the state, women's participation in Buddhism as believers, when seeking asylum in widowhood, and as donors to Buddhist establishments was markedly private. The final part of this chapter is devoted to what must be considered the most private area of a woman's life, the relationship between the empress dowager and her chief minister. Respected modern historians Denis Twitchett and Klaus-Peter Tietze dismiss the story of the empress's liaison with Hann, saying, "Song sources, probably maliciously, suggest that he [Derang] was the empress dowager's lover."[1] However, I want to take a closer look at this aspect of this remarkable woman's life because, contrary to

Twitchett and Tietze's contention, I believe that in the context of Liao conventions regarding sexuality, betrothal, and widowhood, described in previous chapters, the rumored romance may well have been true.

Educated Women

When I began this study of women in the Liao and Jin dynasties, I expected that women would be prominent in marriage alliances. I hoped that the Liao and Jin histories would shed more light on women's lives despite their formulaic conventions. I knew that some Liao and Jin women had led armies. What I did not in any way expect was that these women in a frontier zone on China's northern periphery would have excelled in education and in the study of the Chinese classics. I never anticipated that women of the conquest dynasties would emerge as scholars and poets, or that so many of them would be praised for their piety and quietly exhibit their agency in endowing Buddhist shrines from their own resources.

To be educated in the Liao state was to know Chinese. Although Kitan was the spoken language of daily use and despite the invention of two sets of Kitan characters to express that language, the literary texts that educated men and women studied were written in Chinese.[2] The written forms of Kitan and Jurchen were both based on Chinese characters. Liao tomb steles, for example, often have inscriptions in Chinese on one side and Kitan on the other, but as a literary language Kitan never achieved much scope beyond ceremonial use.[3] Similarly, Jurchen as a written language was confined largely to Emperor Shizong's effort to revive Jurchen culture in the late twelfth century. Meanwhile, members of the aristocratic Xiao and Yelü clans, who dominated Kitan society, wrote much of the poetry and prose collected in the *Quan Liao wen*. Buddhist monks were also frequent contributors.[4] Some of the writings preserved in such compilations are attributed to women, and elsewhere women are praised for their literary skills. Authors of the prose, poetry, and epitaphs collected in the *Jin wen zui*, in contrast, are almost all Han Chinese; Jurchen names are absent.[5] Education numbered among the attributes that made a woman a desirable marriage partner. How women received their educations is less clear.

Liao interest in education began symbolically with culture bearers from the south, including Lady Zhen, who, like Wenji, brought her learning to the northern state, and Lady Chen, who educated her sons in the Confucian classics to become scholars and officials.[6] The honored role of these women speaks to a much broader issue of education generally. Many Chinese women like Wenji, who was educated by her father, received their educations in the southern states and as culture bearers contributed to the cultural trope of bringing civilization to the "barbarians." I have also suggested that the well-educated Kitan lady buried at Yemaotai may have had Bohai connections and thus access to Han culture. As for the books used in this transformation, the Song state, which banned most trade with the Liao, made an exception for Chinese classical books.[7] The Jin first absorbed sinicized Bohai culture and then, after the conquest of the Northern Song, acquired many educational resources in the former Song territory, where schools were found in nearly every prefecture.

The predynastic Kitan had no written language and, one may suppose, little if any education in Chinese. But the establishment of a Chinese-style dynastic government required its officials to be literate and to keep records. Scholars like Hann Yanhui (882–959) can be credited with much of the Kitan leadership's early acculturation, especially with regard to administrative procedures and government structures.[8] According to the tradition preserved in the *Liaoshi*, Empress Yingtian supervised the development of a written form of Kitan with two scripts, thus linking learning and women. But in spite of the invention of Kitan scripts, Chinese was the language of everyday government affairs, record keeping, edicts—at least for the Southern Circuit—and literature. Most government officials were Kitan nobles. How men and women obtained their educations is therefore a crucial question. According to K. T. Wu, who made a study of printing under the Liao, Jin, and Yuan dynasties, the Liao established a national library in 1054, and the next year schools were set up and the classics and commentaries were distributed for instructional use. Historical works were also made available in the schools.[9] Wu's work pertains to Chinese-language printing, not Kitan, all traces of which have disappeared except for stele and tomb inscriptions.[10] The books were almost certainly standard Chinese copies. Wu praises the quality of Liao Buddhist printing and goes on to note that the most famous Liao publication was the Buddhist work *Longkan shoujing*, by the Kitan priest Zhiguang (d. 997).[11] From this evidence, we know that Chinese-language works circulated in the Liao state and that the Liao had establishments to create and print books without depending on imports from the south.

That women were educated is evident from many accounts, beginning with those related to Empress Yingtian, who realized the value of writing. Education has a conspicuous role in the *Liaoshi lienü* chapter. Changge "was so learned in the Confucian classics and well read in historical works that she was consulted and gave advice on political matters. She was adept at poetry and wrote prose in an elegant style."[12] Changge's epitaph also praises her literary skills, lending credibility to the account in the *lienü* chapter.[13] The ill-fated Empress Yide was vulnerable to persecution by Yelü Yixin precisely because she was known to write poetry and songs and enjoy music. One conservative scholar complained that all the trouble came from educating women, for if the empress had not been educated, she could not have written incriminating letters.[14] Of course, we know that the letters were forged, but the point here is that since she was educated, she could plausibly have written them. Many other empresses and concubines were credited with impressive literary skills. For example, Wen *fei*, Emperor Tianzuo's favored concubine, wrote two poems, both of which have been preserved. In the first, she urges the emperor to listen to upright officials instead of putting his trust in irresponsible sycophants. In the second, she cites lessons from the Qin dynasty, more than a thousand years previous.[15] She was clearly familiar with the Chinese classics and histories. Empress Xuan Yi, wife of Emperor Daozong, was praised for "four talents: music, poetry, prose writing, and the study of Buddhism."[16]

The epitaph of another imperial daughter, Princess Qinguo, indicates that "her behavior followed all ethical precedents. She understood [political] matters quickly and thoroughly; she wrote colorful and beautiful prose articles [and] enjoyed reading the sutras."[17] Literary women of the Xiao clan include Xiao *shi*, from Liaoning, who married Yelü Hong. Her epitaph praises her for educating her children, paying respect to the older generation, and Buddhist devotion.[18] Any woman who educated her children had first to be educated herself.

We might expect that some of the most elite and entitled members of Jin and Liao society would have been educated. But epitaphs and inscriptions of less-exalted personages also reveal an unexpectedly high level of educa-

Private Affairs

tion. Testimonies written by husbands, sons, and fathers reflect the degree to which Liao society as a whole valued women's education. Most of the women listed below have no apparent governmental connections and, judging by their names, were from Han or *haner* families. The following inscriptions demonstrate their achievements:

> Zhang *shi* married Zhao [personal name unknown]. Her parents/ancestors came from the lower ranks. . . . She devoted all her energy and concern to her sons and grandsons. One son became a high official in service to the Liao emperor. . . . [She was] possessed of wisdom during her whole lifetime [and] made sure her daughters were educated.[19]

Li Yi donated money to establish a stele for his mother, who was from a noble family in Shandong and "was very famous for her Confucian learning among the scholars in her home [region]."[20] Another inscription commemorates Zhang *shi* who married Liang Yuan:

> As a girl, she was given a Confucian education, had good manners, and was very obedient. She read the national histories [*guoshi*] and always used their moral examples as mirrors to her own conduct. She treated her in-laws as if they were her own parents.[21]

Another scholarly woman, whose surname was also Zhang (no personal name included), is described as follows:

> From an early age, she studied with a Confucian teacher [*ru*] very seriously; when she was grown, she learned feminine skills. Later she met Deng [personal name unknown], a fine scholar and a *jinshi*-degree holder. Both being scholars, they were well suited to each other. Thus they married.[22]

This epitaph also implies that Zhang *shi* was able to meet and choose her own husband, a degree of agency not uncommon during the Liao and Jin periods. This marriage of two scholars in the Liao period predates the more famous marriage between the Song poet Li Qingzhao and her scholar-husband Zhao Mingchun.[23]

Zhang Guan, the wife of Ma Zhiwen, a scholar of note, was another filial and educated woman. She had a literary name, Wen Guo, a custom usually reserved for males in Chinese society. The epitaph praises her as a quick learner and very intelligent. "[She] was beautiful and elegant as well, and qualified to worship the ancestors. Her books and poems were used to teach later generations." Her filial piety was singled out for praise: "she took good care of her parents-in-law."[24]

Li Fei contributed to a Buddhist monument in memory of his parents, where his mother (unnamed) is praised for reading "classics for women."[25] An inscription of 1080 tells of Xiao *shi*, who married Yelü Hongyi. "She educated her children and was respectful. . . ."[26] A Xianyu [clan] woman had two sons, whom she raised and educated. "By the age of twenty, both sons had mastered the classics and history. They passed the exams and attained official positions. She was exceptionally virtuous."[27]

Historical documents, inscriptions, and literary sources contain so many tributes to women's learning that it is impossible to doubt the significance of education among Liao women's accomplishments. The women commemorated in these inscriptions shared the high value placed on education with imperial princesses and women celebrated in the *lienü* chapter. These examples and others like them demonstrate that women were recognized as scholars in the Liao period. They were not unique in this, since literary women also existed in the Song period; however, what is impressive about the Kitan women is that prior to the establishment of the Liao state, the Kitan as tribal peoples lacked a written language and formal education structures. By Chinese standards, they were all "barbarians" and thus by definition uneducated.

Unlike many dynastic histories, the *Liaoshi* contains no section on education. Examinations were set up under the second emperor in the Huitung period (938–947), but only *haner* were eligible.[28] The first regular *jinshi* examination was held in the Southern Capital in 988.[29] Even after the establishment of an examination system, only a few *haner jinshi*-degree holders were recruited into government positions, since members of the Kitan nobility, who were not subject to examinations, monopolized most appointments.[30]

The epitaphs quoted above suggest that women were educated at home by mothers and private tutors, probably together with their brothers, since separation of the sexes was not characteristic of Liao society. Further, some epitaphs indicate that Confucian education was privileged above household skills. The customarily later marriage age for women provided time and opportunity for a more extensive education than would have been the case had women married young. The longer male family members remained at home to study, the longer their sisters also could enjoy access to education. Clearly, part of the high status that women enjoyed in Liao society reflected their education.

The Jurchen, by contrast, adopted Chinese education quite early, probably with Bohai help, and inherited a flourishing system of education including schools, examinations, books, maps, and former Song scholars when their armies took the capital at Kaifeng in 1126.[31] A Chinese-style examination system for the Han population was established in 1123, even before the final conquest of northern China, and the equivalent of an imperial university was set up in the capital in 1132. Thus, virtually from the state's inception, education was institutionalized—and limited to males. A government printing office was set up in 1130, and the National Academy was restored in 1151. Private presses also thrived and put out many kinds of works, including manuals for merchants and medicinal texts in addition to the classics. Works printed by the Jin were, in K. T. Wu's opinion, comparable to the Southern Song's finest products. The Jin also excelled in printing Buddhist works such as the *Tripitaka*.[32] The Jin rulers were proud to think that their learning distinguished them from the Liao, because they were able to use *wen* (literally, "literary," peaceful means), not *wu* (warfare), to rule the country.[33]

Education produced Jurchen intellectuals like the well-known scholar Wanyan Haowen, who when he was seven could compose poems and at fourteen already exceeded his teacher.[34] Biographies of Jin officials bear out the influence of Han scholars on education. Hann Fang, a Jin official hired Hu Li, a scholar from Suzhou who excelled at poetry to teach his children, and Hu became "as if one of the family."[35] Students might study on their own, as did Wang Jue, from Hebei, who became a famous scholar. "When he was young, he always locked his doors and retired to read, never seeing anyone."[36] While girls and young women could not attend academies, they could study at home and with tutors, as did these scholars.

The *Jinshi* has a chapter on education. The state maintained a widespread educational system made up of a combination of private academies, state-sponsored schools, the Capital University, and the formal government examinations, modeled on those of the Song. Jurchen schools were added under Emperor Shizong, using books translated from Chinese into Jurchen. The Capital University had two sections, one for Chinese and the other for

Jurchen, which included training in horse riding and military skills.[37] The Jin state promoted classical education for men of Han descent and others in preparation for the Chinese exams and Jurchen education for tribesmen, especially those from the *mouke* and *meng'an* military units. The greater excellence of the traditional education system inherited from the Song became evident as Han *ren* with classical educations came to dominate government positions.[38] However, hereditary privilege and connections remained the main track to official appointments among the Jurchen nobility and Han elite.

Women's education in the Jin period was probably largely informal. Girls were schooled at home by their mothers or with their brothers as during the Liao but were left behind when boys departed for more formal education. However, at least one formal school for girls existed in the Jin palace according to an entry in the *Jinshi*. Yuan *fei*, who captivated Emperor Zhangzong, was from a lower-class family named Li but because of an injustice done to her parents, was allowed to study in the palace school for girls in compensation. When (male) teachers instructed women, a silk screen was placed between the teacher and the students. Li *shi* stood out among the others for her intelligent questions, but because of the screen, the teacher did not know what she looked like. When the emperor asked which girl was the most promising student, and the teacher replied, "The one who asks questions so loudly," Zhangzong removed the screen and discovered that the girl was not only intelligent but also beautiful. "So the emperor took her as his first-ranking concubine and loved her greatly because she understood his love of literature and poetry."[39]

In this case, Li's moral character and intelligence triumphed over an inauspicious background. Zhangzong reigned in the late twelfth century, by which time Jin society had become thoroughly infiltrated with Confucian values, including, according to this excerpt, separation of the sexes in daily activities such as those of the classroom.[40] The Jin state's Jurchen leaders had become fully sinicized, and as in Song China, the Jin education system channeled young men into institutions outside the home. However, the existence of formal schools for males in the Jin period worked against education for women. Jin girls were expected to learn basic skills so that they could help their husbands and teach their children, but real scholarship was denied to most young women. Han Chinese living under Jin rule continued to follow Song customs in many ways, including early betrothal and marriage.

Finally, a word of caution is in order. Although well-educated women are widely praised in the pages of the dynastic histories, in epitaphs and literary works, such praise is indicative mainly of the value society placed on women's education. It does not necessarily mean that individuals singled out for praise actually attained the education attributed to them. Nor were their poems necessarily their own. The numbers of accolades in praise of women's education does show, at the least, that such education and literary skills were valued in Liao and Jin society and probably indicate that some significant proportion of women achieved literacy in Chinese.

Women's Prominence in Buddhism

Originally the Kitan worshipped the sun as a principal god, but also sacred mountain peaks, notably Mount Muye. A multitude of supernatural spirits inhabited their religious world, one that may generally be called animistic. Shamans conducted ceremonies of many kinds, including funerals. The *Liaoshi*'s annals record frequent visits to Mount Muye and Mount Wu in the reigns of the first several emperors. The cosmic principles related to heaven and earth were also worshipped, as were the spirits of departed ancestors. Divination was conducted using sheep scapulae. Sacrifices of horses and oxen were made at certain times of the year.[41] Human sacrifices were apparently required for imperial funerals, as shown in the dynastic records and archaeological discoveries. At tomb number 1 at Kulunqi, for example, the prone body of a man was interred under the tomb's entry, almost certainly as a sacrifice or guardian. The combination of predynastic shamanistic items, Buddhist culture, and even Daoism, as seen in the tomb of Princess Chenguo, demonstrates that the Kitan combined multiple religious practices regarding the dead. However, the religion for which the Liao and Jin periods are most noted was Buddhism.

Buddhism had been important among Chinese since the late Han dynasty and had reached the height of its popularity in the Tang. Thereafter, especially in the Song period, Buddhism waned among the intellectual elite as Confucianism enjoyed a renaissance. The conquest dynasties, however, following Tang-dynasty precedents, embraced Buddhism, although their support did not mean totally abandoning older religious beliefs, as the mixed nature of offerings in many Liao tombs attests. In supporting Buddhism, the Liao and Jin states carried on the Tang heritage, most notably, as Nancy Steinhardt has demonstrated, in architecture. Steinhardt points to the great surviving Buddhist halls and pagodas, many built with imperial patronage.[42]

Religious belief was an important part of the lives of many women living under Liao and Jin rule, who are praised in epitaphs for their piety. Women who contributed to Buddhist institutions left their names as donors on many inscriptions. In addition to providing evidence of religious belief, these inscriptions provide insights into the Liao economy, regarding especially issues of inheritance and agency in control of money and material assets. Women's names account for as many as one third of all donors on some lists. Thus, this architecture, which expresses so well the imperial and religious power of dynasties, was built—at least in part—with the pious contributions of women. Most of our information on religion, especially as it pertains to women, comes from epitaphs, inscriptions, and burial practices. Typical of government documents, the Liao and Jin dynastic histories, because of their emphasis on official government activities, make little mention of Buddhism. Nevertheless, the Liao and Jin courts sponsored many imperial Buddhist projects, in which the names of empresses and princesses are conspicuous.

Many Buddhist donor inscriptions have been preserved and provide information on the gendered distribution of endowments. Some fifty-seven donor inscriptions recorded in the *Quan Liao wen* and *Liaodai shike wenbian* include over twenty-two hundred names of both men and women. Of these, nearly seven hundred, or over thirty percent, were women, and fourteen hundred, or sixty-three percent, were men, while religious figures, usually of indeterminate gender, accounted for close to one hundred fifty names. Inscriptions usually give a woman's full name if unmarried and her natal surname followed by *shi* if married. Among the women, five hundred sixty-four were married, fifty-eight were unmarried, and another fifty-five were specifically designated as old women or widows. Those with religious titles were usually listed as a group, suggesting that the members of an order raised and donated money together, but sixteen of the women with religious titles were included in the context of family donations. In addition, a number of donations by men were made in memory of mothers or wives.[43] While we know that Kitan nobility and elite Kitan women contributed to Buddhist construction by offering gifts of money and land, the names contained on these donor lists are almost exclusively Han or *haner*. The predominance of Chinese names in Buddhist donor inscriptions for both men and women, taken together with the stronger evidence of Buddhism in *haner* as compared with Kitan tombs (discussed in chapter 2), suggests that in general the *haner* and Han population in the Liao state may have embraced Buddhism more fervently than the Kitan, who practiced an eclectic combination. This observation of the significance of *haner* and Han participation in Buddhist works and piety is supported by Dieter Kuhn's observations on the contributions of Han Chinese architects and craftsmen to Liao Buddhist constructions.[44]

These lists are interesting for several reasons. First, these donor lists underscore the popularity of Buddhism in the Liao state. Second, that a significant proportion of the donors were women reflects the importance of faith in many women's lives. Third, these donations show that women could bestow money or material property in their own names and that they had both the will and the independent agency to do so. This fact further implies that women in the Liao state had some latitude in controlling family finances, and since these finances did not—at least in pastoralist families—come through dowries, the resources must have come from women's initiatives within or outside the family structure. In the case of Han or *haner* women, the money might have come from dowries. The great majority of the women listed have Han names.

Certainly a great many Liao women were devout Buddhists, as both epitaphs and donor lists attest. The same had been true in the Tang dynasty, at the height of Buddhist popularity in China; the only woman to reign as emperor, Empress Wu (Wu Zetian), was a dedicated Buddhist. Like its predecessor the Tang and contemporary the Xi Xia, the Liao state sponsored great Buddhist monuments, which in turn bolstered the state's legitimacy.[45] It may be significant, however, that the majority of Buddhist monasteries, temples, and pagodas in the Liao capital Shangjing were located in the Chinese rather than the Kitan city.[46] The Guanyin Pavilion (dated 984), still standing at the Dule monastery, was constructed through the patronage of Hann Kuangsi and his son, Hann Derang. The monastery and pavilion are located in modern Jixian, Hebei province (Liao Jizhou prefecture), some fifty-five miles from the Southern Capital and near the Hann family home at Yutian.[47] While the pavilion's construction might be considered a private family matter, the line separating official, imperial, and state sponsorship and private contributions was never well defined. What does seem apparent is that the *haner* population of the Liao state played a large part in its Buddhist faith and institutions and that women, in turn, had an important role in funding these institutions. To the extent that women from Chinese backgrounds were given dowries, dowry funds might have been used for Buddhist contributions.

Little is known of the predynastic beliefs of the Jurchen, a result in part of the absence of a more extensive archaeological record. The Jin adopted Buddhism, probably from the Bohai, along with other aspects of Chinese culture, and during the course of the dynasty constructed many temples, some of which are still extant.[48] However, none of the Jurchen tombs discussed in chapter 4 had any religious content, although from other sources we know that Buddhism permeated the religious beliefs during the Jin period. At least one burial urn at the Jin imperial tomb site contained ashes, suggesting that it was a Buddhist interment.[49]

Information on Buddhist piety in the Jin period is limited. I have not been able to discover Jin Buddhist donor lists comparable to those from the Liao. With the exception of the extensive Buddhist murals at the Yanshan temple at Fanzhi in Shanxi, which do have a decidedly female slant, sources for the Jin period are in general thinner and less informative than those for the Liao.[50] However, epitaphs continue to be a useful source for information on women. One example of imperial piety comes from an inscription concerning the mother of the Jin emperor Zhangzong, who was Bohai. The emperor and his concubine attended the empress dowager on her deathbed. The empress dowager said to Concubine Dian, "I want to establish a temple [at Helong] for the souls of my family. I have seven hundred thousand cash of my own. Use my money to build the temple." Dian *fei* then built the Daming temple according to her request.[51]

Another source of information about the participation of women in Buddhist piety comes from the wall paintings in the Yanshan temple. The marketplace scene has been discussed earlier in relation to women's presence on the streets of Jin towns (chapters 3 and 4). The temple was established by the first Jin emperor in modern Shanxi at a point along the Wutaishan pilgrimage route.[52] According to art historian Susan Bush, the murals were sponsored by local families, and the donor inscriptions name "at least nine widows with sons and series of married couples." The artist who supervised the murals, Wang Gui (active ca. 1200), may have been trained at the Northern Song capital, which would account for the resemblance in style of these murals to Northern

Song painting.[53] The temple's entire decorative scheme shows an interpenetration of Buddhism with daily life at all levels of Jin-dynasty society, from deity to peasant. One large scene is dominated by tableaux of vast palaces. Women are conspicuous in many scenes, including the depiction of Prince Siddhartha's Great Departure, which is set in the gardens of the prince's palace depicted in the painting. No effort is made to reproduce Indian-style costumes or settings. Instead, elegantly attired palace ladies in Song-style attire appear to move freely inside and outside the grounds of sumptuous Chinese palaces and mingle with men, also in Chinese dress. The artists of these murals did not separate men from women. Furthermore, all social classes are depicted, from palace ladies to Buddhist nuns to prostitutes, peasants, and even beggars. In Buddhist terms, both high and low are equally capable of enlightenment—from an emperor down to a lowly cowherd. Men, women, beasts, and even ghosts alike partake of the Buddha's message.[54]

The main illustrations are related to Buddhist sutras, especially a Pali sutra involving Sumeda, an earlier Buddhist female avatar.[55] Street scenes show ordinary people going about the day's business, and genre scenes show peasants and other commoners. Hunters shoot at targets; peasants plow and sweep while others milk cows.[56] Tigers and hungry ghosts are shown worshipping at a Buddhist shrine. In one scene, an emperor holds informal court in his garden.[57] Another scene shows a mill for grinding flour.[58] An elaborate pagoda not unlike existing Liao pagodas is shown in the background of a landscape setting.[59] Another theme, shown in the palace scene, involves temptation, represented by the Buddhist devil Mara. The marketplace scene offers a glimpse of some of the erotic temptations of daily life. The Buddhist figure of Blue Robe stands on the riverbank leaning on a balustrade below the pavilion with the erotic "wildflowers."[60] The murals revolve around the legend of the goddess Hariti. Bush suggests that scenes featuring Hariti were placed near the doorway to the temple, "presumably as a model for women pilgrims." Bush points out the significance of women's roles in the murals at the Yanshan temple. The subject matter in these works seems particularly responsive to the concerns of women patrons and viewers.[61] Her observations point to another role for women in Buddhism, as pilgrims on the road to Wutaishan, which was located in Shandong, in the Jin state.

Donor lists, epitaphs, tombs, and wall paintings all show that women were active and prominent in Buddhist activities. Moreover, as discussed in chapter 5, Buddhist retreat appealed to women on more grounds than piety alone since widows could avoid following in death or levirate remarriage by taking vows. Others could commemorate loved ones with endowments to religious institutions, as the varied dedications reveal. Women might well have gone on pilgrimages. Above all, Buddhism, with its emphasis on saving female as well as male souls, offered women significant choice and greater agency than marriage rules alone would suggest.

The Romance of Empress Chengtian

Empress Dowager Chengtian has been portrayed in these pages as an educated woman, a skilled administrator who inspired loyalty in her ministers, and a warrior woman who led Liao troops to victory over the Song. But her staid official biography in the *Liaoshi* does not hint at the drama and intrigue behind her accomplishments. The following account was written by the Song writer Liu Bin, mentioned in chapter 6, and recorded in the *Ban Song shi xintan xiaoer*, now preserved in the *Quan Liao wen*:

> When the empress was young, she was betrothed to Hann Derang, but for a long time they did not marry. Then the imperial clan requested that she marry the emperor [Jingzong], so the Xiao family cancelled the betrothal and married her to the emperor.[62]

The future empress would have been about sixteen when she became the emperor's principal concubine, and since Jingzong reigned for fifteen years and she was twenty-nine or thirty at his death, her betrothal to Hann must have been made at an even earlier age, a point of interest in terms of women's sexuality. Upon her elevation to empress, she received the title Ruizhi.

> [Ruizhi] gave birth to Longxu who came to the throne as a child. She was then a young widow, regent for Longxu, and head of military affairs. But she feared that her son might be overthrown. So she went privately to Hann Derang and asked him to resume relations with her . . . [so that] the emperor would be his son as well. From then on, Hann Derang frequented the inner quarters.[63]

Hann Derang came from an illustrious *haner* family. His grandfather, Hann Zhigu, had been captured by the first emperor and became a trusted official in the early Liao government. When Hann Kuangsi, Derang's father, was disgraced for losing a major battle to the Song in 979, only Empress Ruizhi's intercession on his behalf saved him from execution. Subsequently, Kuangsi was appointed to the important post of southwestern military commissioner, in which capacity he served until his death.

Derang's career prospered under Jingzong. The two had been childhood friends. According to his official biography in the *Liaoshi*, "[Derang] was famous for his prudence." He served first as viceroy of the Supreme Capital, then as viceroy of the Southern Capital, Nanjing [Yanjing], and "was powerful in controlling capital affairs and had a good reputation." He led the defense of the city against Song invaders in 979. "When Jingzong lay dying, he appointed Derang and Yelü Xiezhen to take charge of his will and safeguard the heir apparent." Hann Derang was forty-two at the time of Jingzong's death and held the post of southern military commissioner. With Xiezhen's and Derang's help, the young Longxu became emperor and Empress Ruizhi became empress dowager, taking the title of Chengtian. Xiezhen was elderly, and after his death, Derang was appointed head of military affairs, and the *Liaoshi* records that "the empress dowager trusted him increasingly." He was appointed commander in chief of the Northern Administration and, after Yelü Xiege, the northern military commissioner, died in 998, Derang succeeded to that position, which he held concurrently with his other appointments. These positions are significant because the Northern Administration was normally the exclusive prorogation of the Yelü and Xiao nobles. *Haner* like the Hann and Zhang families normally served only in the Southern Administration. The empress appointed Derang grand counselor in 1001.[64] According to modern historians, "Hann held more complete civil and military control over the Liao government, both of its Chinese and Khitan [Kitan] components, than any minister had before or after him."[65]

Hann's biography is recorded in both the *Kitan guozhi* and the *Liaoshi* under the name Yelü Longyun. The entry in the *Liaoshi* notes that he received the honorary surname Yelü and the personal name of Chang in 1005 after the Battle of Chanyuan vanquishing the Song.[66] In receiving the name Yelü, an exceptional award, Hann became an honorary member of the imperial clan.

In the third month of 1008, he was given the new personal name Longyun.[67] The personal name Longyun was an even greater distinction, for it enrolled Hann in the empress's immediate family, since "Long" was the generational name of her sons Longxu, Longqing, and Longyu.[68] But another son, who receives no mention in the *Liaoshi*, held the title Prince of Chu. Song sources identify him as the son of Hann and the empress.[69]

Derang's romance with the empress dowager began during his stewardship after the emperor's death. His protection was crucial in securing the throne for the child emperor. Their relationship appears to have been quite open. In Liao society, a betrothal could be broken, but such an action was viewed very seriously. The significance given their earlier betrothal in this account is consistent with what we know about conquest-dynasty customs regarding betrothals, described in chapter 4. Liu's tale continues,

> Hann was married to a woman of the Li family. So Hann and the empress poisoned Li *shi*. Thereafter, they were totally together every minute of the day and often went hunting. Before long, the empress gave birth to the Prince of Chu, who was acknowledged to be the son of Hann Derang. They loved this son very much and granted to him the surname of Yelü. [He] was the object of great affection and was spoiled by his parents.[70]

The indictment that Hann murdered his wife in order to be with the empress and that Chengtian connived in this crime is first mentioned here, and it may be this murder rather than the romance that was concocted by Song reporters to castigate the empress.

Liu prefaces the story of the empress's romance with an account of her second son's behavior: As the younger brother, Longqing was spoiled by his mother; he had "a huge palace and more things under his command than the emperor." Every year, he "went hunting for girls" and abducted young women, the "best of whom he chose for his concubines and wives." Longqing's behavior was so arrogant that he made his mother, Empress Dowager Chengtian, "walk behind him, and he quarreled with the grand counselor, Hann Derang, to such an extent that there existed a deep enmity between the two."[71]

If Liu's story were the sole account of the empress's romance, I would join Twitchett and Tietze in dismissing the story as a salacious concoction. However, Hann's biography speaks at various points of his services to the empress as her chief minister. From information in Chengtian's biography, Hann was clearly the empress's "favorite" in the Elizabethan sense. But an enigmatic entry in the *Kitan guozhi* gives further support to the romance theory: "[Hann] received full powers and enjoyed the pleasures [accorded to] the Duke of Piyang," who was the reputed lover of Empress Lü in the Han dynasty.[72] Liu Bin's account is supported by a second contemporary and more authoritative report by the Song official Lu Zhen, who was sent as an ambassador to the Liao court at Zhongjing in 1006 to celebrate Emperor Shengzong's birthday. Lu's report describes his trip to the Liao capital in great detail, providing many acute observations of intelligence value for the Song.

He retold the story of Empress Chengtian and Hann Derang in somewhat different words. "When the Xiao empress [dowager] was young she was betrothed to Hann [Derang].... The Xiao clan stole Hann's wife and offered her [to the Liao emperor]. Longxu was born [of this union]." Lu continues,

> When the Yelü emperor died, Longxu inherited the throne . . . while still young. The Xiao empress was [thus] widowed at an early age. Fearing that [this situation] would be disadvantageous to [her] child, [she] said privately to Derang, "I was once betrothed to you. I would that we made harmonious our former amicability.... Then the young lord who rules the nation will be your son also." Henceforth Derang entered and exited [her] personal quarters as he pleased. Following this, Derang's wife, Li *shi*, was killed with poisoned wine. Every time [the empress dowager] went out to hunt, [she] always abided with Derang in the same round tent. Before long the Prince of Chu was born; he is Hann's son. [The empress] and Derang loved him deeply and bequeathed to him the [imperial] surname of the Yelü clan.[73]

Whether sexual relations were condoned during betrothal is unclear, but the empress's request to Hann, as reported in Liu's account, implies that they had previously enjoyed such relations.

The stories told by Lu Zhen and Liu Bin are sufficiently similar that Liu's tale might have been based on Lu's account, but in fact Liu Bin's story appears to be the earlier of the two. It is not dated but was probably written around 1005, while Lu's version, based on a visit in 1006, was not published until 1010–1016.[74] Lu and Liu agree that Hann and the empress were responsible for the death of Hann's wife and that the Prince of Chu was the son of the empress and Hann Derang. Although Emperor Jingzong had four sons, three of whom were born to Empress Ruizhi, there is no listing for a son with the title Prince of Chu in the *Liaoshi*.[75] While Liu Bin's tale may have been based on hearsay, Lu's account, which was part of an official report on his visit to the Liao state, has the ring of authenticity.

Lu goes on to describe the principals at the Liao court as he met them. He was first met at the Southern Capital by envoys from Longqing, Prince of Qin, who commanded the realm of Yan. Lu met Longqing later at a reception for the Song officials at the capital, Zhongjing. In describing the emperor's brother, Lu comments that "at one time he annually registered the sons and daughters of the people [of Yen] and personally chose [from among them]. The best . . . he made his wives, and the next [best] were made concubines and servants." This description of Longqing's activities is much closer to the Manchu *xiunü* practice than the brutal abductions Liu describes. Lu goes on to add that Longqing frequently accompanied his mother, the empress dowager, on summer excursions, "and the caitiff grand counselor is especially envious of him, so he does not get along with Hann Derang."[76]

The Song embassy was received at an official court reception by Emperor Shengzong and Hann Derang. Lu describes the emperor as a man of "thirty or more years old," wearing Chinese-style clothing. Grand counselor in chief and Prince of Jin, Hann Derang, Lu notes, was a man of about sixty. With him was the Prince of Chu, "the son of [Hann] and the empress."[77] The empress dowager was not present at this audience, but the Song ambassadors had an audience with her the following day. Lu describes her as a woman "[of] approximately fifty, wearing a cap of kingfisher-feather adornments . . . a small solid yellow brocade robe drawn in [at the waist] with a white brocade sash . . . and a brocade skirt." Also present was a boy of ten or so, who "wore a barbarian cap and brocade clothing and frolicked about playfully. . . . In appearance he resembles Grand Councilor Hann. In all probability he is the son of Hann borne by the empress dowager." The boy is mentioned several times in Lu's report, and this description coincides with the historical notation that the empress bore a son named Diange, who did not live to adulthood. Lu saw Chengtian at several other events, including the emperor's birthday celebration and the New Year's banquet. The envoys took their leave of her when they departed the capital on the eighth day of the new year.[78]

Lu's account was an official report designed to provide an accurate picture of the geography of Liao roads, towns, and fortifications and the customs of its people, especially the government. He spends much of his report describing the foreign customs at the Liao court, for which he uses such demeaning epithets as "caitiffs" [*lu*] to describe the Kitan. However, Lu does not appear to criticize the behavior of the empress dowager and Hann directly, although he may have relished telling a risqué tale to the moralistic scholars back at the Song court.[79] The story of the empress and her minister might have been intended to denigrate the "caitiffs" by showing how far their morals strayed from Chinese standards, or it could simply be descriptive. More important for our purposes is that Lu Zhen's report provides an independent source supporting Liu Bin's tale, written earlier. In both accounts, Longqing acts arrogantly and is antagonistic toward Hann. The Prince of Chu is mentioned in both sources as Hann's son, and Lu encounters what he takes to be a second son of Hann and the empress in her quarters.

In retelling the romance, Lu states that the Xiao clan "stole" Hann's wife. Both accounts imply that the empress's earlier betrothal was an important factor in justifying her liaison with Hann Derang. As seen in chapter 4, betrothals in Liao society were very nearly as binding as marriage and may have included sexual privileges.

One point bears further investigation. Why was marrying fifteen-year-old Xiao Yanyan to the new emperor, Jingzong, so important that it justified breaking her earlier betrothal? Political reasons may well have hinged on the history of the imperial succession and Yanyan's lineage. When Empress Yingtian had negotiated the compromise that put Deguang on the throne, the brothers pledged that Bei's son would succeed Deguang and that thereafter the two lines would alternate. Thus, Bei's son, Emperor Shizong, succeeded Deguang, while the fourth emperor, Muzong (r. 951–969), was Deguang's son.[80] Shizong was assassinated in an attempted palace coup, and Muzong was murdered in his bed by his own servants.[81] Various political intrigues against Prince Xian, the future emperor Jingzong, made him flee for his life, because Muzong saw him as a threat to his own succession. However, Muzong had no heirs, and so Jingzong succeeded him. When Jingzong, Shizong's son and Bei's grandson, succeeded to the throne he must have felt quite insecure. If indeed he was the son of Lady Zhen, he would have been half Chinese—even more reason to find an empress of unimpeachable pedigree to bear his heirs.

Yanyan was descended from an uncle of Yingtian's mother's second husband from the Yishisi lineage, according to Jennifer Holmgren.[82] Karl

Witt-fogel and Feng Chia-sheng state that she was a great-granddaughter of Yingtian's brother or uncle.[83] As Yingtian's grandniece in the fifth generation, she must have represented a combination of earlier Xi nobility with the Xiao and Yelü lines, which had the power to dampen the rivalry between the heirs of Prince Bei and Emperor Deguang. She was also of a senior generation to Jingzong, who was descended from Abaoji in the fourth generation. The practice of alternating the throne between the two lines and the bloodshed it engendered ended with Jingzong. The subsequent birth of a son who would inherit the throne as Emperor Shengzong sealed the pact.

Empress Ruizhi became a widow when Jingzong died in 982. Widows in Liao society had limited alternatives. Levirate was not an option for Ruizhi; to have married one of the emperor's younger kin would have been tantamount to handing over the throne to young Shengzong's rivals. As a Kitan widow, she could not marry again, but chaste widowhood had not yet become customary even among the Han sector of society as early as the 980s. As a young widow caught in perilous circumstances, support from Yelü Xiezhen and Hann Derang was crucial to Chengtian's appointment as regent and her son's succession. Both men were sufficiently important that they are mentioned prominently in Empress Chengtian's official biography as well as in unofficial sources, and they feature in detail in the chapters on meritorious officials as well as in the standard chronicles of Jingzong's and Shengzong's reigns. Did remaining widowed and functioning as regent for her son and head of the imperial family under these circumstances require sexual abstinence? What did widowhood mean in the context of an earlier betrothal?

Did this betrothal justify renewing her relationship with Hann Derang, as the sources not so subtly imply? Kitan girls enjoyed a period of sexual freedom prior to marriage. According to both Song accounts, Chengtian took the initiative in going to Hann Derang and asking him to resume their relationship. In so doing, she was being assertive in a manner reminiscent of the girls who sang of their attributes on street corners. Did the sexual freedom that unmarried girls could exercise in any way influence the empress's actions? Did the granting of the imperial surname to Hann in some way justify their relationship? One might argue that this made him eligible to take Jingzong's widow in a levirate union since Hann was younger than the deceased emperor. But that excuse does not seem plausible because Hann received this honor only a few

Private Affairs

years before Chengtian's death, when their affair had already endured for over twenty years and had produced at least one, probably two, sons.

We may never know the answers to these questions. Chengtian's romance was clearly exceptional. But, taking into consideration the accepted Liao norms for female sexuality, as discussed in chapters 4 and 5, I find the story of the romance between Chengtian and Hann Derang plausible. It is consistent with the sanctity the Liao accorded betrothals, with Liao concepts of sexuality, marriage, and the restraints placed on widows. It also accords with the remarkable degree of agency that imperial women exercised in the Liao period. Courage and assertiveness seem to be common characteristics of warrior women, whether couched in political or personal terms.

Furthermore, the accounts by both Lu and Liu must be set against contemporary Song standards of women's conduct and widow chastity that formed these authors' cultural contexts. Both men whose accounts tell this tale were products of the Northern Song period, when a new Confucian orthodoxy with its stricter moral standards was developing. Premarital sexual liaisons implied by the betrothal between Yanyan and Derang would have been scandalous in Song China, where young women were carefully sequestered prior to marriage and virginity was a prerequisite. Moreover, for a prominent widow like Empress Chengtian to openly have a lover would have been equally appalling. In Song China, a woman's chastity after being widowed was highly valued, and while widows often remarried—a privilege denied Kitan women—to conduct an illicit affair would have been an even greater disgrace.[84] Thus, while criticizing the shameful behavior of "barbarians," the Song accounts illustrate the ways that women's sexuality and chastity in Song society differed from those of the Liao. What may have been intended by the Song authors to be a salacious piece of slander was more probably grounded in Kitan customs concerning betrothals and widows.

Finally, a Ming-dynasty version of the story, which implicitly assumes Chinese standards for women's comportment, labels their affair outright adultery.

> Xiao *taihou* [Empress Dowager Chengtian] died in [1009]. She was very clever and good at cajoling ministers and high officials [to the point where] they were all willing to die for her in battle. [She] led the troops and joined

in the battles.... She lived in adultery with Hann Derang, and after she started this affair, she granted him the name of Yelü Longyun. Not long after [the empress's death], Derang also died. He was buried alongside her.[85]

In this version, the empress is praised for her military leadership, as she is in her official biography and in the Song sources. This Ming source explicitly points out that she led troops and joined in battles and is critical when accusing her of being clever and good at "cajoling ministers and high officials." Cajoling and cleverness were not qualities that Ming Chinese admired in women.[86] Following these criticisms, the author accuses the empress of adultery—even worse! But this Ming account is the only source mentioning the burials of Chengtian (d. 1109) and Hann (d. 1111), since the Song accounts were written prior to their deaths. It also adds a detail regarding their respective burials that has recently been confirmed by archaeological discoveries. The identification of a group of tombs belonging to emperors Jingzong, Shengzong, Chengtian, and Hann Derang was announced in 2005. Just as reported in the Ming source, Hann Derang was discovered to have been buried beside his empress.[87] Since empresses were normally buried in the tomb with the emperor, which would have been reopened for this purpose, this announcement probably indicates that Hann's tomb was located next to Jingzong's imperial mausoleum. This discovery, to me, is a final confirmation that the romance reported between the empress and her minister was in fact true.

As a footnote, relics from Hann's tomb, including artifacts of solid gold and others with gold inlay or gold and silver leaf, were on sale on the international antiquities market in the early 1990s.[88] The vandals who robbed the tomb destroyed valuable contextual evidence and probably prevented archaeological publication related to this important tomb.

Conclusion

Education, religion, and romance were all essentially private activities for which the sources are disappointingly indirect. We have the words of others praising women's literacy, reading, study, and writing in biographies and epitaphs, but no writings that can be reliably attributed to women themselves.

We have vignettes and epitaphs regarding women's Buddhist devotion and donor lists of those who contributed to Buddhist constructions and institutions, but again no personal accounts of piety. Romance is an even more shadowy area. The Liao dynastic and private histories carry hints of a special relationship between Empress Chengtian and Hann, but they were written one hundred to two hundred years after the event. Travelers' accounts are more timely and more specific but were written by Song observers with implicitly Confucian standards for feminine behavior. Some were openly critical and demeaning. But historians also have the contemporaneous context to inform their narratives, and the context of women's daily lives, the *lienü* chapters, archaeological discoveries, and the social customs regarding sexuality, marriage, widowhood, and chastity provide a rich contextual setting for these private activities. Added to this picture are known patterns of women's agency and assertiveness in the Liao and Jin periods.

I argued in the previous chapter that Yang Miaozhen should be seen not as an aberrant example of a Song woman whose actions went against all conventional Song feminine standards but rather in the context of Jin society, where she follows on the heels of militant Liao empresses and heroic Jin *lienü*. In this setting, hers is the final chapter in a sequence of warrior women of the Liao and Jin dynasties. Similarly, if Empress Chengtian's romance is seen as more than a singular and unique occurrence at odds with the rest of society, it too should be evaluated against the context of Liao history. Given the flexible attitudes toward women's sexuality, the strictures against widow remarriage, and the common use of levirate, a young widow's accommodation with a lover may indeed not have been all that unusual in tenth-century Kitan society.

The women in this chapter negotiated in different ways between steppe and Confucian societies. Kitan and Jurchen women who gave money or resources to support Buddhist temples had adopted some of the conventions of Tang and Bohai society. Han and *haner*, who, to judge from their names, made up the vast majority of the women supporting Buddhism, were adhering to the religion of their conquerors in a sense or to remnants from the Tang period, for Buddhism was in decline in the Song and Southern Song states. Kitan and Jurchen women who pursued education in the Chinese language and classics and who wrote prose and poetry clearly had adopted Han culture, although not to such an extent that they altered their fundamental identity. The *haner*, Han, and Bohai women who also embraced education were both benefiting from the social context of Liao society and reinforcing their Confucian cultural values. Chengtian was first and foremost a Kitan woman, as her military achievements and sexuality demonstrate, but in terms of education and administrative skills, she too negotiated aspects of Han Confucian culture to her advantage.

Conclusion

THE PRECEDING CHAPTERS have been organized topically, each dealing with a single issue, such as women's daily lives, aspects of betrothal and marriage, widowhood, warrior women, and so forth. The internal organization of each chapter attempts to follow persons or topics sequentially, but the data is often imprecise in terms of date or relative chronology. The range of the book is broad, covering over three hundred years, and the synchronic method is not ideal for attempting to answer questions of how changes occurred over time and what factors influenced or precipitated change. At the same time that Liao and Jin women acquired new cultural attributes, they often maintained traditional attitudes as well, notably with regard to martial skills, horsemanship, marriage, and widowhood. Historians may therefore not be satisfied with a topical approach—and I have found this a difficult book to write—since they (we) like to ask diachronic questions about time, historical context, and change and analytical questions regarding causality and outcome. Thus a chronological review is appropriate at this point, followed by a final word on the significance of conquest-dynasty women.

The Women

Women of the Liao and Jin states who figure in the preceding chapters were daughters, wives, mothers, widows, empresses, warriors, and outlaws. We have been engaged with four different constituencies: Kitan women, *haner* women living under Liao control, Jurchen women, and Han or *haner* women under Jin domination. Many of the changes women experienced across this time span involved tensions between maintenance of indigenous cultural values or lifestyles and adoption of Han Chinese culture in a process generally referred to as sinicization. These changes, or more precisely adaptations, involved negotiating values as selected aspects of Han culture were added while others were ignored. Adopting the Chinese language in both its spoken and written forms was one issue, but the invention of written forms of Kitan and Jurchen to compete with Chinese underscored the significance of tradition. Maintaining martial prowess on the battlefield supported by pastoralist lifestyles involved traditional values of steppe, field, and forest. Adoption of certain Han Chinese customs and Confucian ethical principles but not others was one aspect of adaptation. Development of a written language was another, since both the Kitan and the Jurchen had only oral traditions prior to establishing states. Buddhism was a third aspect of adaptation. The warrior women described in the introduction to the chapter on Liao empresses not only embraced martial skills but they were also literate and sometimes pious. Many women had the agency and ability to construct their own identities in Liao and Jin China.

The first woman in this chronological survey is Empress Yingtian, in the tenth century. Her life and identity might be taken as a starting point in terms of cultural values. A woman of the steppes, she was as skilled in political intrigue as she was in military leadership. She worked closely with Abaoji, helping to strengthen his position, aiding in military matters, and helping to put down rebellions. She commanded her own military forces. The Chinese imperial model that Abaoji adopted required political structure, literacy, and record keeping. His *haner* advisers undoubtedly used their literary skills for these purposes. Yingtian was also aware of the value of literacy and promoted the invention of a written version of the Kitan language, perhaps with the intent of preempting extensive sinicization that dependence on Chinese might have promoted. Thus, from the beginning of the Liao state in the tenth century, adoption of Chinese models competed with traditional values.

Empress Yingtian established another precedent by initiating the imperial marriage tradition in which Abaoji's Yelü clan married exclusively with her own originally Shulü clan, renamed Xiao. In her most celebrated moment, Yingtian refused to follow the steppe custom of widow suicide and instead cut off her hand to accompany the emperor in death until she might join him later, thus abrogating widow suicide and offering widows a new alternative to the unhappy choice between following in death and levirate. Yingtian was also the first warrior woman in the Liao dynasty, an aspect of conquest society that endured not only through the Liao but also until the end of the Jin and on into the Yuan.

Yingtian was followed in the reign of her son, Deguang, by two culture bearers, both of whom came from the Latter Tang state. Lady Chen of the *lienü* chapter came from the Latter Tang but resided in Liao territory. She educated her sons in the Confucian tradition to become government officials. Lady Zhen, also from the Latter Tang, was obtained by the prince who would become the third emperor, and he made her his empress. She may have been the mother of Emperor Jingzong. Both women can be seen as emblematic of the penetration and adaptation of Han learning and education. Although Han officials serving the Liao played leading political parts and no doubt facilitated acculturation, women also engaged in literary study.

The elderly woman occupant of the remote tomb at Yemaotai discussed in chapter 1, together with the contents of her tomb (dated 960–980), illustrate intriguing aspects of the ways in which Han adaptations and Kitan identity had become interwoven by the latter part of the tenth century. The unnamed lady is dressed in Kitan clothing and boots. The tomb furnishings include saddles, horse equipment, and weapons, emblematic of pastoralist culture. However, she was buried in a Han-style marble sarcophagus with carved Chinese directional symbols and floral decorations. The two paintings buried with her were done in the style of the late Five Dynasties, and the many books and manuscripts stuffed into her tomb were almost certainly written in Chinese. Thus, the combination of Han learning for women together with Kitan cultural identity is evident from early in the dynasty.

Further aspects of negotiated values are evident in the reign of Emperor Shengzong (r. 982–1031) and his mother, who was first Jingzong's Empress Ruizhi and after his death Empress Dowager Chengtian. She combined the martial prowess of Yingtian with administrative skills and political acumen that argue for a high degree of proficiency based on education and literacy. If, as Daniel Kane has suggested, by the early eleventh century the Kitan elite generally spoke Liao Chinese while the court language had become the more sophisticated Song Chinese, Chengtian must have been adept in both, as well as Kitan.[1] The empress dowager was observed by the Song diplomat Lu Zhen wearing Chinese silk brocades, another sign of selective accommodation. Her efforts to secure her son's succession to the throne and her own skill in administrative affairs were paralleled by empress dowagers in the Song state. But her exceptionally able military leadership and assertive sexuality in going to Hann Derang for support reflected steppe traditions. That the Liao court accepted her long liaison with Hann also rested on traditional precedents, including the significance of betrothals in Kitan society and a relatively more open attitude toward sexuality evidenced in steppe cultures.

Although Chengtian's life may have some similarities with that of Yingtian, it was fundamentally quite different. Yingtian supported Abaoji, accompanied him on military missions, and dominated the government after his death, but only briefly, until she had seen her son Deguang, a forceful emperor, on the throne. She was a woman of the steppes; she must have spoken Kitan, a language for which she also recommended the creation of a script even if she probably could not read it, and acknowledged steppe customs even when refusing to follow them. Fifty-six years later Empress Chengtian showed herself to be an educated and literate woman. She enjoyed the hunt and, like Yingtian, excelled in the military field. But unlike her, Chengtian was a working administrator. Her leadership was respected and her decisions accepted by the high ministers of state. She ran the Liao Empire for thirty years, a far more complex administrative job than it had been in Yingtian's time.

The archaeological discovery of the burial of Princess Chenguo (d. 1018), niece of Emperor Shengzong, sheds a different light on mid-Liao culture. Her tomb emphasizes pastoralism, with horses depicted on the walls and actual saddles and other equipment among the artifacts inside. Archaeologists found evidence that she had been in poor health, but her tomb portrays a robust feminine culture. She wore the accoutrements of a Kitan woman on her belt and seemed ready to mount the horse portrayed on the entry wall and ride across the steppes. The only Chinese intrusion in the tomb is evidence of Daoism, but animistic rites clearly took place as well.

Several decades later, Yelü Changge, of the *lienü* chapter, who lived in the reign of emperors Xingzong and Daozong, also combined selected aspects of Han culture with Kitan tradition. Changge was skilled in literary matters, wrote poetry—again, almost certainly in Chinese—and displayed Confucian virtues, including loyalty and filial devotion to her brother. While filial piety was intrinsically Confucian, loyalty was not confined to Confucian ethics. In circumstances of shifting allegiances and affiliations on the steppes or in sophisticated political intrigues, loyalty was a prime consideration among the people of the Liao, whether Kitan or *haner*. Changge thus entwined customary Kitan values and selected Confucian ethics with aspects of Han learning.

Of about the same time, Concubine Xiao's epitaph shows that she excelled in the typically Kitan skills of riding and hunting, but she also wrote poetry and decorated her home with paintings in her own hand. She was skilled in debate and gave astute political advice. Like Chengtian, Changge, and the unknown lady at Yemaotai, she combined the best of both cultures.

The late eleventh-century tomb at Kulunqi, in contrast, emphasizes steppe culture, depicting the wedding of a princess with all the pastoralist accoutrements described for such a ceremony in the *Liaoshi*, including the camel carriage, burial cart, and a woman holding a mirror facing the bride. Human and animal sacrifices found in the tomb reinforce the steppe model, but Buddhist décor dominates the inner burial chamber. While Buddhism may have been the professed religion of the Kitan aristocracy, in the afterlife, the elite wished to be reunited with steppe culture as well.

Three Xiao women in the *Liaoshi lienü juan*, discussed in chapter 1, Erliben, in the reign of Daozong, Yixin, and Nuolan (d. 1115), all followed their husbands in death, a profoundly Kitan gesture. In spite of the education and filial piety attributed to them, following in death was the ultimate pastoralist statement. While Yingtian's sacrifice may have made widow suicide no longer mandatory, it was clearly still honored in practice, as these three women's biographies demonstrate.

What then can be said of the pattern of changes in the Liao dynasty? As sketched above, Han Chinese influence came early to the Kitan, since it is already visible in Abaoji's construction of the state that came to be known as Liao. Over the next two hundred years, Kitan women adopted Chinese literacy and selected Confucian values, but periodically the pendulum swung back toward the pastoralist tradition, repeatedly reinforcing steppe values and customs. These trends produced a tension between traditional steppe customs and adoption of Han culture.

The Jin period, by contrast, was marked by significant and increasing sinicization among both men and women. A meaningful analysis of diachronic change among Jurchen women is impeded by the absence of archaeological data on anything resembling the scale provided by the many tombs of the Kitan elite. Written records and paintings therefore become all the more important in depicting cultural differences. The *lienü* chapter in the *Jinshi*, arranged chronologically, tells an interesting story. Jurchen women were active as warriors from early in the dynasty to its end. The first woman mentioned in the chapter, Shalizhi, organized people to fight and led them in defeating rebels, and another, Aluzhen, late in the dynasty, defeated enemy troops. Women with Bohai or Han surnames married to men of the Jurchen elite defended the family reputation but were less assertive militarily than Jurchen women. Han women, meanwhile, reflected Chinese values, such as avoidance of remarriage, a trait that may predate the later development of widow chastity in Yuan and Ming China. But the final woman described in the *lienü* chapter, Zhang Fengnu, a prostitute, acted courageously in encouraging the troops to defend the city against the Mongols. The celebration of these activities in the *lienü* chapter reflects the values of Jurchen and Jin society more generally rather than necessarily representing actual biographies. One must of course always remember that biographies and even epitaphs cannot be taken literally but are emblematic of societal values.

The list of valiant Jin-dynasty women would not be complete without Wulinda (d. 1160), wife of the future emperor Shizong, who bravely sacrificed her own life rather than compromise her husband and thus indirectly ensured Shizong's accession to the throne. As emperor, Shizong instituted a reform movement to bring back the old Jurchen martial prowess and cultural values, including revival of the Jurchen language. The burial of Prince Qi and his wife in Jurchen costumes near the ancient capital in the Jurchen homeland is evidence of that movement in the late twelfth century. Although the prince and princess were attired for burial in Jurchen-style clothing, the materials for these antique styles included fine silks and gold thread, an apparent contradiction to the traditional customs and culture that Shizong was trying to revive. Chinese had already become the common language for the Jin state. Chinese influence prevailed, and the emperor's efforts to revive Jurchen culture and prowess were ultimately unsuccessful.

The most famous of Jin warrior women, Yang Miaozhen, lived at the end of the dynasty. As described in chapter 6, she was a warrior woman who led her own and her consort's troops. Although Miaozhen came from an ostensibly Han family, she clearly subscribed to a Jurchen martial identity in spite of Jin society's increasing reliance on Han Chinese language, customs, ethics, and values.

Turning to art, we see women portrayed in the Yanshan temple paintings, of about 1150, walking freely on the streets, but whether they are Han or Jurchen is unclear. Fan Chengda's description of women in the former Song capital as preserving antiquated Han styles accords with these paintings. Perhaps the most interesting Jin painting is the representation of Lady Wenji's return, created for the Jin court around 1200.

Lady Wenji, who has become a leitmotif for the women of the conquest dynasties discussed in this book, is portrayed as a Jurchen matron in the painting (featured at the beginning of this book). She was probably intended as a moral exemplar. But the *Wenji* painting also carried a double message, since the Jurchen warriors following her are represented as "barbarians" cringing from the wind, hardly admirable stances. While the female servants appear stoic, Wenji alone is portrayed as heroic. In depicting Wenji as mounted and resolute in Jurchen costume, the painting also shows her as a warrior in the old tradition. She is returning to civilization—the sinicized civilization of the Jin capital—and her tale of capture and return emphasizes the virtue of loyalty.

Thus this work of art, like the Prince Qi burial and Shizong's efforts to revive the Jurchen language, carries a complex set of messages, on the one hand affirming warrior culture and on the other reinforcing Confucian concepts. Wenji, as culture bearer, literary lady, loyal daughter, and warrior woman resonates throughout the pages of this book. Like Wenji, Lady Zhen and Chen *shi* were culture bearers. Changge and other educated *lienü* selectively adopted Chinese culture and Confucian ethics in their wake. *Haner* and Han women under Liao and Jin rule who carefully preserved Chinese dress and culture in their homes mirrored Wenji's longing on the windswept grasslands for her home in Chang'an. For others, like the Jin imperial women who viewed the painting, Wenji exemplified loyalty above all, a virtue shared by both Confucian and steppe cultures.

Han and *haner* women living under Jin rule also maintained cultural continuity. Unlike the men, who, to borrow the words of Fan Chengda, became "barbarized," wearing Jurchen clothing and boots and even hairstyles, the women wore Han silk dresses and drank tea. The outer chambers of their tombs conform to Kitan cultural rhetoric, with horses, camels, and steppe vehicles conspicuously displayed, but the inner chambers, the domain of women, reflect Chinese styles in dress and comportment and often display Buddhist attributes. The women preparing tea as shown on the walls of Hann Shixun's tomb late in the Liao period wear silks in Song-dynasty style; "Grandma" too is clad in silk, but she is entertained by Kitan dancers and koumiss jugs appear under the tables. No immediate changes in *haner* tomb contents and decoration appear with the arrival of the Jin.

Liao and Jin women did, over time, evolve toward a greater degree of cultural adaptation to Han Chinese customs. The contrast between Empress Yingtian and Empress Chengtian shows how great a change had occurred in a short period of time, and while Chengtian had not become sinicized, much of the transformation that included language and administrative skills was mandated by the adoption of Chinese methods of government. Chengtian, Changge, the lady in the tomb at Yemaotai, and Concubine Xiao demonstrate the combination of Kitan tradition and Chinese adaptations that may well have represented an ideal for elite Liao women in the eleventh century. But this brief chronological review of Kitan women discussed in this book implies no march toward sinicization. Rather, such women strove to maintain Kitan traditions at the same time that they adopted selected aspects of Chinese culture.

As for Jin women, the situation is less clear. The influence of the Bohai brought sinicization early, and Chinese culture was more thoroughly incorporated. The absence of archaeological evidence for Jurchen women leaves a major gap. Nevertheless, Jurchen women in the *lienü* chapter of the *Jinshi* maintained martial skills, as did—most famously—Yang Miaozhen at the end of the dynasty. The painting of Lady Wenji in Jurchen costume portrays a nostalgia for the old ways even as she is shown returning to Chinese-style Jin civilization.

Cultural Change and Adaptation

The pattern of preservation and adaptation is also evident in the major institutions of the Liao and Jin periods affecting women, such as status, education, marriage, widowhood, and burial. Girl babies were welcomed in Liao and Jin society, for under the bride-price system their marriages would enrich the family. Marriage was not, however, universal, and the biography of Changge as well as evidence from tombs where individual women were buried supports this point. Girls brought up in the natal home could remain unmarried and even set up their own households, although the details of what circumstances allowed this are not yet clear. Moreover, the frequency of women as the main occupants—often the only occupant—in impressive Liao mausoleums underscores the prominence of women in Liao society. Such a relative degree of preeminence reflects steppe, not Han, culture.

One aspect of women's lives that does show increasing incorporation of Han influence over time is education. Beginning with the culture bearers at the opening of the dynasty, Liao women increasingly appear in the records and archaeological materials as educated and literate. They read the classics and adopted aspects of Confucian ethics, including loyalty and sometimes filial piety. Although educated Kitan women, such as the lady of Yemaotai, show up early in the dynasty, evidence suggests that female education became more common and more highly valued later on. Facility in Chinese also increased in the early part of the dynasty, whether the dialect was Liao Chinese or the more sophisticated Song speech that Kane has attributed to the Kitan elite, so that by the twelfth century it may have replaced spoken Kitan among the elite. The Kitan script remained in use, probably largely for ceremonial inscriptions, since surviving inscriptions are found only in tombs or on steles.[2] The Kitan written language persisted into the Jin period, and although the Jin developed a Jurchen script, it seems to have been lost by the time of the Mongol conquest. The last person recorded to have been fluent in Kitan, both written forms and as a spoken language, was Yelü Chucai in the early Yuan period.[3]

Marriage customs of the Kitan and Jurchen, including primary brideprice marriages, sororate, and levirate seem to have undergone little change, although the practice of taking concubines, adopted from the Chinese, increased over time. Generation-gap marriage was practiced by both the Kitan and Jurchen elite. Meanwhile, following in death continued to be honored. Levirate was among the most distinctive marriage customs and remained so throughout both dynasties. Edicts alternately prohibiting and allowing *haner* families to practice levirate in the Jin period suggest that pastoralist "barbarian" customs were sometimes adopted by the Han population, especially, no doubt, by in-laws wanting to keep a widow's property and resources in the family. Toward the end of the Liao dynasty, retreat for widows into a Buddhist sanctuary or chaste widowhood became acceptable, although most of the evidence for Buddhist piety involves Han women. The early Kitan and Jurchen had multiple wives but not secondary wives. The first Liao emperor to have recorded concubines rather than or in addition to multiple wives was Shizong in the mid-tenth century.[4]

Liao burial customs changed dramatically early in the dynasty. Whereas the Kitan elite had once set corpses in trees and buried the dead under the open sky, tombs of the elite from as early as the 920s show that the Liao court had adopted Tang-style mausoleums almost immediately and continued to construct ever more elaborate tombs throughout the dynasty.[5] Tomb architecture was based on Tang-dynasty precedents, not influences felt from the Song.

The Jurchen seem to have rejected Han burial practices. The few Jurchen tombs discovered so far are simple shafts or wood or stone coffins without a tomb, a custom dating from predynastic times. Even the Jin imperial burials, located outside the Central Capital (modern Beijing), which were established in the mid-twelfth century during the reigns of the third and fourth emperors, are far simpler than their Liao counterparts. Thus, although the Liao elite adopted Han funeral architecture, the Jurchen were reluctant to do so and maintained predynastic practices. The tension, it can be seen, between adoption of Chinese culture and preserving indigenous traditions continued.

The progression of the Buddhist faith among women in the Liao and Jin empires is not easy to trace. Evidence of Buddhism is scant in early Liao tombs, where animistic sacrifices or Daoist imagery predominate. Even later in the dynasty, burials continued to be eclectic, containing evidence of shamanism and emphasizing pastoralist culture but often having Buddhist paintings and relics in the burial chambers. Most of the data on women's engagement with Buddhism, such as epitaphs and donor records, come from the end of the Liao period. Even the tombs of the Han elite late in the Liao period, which might be expected to adhere more closely to Buddhist beliefs, are not unmixed with animistic or other outside influences. Mention of Buddhist piety occurs more frequently with *haner* and Han than with Kitan women, and almost all the Buddhist donors on inscriptions have Han names. From this admittedly partial evidence, it would seem that Buddhism was stronger among the Han population than among the ruling elite, in spite of the great Buddhist monuments the Liao state erected.[6]

Distinctions between Kitan and Jurchen women on the one hand and Han and *haner* women on the other has been a concern throughout the chapters of this book. In the *haner* population the pressures were to conform to Kitan or Jurchen customs. Men wore a version of Kitan or Jurchen clothing, and evidence, both literary and pictorial, indicates that during the Jin period they were required to shave their foreheads and wear a queue. The differences between male and female acculturation suggest *haner* women spoke Chinese in the home, just as they dressed in Chinese styles, while men more likely spoke Liao Chinese or Kitan. Curiously, however, among the Han and *haner*, Kitan or Jurchen attire indicated subservient social status and appears in tombs to have been worn by servants, possibly slaves, and children, while adults wore Han-style clothing.

The situation regarding acculturation over time was quite different for the Jurchen. Early contact with Bohai culture jump-started Jurchen women's literary culture. Records regarding elite Bohai and Jurchen women uniformly depict them as literate, following Confucian virtues for women, and devoutly Buddhist. It is generally accepted that the Jurchen adopted Chinese culture rapidly under the first four emperors. Chinese replaced Jurchen as the spoken language of the dynasty well before Emperor Shizong's attempts to recapture Jurchen culture. Overall, Jurchen women converted to Chinese culture much more readily and rapidly than did their Kitan counterparts, but they nonetheless respected the warrior tradition even to the end of the dynasty. Further developments in the Jin period show new evidence of a growing emphasis on conjugal relations, as seen in burials and wall paintings, and, late in the Jin, a trend toward depicting drama appears in tomb iconography.

Some of the enduring characteristics of women in the conquest period include the high social status accorded women, the degree of independent agency they exercised, and the tradition of warrior women. Warrior women, including empresses Yingtian, Chengtian, and Xiao, Jin *lienü* with Jurchen names, the representation of Lady Wenji in Jin art, and finally the story of Yang Miaozhen, figure in this account from the beginning of the Liao to the end of the Jin. Kitan, Jurchen, and Han women who had adopted steppe patterns of martial behavior did not have to don men's clothing or act as surrogate males; women were respected as warriors in their own right. The agency these women exercised in their lives and especially in martial activities is truly remarkable. In this relatively open society of the north, women had freedoms and choices unknown in the south, but also restrictions. The social context in which Liao and Jin women lived and the customs and patterns they developed and maintained influenced women of later dynasties, for the Liao and Jin were the forerunners of the Yuan and Qing, respectively.

Cultural Identity

One of the main purposes of this study has been to examine how women constructed their individual identities in different times and places and how these constructions changed over the three-hundred-plus years covered in this book. Patricia Ebrey has suggested that the literati ideal for Song-dynasty males required a more elegant, refined, but physically weaker image, and women became more feminized and fragile to complement this shift. The robust and capable women of Tang art vanished, replaced by slender, small, elegant Song women.[7] Additionally, the "civilized" Han Chinese literati of the south contrasted with the rough, martial "barbarian" Tanguts, Uygurs, Kitan, and Jurchen of the north, accentuating the superiority of the Chinese. By contrast, the more macho and martial conduct of conquest-dynasty males allowed female identity to develop in more independent, martial, and assertive ways as well.

Men of Han Chinese origin serving the Liao and Jin governments apparently adopted the culture of their rulers to a large extent.[8] But cultural identity was a more sensitive concern for women, who conserved Han traditions in their homes and in their tombs. Living in the shifting frontier zone, they subscribed to varying degrees of adaptation. Identity in this zone was malleable and constantly subject to a changing environment. Liao and Jin women resisted a number of gendered traits commonly associated with southern women of Confucian backgrounds, including separation of the sexes, foot binding, sequestering inside the home, dowry marriages, and remarriage for widows. Many ostensibly Han women living under Jin rule acquired additional agency in the north's more open society and moved easily in public so that, in Susan Bush's words, they became "protagonists."[9] A prime example is Yang Miaozhen, who took on a Jin cultural identity even though she was from a family with a Han surname.

The kind of life a woman lived, whether as a pastoralist horse rider, a culture bearer, or a preserver of culture, was conditioned by geography, cultural heritage, social context, and by her own choices. Kitan women adopted literacy and selected Confucian virtues but never totally relinquished their identities as pastoralists and warriors. Jin women's cultural identity was shaped from the beginning of the dynasty by close contact with the Bohai elite and the incorporation of the northern half of Song China together with its population. Economically, women had their own resources to some degree and used them to contribute to Buddhist institutions. Meanwhile, the poignant tombs of the *haner* suggest that many women under both Liao and Jin rule carefully conserved their cultural heritage and practiced Buddhism in the home.

Sexuality, marriage, and widowhood are widely accepted by modern scholars as touchstones of women's lives. At each of these points, conquest women differed significantly from the Han Chinese conventions south of the frontier zone. Teenage girls apparently appeared freely in public, were sexually active, and enjoyed some degree of choice in the selection of marriage partners. Women were not sequestered, as became increasingly true in Song China. Some Liao empresses wielded great power as regents, while Jin-dynasty Bohai mothers quietly brought up their sons to become scholars and emperors. One might argue that the agency exhibited by Liao and Jin women signified a greater degree of freedom. But such freedoms were balanced by restrictions that included bride-price marriage and harsh choices for widows such as following in death and levirate.

Bride-price marriage meant that a woman effectively became the property of her husband's family. Edicts and laws against intermarriage between the Kitan, *haner*, and Han populations limited marriage choices. The frequency of edicts forbidding intermarriage testifies to its continued practice. Widows were subject to harsh conventions. Following in death was honored throughout the conquest period, and the custom persisted even into the Qing dynasty, when edicts were issued forbidding it.[10] Levirate must have been distasteful to many women, but it was widely practiced and laws forbidding Han and Bohai to practice it attest to its popularity—at least among in-law families, which stood to gain by the custom.[11] Buddhist retreat and widow chastity gained increasing momentum among the *haner* and Han populations across the span of the three hundred years covered in this study.

Thus, we see a very mixed picture of women's cultural identities, much like the changing geography in the frontier zone during the Liao and Jin periods. Women may have read the Confucian classics, but to what degree did they subscribe to Confucian hierarchies? The *Liaoshi* notes that imperial women "followed their husbands," which might be taken to refer to Confucian hierarchical precepts that subordinated women, but it could also refer obliquely to following in death, a quintessential steppe practice.[12] Warrior women followed their fathers, brothers, and husbands in battle and learned their skills. These women did not observe "thrice following," as recommended by Ban Zhao, by which a girl followed her father's wishes, wives were subordinate to their husbands, and widows to their sons. Kitan empresses were assertive in directing their imperial sons and husbands, although Jin empresses seem to have used more subtle means. Yelü and Xiao women who married down to younger males in generation-gap unions must often have bossed their young husbands around. Liao and Jin women may have been subordinate to men in the Confucian sense—but not very subordinate.

Loyalty is the most frequently mentioned Confucian virtue, probably because it coincided more closely with steppe values than concepts like filial piety and benevolence. As Naomi Standen has demonstrated, loyalty by men of Han Chinese background to the new Liao emperor and state was a crucial component of early Liao success.[13] The story of Lady Wenji was appealing to a Jin audience because of her loyalty. The wisdom embodied in education, literacy, writing, and teaching also reflects the Confucian values espoused by women of the conquest dynasties. Some attributes, such as horsemanship, bride-price marriage, widow practices, and neglect of filial piety were apparently shared with other steppe people such as the Tanguts of the Xia and the Mongols—as far back as Sima Qian's descriptions of Xiongnu. Others, including literacy, Buddhist piety, and the trend toward chaste widowhood, were shared with southern Chinese women's culture.

A Kitan or Jurchen woman might identify wholly with the culture of her birth or add selected aspects of Chinese culture such as literacy and ethics. Meanwhile, Han Chinese women became, to a greater or lesser degree, "barbarized." In the context of the middle period of Chinese history, the women of the Liao and Jin dynasties stand out for their vivid lifestyles and the manner in which gender relations were constructed, for their martial achievements as warriors, and for their education, literacy, and Buddhist piety. All this indicates that the women of the frontier zones occupied a true middle ground, adapting their cultural identities in a constantly shifting geography.

Significance of Conquest-Dynasty Women

What is the significance of studying women of the Liao and Jin dynasties in the context of Chinese history as a whole? First, these women offer an alternative model of womanhood in the Chinese sphere to set against conventionally understood images of Song and later women. Kitan and Jurchen women had more agency, physical skills, and evident courage than the conventional understanding of women in the mid-to-late imperial periods suggests. Second, the definition of gender and gendered divisions of labor were constructed differently in the Liao and Jin states than in Song China. The discussions offered here regarding sexuality, marriage customs, daily lives, female education, Buddhist piety, and aspects of widowhood provide a distinctly different construction of the role of gender in the northern states that contrasts with Confucian/patriarchal domination in the south in a number of ways. Conquest-dynasty women may have more similarity with women from the Tang dynasty than those from the Song, but to establish this we need more information on Tang women. Third, the lives of empresses like Yingtian and Chengtian, the tombs of Princess Chenguo and the lady of Yemaotai, the epitaph of Concubine Xiao, and the tale of Yang Miaozhen all reveal differing aspects of women's identity. These women were remarkable individuals whose stories should be brought to modern audiences.

But were Liao and Jin women unique? Xia women were also brought up in a martial society. In her study of the Xia state, Ruth Dunnell notes that women were prominent as regents in the eleventh century and "exercised active military leadership." One in particular was the empress dowager and regent Liang, who was trained in military affairs and inherited the prerogatives and military authority of the previous empress. In 1082 she personally led Xia troops into a conquered Song city.[14] Dunnell remarks that the Xia empress "challenged the conventions for 'women.'"[15] The conventions she and women like her challenged were essentially Han Chinese, not the customs of the steppe and forest.

In the Mongol tradition, the widow of a ruler was eligible to serve as regent, and on several occasions, the Mongol Empire was ruled by imperial widows or dowagers. Töregene, the widow of Ögödei, son of Chinggis Khan, and regent for Güyük Khan, ruled the empire from 1241 to 1246 and managed the succession, much like Yingtian, until her son Güyük became khan.[16] Sorghaghtani Beki was another assertive woman, who skillfully and patiently maneuvered in sensitive political matters dominated by forceful warriors to put two sons, first Möngke and, after his death, Khubilai, on the Mongol throne.[17] The activities of Liao women were not as unprecedented as the *Liaoshi* claims but may well be embedded in deeper strata of inner Asian tradition, much like the tradition of following in death. Thus, contrary to the quote from the *Liaoshi* with which this book begins, Liao warrior women were not unique. Clearly, more research is needed on the lives and roles of central Asian women.

Even Song empresses were active as regents and rulers in the eleventh century. The most conspicuous were Empress Dowager Liu and Grand Dowager Xie. Empress Liu, a contemporary of Empress Chengtian's, controlled the government during the illness of her husband, Emperor Zhenzong (997–1022), and the minority of her son, Emperor Renzong (1022–1063).[18] At the end of the dynasty, with children as emperors, Empress Dowager Quan and Grand Dowager Xie were extremely influential, and it was Empress Xie, as regent, who, at the end, surrendered to Mongol rule.[19]

Warrior women were not confined to China. In Japan at virtually the same time, Hōjō Masako, widow of Minamoto no Yoritomo (d. 1199), was the first and only woman to rule the *bakufu* military government as shogun. She too is credited with armed warfare and military leadership.[20] In twelfth-century Europe, Eleanor of Aquitaine possessed vast lands in her own name, rode in the Second Crusade, and audaciously divorced Louis VII of France and chose as her husband a martial prince, who became Henry II of England; she, like Empress Chengtian, also dominated the reigns of two of her sons.

This study suffers from omissions, the most striking of which is the absence of women's voices. A few poems included in the *Quan Liao wen* collection are ascribed to empresses, such as Yide and Xiao *taihou*, or to imperial concubines, such as Wen *fei*.[21] But we have no way of being certain these writings are in fact women's voices, and this book is the poorer for their absence.

Another curious omission in the records of women's lives is the issue of children. Names of children are routinely listed in formal biographies, but not in the *lienü* chapters. Information on childhood is also scant. In contrast to the Chinese biographical entries, rarely are the distinguished achievements of fathers and grandfathers mentioned in the biographies of notable men. While Liao and Jin societies valued women's education, we have very little information about how they were educated.

What did their contemporaries and subsequent Chinese women make of the warrior women of the Liao and Jin? When seen through a culturally Chinese lens, these women may have been perceived as negative examples and used to reinforce conventional feminine mores. No issue is more subjective than customs surrounding women's sexuality, including marriage, and the status of widows. Was the seclusion of girls and women that followed in the Song and Ming periods prompted in part by male desires to control their daughters and wives lest they follow the more independent ways and sexually assertive conduct of northern women of the conquest dynasties? Did the grannies and nursemaids of the Song and Ming eras frighten their charges into behaving like good girls with examples of uncivilized, big-footed warrior women of the north? Were the mythic heroines of Ming fiction who rode astride, fought in hand-to-hand combat, and could fly through the air reminiscent of warrior women? Perhaps today's cinematic crouching tigers, hidden dragons, and flying daggers are faint echoes of a tenth-to-thirteenth-century past.

Notes

Introduction

1. Toghtō et al., *Liaoshi*, 71:1199 (hereafter *LS*).
2. Fiskesjö, "On the 'Raw' and the 'Cooked' Barbarians of Imperial China."
3. *LS*, 71:1199–1200.
4. Ibid., 1201–1202.
5. Ibid., 1204.
6. Alutu et al., *Songshi*, 476:13810–13850; Alutu et al., *Jinshi*, 17:383 (hereafter *JS*).
7. Fang Xuanling, *Jin shu*, 97:2534. I am indebted to Dr. Shuo Wang for bringing this citation to my attention.
8. Franke, "Women under the Dynasties of Conquest." Franke used many of the primary sources consulted in this study to list these characteristics but did not attempt to situate them in the context of Liao social history.
9. Birge, "Levirate Marriage"; Birge, *Women, Property, and Confucian Reaction*; Birge, "Women and Confucianism."
10. De Pee, "Till Death Do Us Unite."
11. The iconic depiction of the "barbarians" of China's borders was established by the great historian Sima Qian writing during the Han dynasty in the reign of Emperor Wudi (r. 140–86 BCE) (Sima Qian, *Shiji*, juan 110). Sima Qian's depiction of the Xiongnu affected all later descriptions of non-Han pastoralists. See also Gungwu Wang, "Rhetoric of a Lesser Empire," 47–50; Jing-shen Tao, "Barbarians or Northerners."
12. Mann, "Presidential Address," 854–856.
13. For an overview of central Asian peoples, see Lattimore, *Inner Asian Frontiers of China*, 115 ff.; Fletcher, "Mongols."
14. With apologies to Richard White, *Middle Ground*.

15. Sima Qian famously wrote, "Zhu shui cao qian xi" 逐水草遷徙 (*Shiji*, 110:2879).
16. Lattimore, *Inner Asian Frontiers of China*, 3.
17. On the myth of the Great Wall in Song times, see Waldron, *Great Wall of China*, 24–26. More recently, Nicholas Tackett has shown that while walls and remnants of walls crisscrossed Liao and Jin territories, they were not consolidated as a "great wall" and did not constitute boundaries. See Tackett, "Great Wall."
18. *LS*, 69–70:1077–1196. Chapter 69 is devoted to tribes, *bu* and *zu*, who sent gifts and tribute and with whom the Kitan had frequent contact. Chapter 70 concerns tribute states (*shuguo*), with which the Liao court had more formal tribute relations.
19. This terminology is examined in Gungwu Wang, "Rhetoric of a Lesser Empire," and in Jing-shen Tao, "Barbarians or Northerners."
20. Liu Pujiang, "Shuo 'hanren.'" These definitions based on ethnic and geographic origin are examined further in chapters 2 and 3. See also Liu Pujiang, *Liao Jin shi lun*, 38.
21. Kane, *Kitan Language and Script*, ix–x.
22. Ibid., x, 266; Greenberg, *Indo-European and Its Closest Relatives*, 17, 281.
23. Kane, *Kitan Language and Script*, 227–264.
24. Greenberg, *Indo-European and Its Closest Relatives*; Menges, *Tungusen und Ljao*.
25. Ethnicity and its characteristics in northeastern China is a contested issue among current historians. See Elliott, *Manchu Way*, for the view that "ethnicity," when carefully defined, is useful in discussing peoples of the northeast, and Crossley, "Thinking About Ethnicity," for an opposing view.
26. Levirate was a widely practiced steppe custom that required a widow to marry her late husband's younger brother or nephew. The term is based on, in the *Old Testament*, Deut. 25:5–10, Levi's marrying Ruth, his deceased brother's widow. Levirate is often contrasted with the Chinese practice of exogamy, where a widow, when she remarries, contracts the marriage outside both her natal and husband's families. In the Liao and Jin context, a further constraint was that the new husband had to be younger than the deceased. Levirate has been known in many cultures, as the reference to the early Hebrews shows.
27. Patricia Ebrey studies Song women extensively in her classic work *The Inner Quarters*. She finds that from childhood women and men were separated in Chinese households and that women increasingly confined their activities to the inner quarters over the course of the Song dynasty.
28. The Bohai state existed in eastern Manchuria between the Liao River and Korean borders from 719 to 926. The population absorbed a great deal of Tang Chinese culture and served as a mediator and conduit between China to the south and Korea to the east. Its principal capital became the Liao Eastern Capital when it was taken over by that state in 927 and became a semi-independent appanage of Dongtanguo, ruled by the eldest son of the first Liao emperor, Prince Bei. After his death, it became the Eastern Circuit of the Liao Empire. But the Bohai sought independence and frequently rebelled, aided by their allies, the Jurchen of the region. The final rebellion in 1125, led by the Jurchen with Bohai

assistance, overthrew the Liao state. See Franke and Twitchett, *Alien Regimes and Border States*, 3–5, 28, 31, 36, and passim.
29. Standen, *Unbounded Loyalty*.
30. Nienhauser, "Ballad of Mulan," 77–80.
31. *Hou Hanshu*, 84:1891–1893. The two poems in the *Hou Hanshu* are attributed to Cai Yan, but whether in these poems we have the authentic voice of a late third-century Han woman is open to question.
32. The sources describe Xiongnu, but the actual raiders are more likely to have been Xianbei tribesmen, who replaced the Xiongnu as the dominant power of the steppes in the first century CE. See Bielenstein, "Wang Mang," 268; Yu Yingshi, "Han Foreign Relations," 442–444.
33. *Hou Hanshu*, 83:1892–1893.
34. See Leung, "Frontier Imaginary in the Song Dynasty," for a discussion of the four album leaves in the Boston Museum of Fine Arts depicting the Wenji story; Wang's poem is found on p. 251.
35. Murray, "Southern Sung Painting Regains Its Memory"; Xu Bangda, "Song ren hua renwu gushi ying ji 'Yingluan tu' kao." The empress was the mother of Southern Song emperor Gaozong (r. 1127–1163).
36. Bush, "Five Paintings of Animal Subjects," 194–196; Johnson, "Art of the Jurchen Revival," 24–39. This painting was first published in Guo Moruo, "Tan Jin ren Zhang Yu," and in Su Xingjun, "Ji Jin ren." A full color illustration has been published in Jilin sheng bowuguan cangpin zhuanji, *Yi yuan duo ying*. The painting has a brief inscription giving its title, the artist's name, Zhang (the second character of the name is illegible), and the title of an office, *zhiyingsi*. This office functioned in the Jin imperial household between 1201 and 1209.
37. Guo Moruo has interpreted the second character of the artist's name as Yu 瑀 and the artist's full name as Zhang Yu, but the name Zhang Yu does not appear in lists of Jin painters. Zhang Gui 珪, however, was a well-known Jin painter (fl. 1150–1161), and at least one of his paintings still exists (Bush, "Five Paintings of Animal Subjects," 183–185). Zhang Yu was likely a younger member of the family of court painters.
38. The remainder of the scroll shows mounted tribesmen and a haughty Chinese official; this aspect of the painting is discussed in chapter 3.
39. The fierce wind may be read literally or allegorically. Here I differ with Guo Moruo, who calls the wind the "north wind of the steppes." See "Tan Jin ren Zhang Yu," 2.
40. Selection of one of the five elements and its accompanying color was a matter of much debate at the Jin court, which had finally been decided by Emperor Zhangzong in 1202. See Rogers, "Late Chin Debates on Dynastic Legitimacy," 58.
41. Bush, "Five Paintings of Animal Subjects," 196; Guo, "Tan Jin ren Zhang Yu," 1–4.
42. *LS*, 71:1201; *Kitan guozhi*, 13:141.
43. *Quan Liao wen*, 92.
44. Compilation was begun in 1343 under the direction of the Mongol minister Toghtō.

Both were hurriedly compiled from surviving records, perhaps with the intention of legitimizing the Yuan dynasty. Although the *Jinshi* may be considered the better of the two, both these two histories and the *Songshi*, compiled at the same time, have many errors, contradictions, and omissions. The *Liaoshi* was completed in April 1344, the *Jinshi* in November of the same year, and the *Songshi* was finished in December 1345. See Hok-lam Chan, *Historiography of the Chin Dynasty*, 3–65.

45. LS, 107:1472; *Quan Liao wen*, 409.
46. Although a number of works illustrating "barbarians" purporting to be Kitan or Jurchen or Chinese variations of such "barbarians" exist in various Western and Chinese collections, the only ones that I have used in this study are those few whose authenticity can be demonstrated through comparisons to wall paintings in tombs or other unquestionably authentic contemporary sources.
47. The sources are varied and include dynastic histories, tomb epitaphs, and travelers' reports by Song envoys like Lu Zhen, who visited the court of the Liao emperor Shengzong; Hong Hao, who was a captive at the early Jin court; Fan Chengda, who visited the Jin in the mid-twelfth century; and Cheng Zhou, who made a journey through the Jin empire in the early thirteenth century. Their reports were essentially intelligence briefs and contain many astute observations.
48. Kane, *Kitan Language and Script*. Kitan, Khitan, and Qidan are all currently in use in the English-language literature on the Liao period.
49. Twitchett and Tietze, "Liao," xxii, 76–80.
50. The Sixteen Prefectures were ceded to the Liao in 936, but in 959 the Song took back the region of Guannan, leaving only fourteen prefectures, including Yanxian, where Yanjing city was located, and Yunxian and areas along the border as far as modern Datong. This region, which includes the site of modern Beijing, is especially important in this study since the majority of the Han and *haner* populations lived in this region. See Nap-yin Lau, "Waging War for Peace?".
51. Twitchett and Tietze, "Liao," 79.

ONE
Womanly Ideals in the Liao and Jin Periods

1. With apologies to Laurel Thatcher Ulrich ("Vertuous Women Found," 20).
2. Davis, "Chaste and Filial Women," 212.
3. Dong Jiazun, "Lidai jiefu, lienü de tongji," 112.
4. *JS*, 130:2804.
5. Ouyang Xiu, *Xin Wudaishi*; Ouyang Xiu, *Historical Records of the Five Dynasties*, xliv; Davis, "Chaste and Filial Women," 204–218; Xue Juzheng, *Jiu Wudaishi*, 36.
6. Since the Liao, Jin, and Song histories were simultaneously under construction, the *lienü* chapter in the *Songshi* would not have been an available model.

7. I have relied in part on discussions in Raphals, *Sharing the Light*, 111–117.
8. Ibid., 5–6, 20, 22.
9. *LS*, 107:1471.
10. *Xiucai*, "one of cultivated talents," and as applied to males, title of the holder of the first literary degree in the examination system, from which women were of course excluded.
11. *LS*, 107:1471–1472. According to the biography of her son, Xing Baopu, Lady Chen was probably born in the 940s about the time that the Liao took over the Sixteen Prefectures. See *LS*, 80:1278–1279.
12. See Standen, *Unbounded Loyalty*, regarding recruitment of Latter Tang and other Han officials to ranks in the Liao government.
13. *LS*, 107:1471.
14. *LS*, 80:1278–1279.
15. Baozhi does not have a separate biography.
16. *LS*, 107:1472.
17. Ibid.
18. Kane, *Kitan Language and Script*, 227, 229, 260.
19. Ibid., 229.
20. *Quan Liao wen*, 409.
21. Part of the epitaph is identical with the *LS* entry, suggesting that the *LS* editors quoted the epitaph.
22. *LS*, 71:1200.
23. Wittfogel and Feng, *History of Chinese Society*, 200–201.
24. The tomb of Yelü Nu has recently been discovered by archaeologists at Fuxin, in Jilin province. The discovery was announced at http://www.ylwh.com/ylwh/qd/4.htm. Yelü Nu was buried in a small cemetery with other members of the nobility; his wife, Lady Xiao, was buried with him.
25. *LS*, 107:1473–1474; Wittfogel and Feng, *History of Chinese Society*, 265.
26. *LS*, 107:1474.
27. Ibid., 1475.
28. Carlitz, "Social Uses of Female Virtue," 122; Davis, "Chaste and Filial Women," 206–209.
29. Dong Jiazun, "Lidai jiefu, lienü de tongji," 112–113.
30. Neither the Liao nor Jin scripts has been fully deciphered, but see Kane, *Kitan Language and Script*.
31. *Quan Liao wen*, 125–127; the title Princess Qin-Jinguo was reserved for imperial daughters of the first rank. See Tang Tongtian, "Liaodai de mingfu," 103.
32. *Liaodai shike wenbian*, 248.
33. *Quan Liao wen*, 192–194. The notation that she had no children may mean that none survived infancy. Given the high status of Kitan women, it probably does not mean that she bore only girls.
34. Ibid.

35. Kroll, "Life and Writings of Xu Hui."
36. Liaoning sheng bowuguan, Liaoning Tieling diqu wenwuzu fajue xiaozu, "Faku Yemaotai Liao mu jilue"; Feng Yongqian, "Faku Yemaotai Liao mu chutu de taociqi."
37. Observations based on a visit to the Liaoning Provincial Museum in 2001. When I viewed these boots, they had fallen virtually to dust.
38. Liaoning sheng bowuguan, Liaoning Tieling diqu wenwuzu fajue xiaozu, "Faku Yemaotai Liao mu jilue." An archaeological report suggests that the lady may have been associated with one of the enfeoffed princedoms in Anting or Liaozhou that were located near the site of the tomb in the Liao period. She had no gold or silver face mask as did most members of the imperial clan so far found in unlooted tombs.
39. Liaoning sheng bowuguan, Liaoning Tieling diqu wenwuzu fajue xiaozu, "Faku Yemaotai Liao mu jilue."
40. Photos of the interior of the tomb on view at the Liaoning Provincial Museum (April 2001) show a ledge packed with scrolls.
41. Yang Renkai, "Yemaotai Liao mu chutu guhua de shidai ji qita."
42. Ibid.
43. I viewed this small house at the Liaoning Provincial Museum. For this and similar constructions, see Steinhardt, "Architectural Landscape of the Liao," 47–48. A similar coffin chamber, in this case made of stone, was discovered in 2000 near Xi'an, dated 579 CE, in the Northern Zhou period. See Xi'an shi wenwu baohu kaogusuo, "Xi'an beizhou Liangzhou Sabao Shi jun mu fajue jiangbao."
44. *Quan Liao wen*, 192–194.
45. Google Maps, http://maps.google.com/ (accessed April 2009). Even today with highways and toll roads, it is a three-and-a-half-hour drive.
46. *Liaodai shike wenbian*, 142–143.
47. Lisa Raphals shows that earlier *lienü zhuan* particularly eulogized women as learned instructresses and moral advisers, as mothers who gave maternal instruction by educating young sons and admonishing grown sons, as wives who corrected their husbands' faults, etc. See *Sharing the Light*, 54–55. Although these types occur in the Jin *lienü* chapter, the examples are not grouped by type.
48. Liu Pujiang, "Shuo 'hanren,' " 6:57–61.
49. *JS*, 130:2798.
50. Ibid., 2800–2801.
51. Judge discusses Confucian representations of martial women as surrogate males in *Precious Raft of History*, 151–152.
52. *JS*, 130:2802.
53. Ibid., 2802–2803.
54. Ibid., 2803.
55. Raphals, *Sharing the Light*, 28–41, 55.
56. *JS*, 130:2801.
57. Raphals, *Sharing the Light*, 55.

58. *JS*, 130:2801.
59. Ibid., 2805.
60. Ibid., 2799.
61. Ibid., 2798.
62. Ibid., 2799–2800.
63. Ibid., 2802.
64. The cutting of human flesh to cure an illness is a common trope in Confucian tales of filial piety from later dynasties—but is nearly always done by daughters-in-law attempting to save their husbands' ill parents.
65. *JS*, 130:2804.
66. Ibid., 2798–2799.
67. Ibid., 2799.
68. Raphals, *Sharing the Light*, 54–55.
69. *JS*, 130:2805.
70. Birge, "Levirate Marriage," 107–146.
71. Raphals, *Sharing the Light*.
72. Birge, "Levirate Marriage," 107–146.
73. Bol, "Seeking Common Ground"; Jing-shen Tao, "Jurchen *Chin-shih* Degree."

TWO
Liao Women's Daily Lives

1. This painting is in the National Palace Museum, Taipei, where I had an opportunity to view it closely in 1986. It is reproduced here with special permission from the museum. The authenticity of the *Fan ma* scroll is strongly supported by close comparison between the painting and unquestionably authentic materials such as wall paintings and tomb artifacts.
2. Here I am not concerned with the attribution or authorship of the painting but rather with its content. Other paintings depicting Liao life, often associated with Lady Wenji's sojourn with the barbarians, lack the range of representations found in this scroll. (See note 5 below.)
3. The landscape style, with folded "oyster-shell" rock and mountain landscape formations and hills shown without depth (as if cardboard props, out from behind which figures suddenly appear) is consistent with pictorial landscape conventions of the late Five Dynasties period. The date of the work is probably tenth century, allowing for a certain degree of stylistic time lag. In any case, the time frame of the painting is well within the Liao period.
4. For a discussion of the painting and its authorship, see Cao Xingyuan, "Chuan Hu Gui 'Fan ma tu' zuozhe kaolue."

5. Because of questions of authenticity and interpretation, I am not making use of paintings depicting pastoralist life that are attributed to Song or later artists, such as the album leaves in the Boston Museum of Fine Arts entitled *Lady Wen-chi's Return to China* and the *Eighteen Songs of a Nomad Flute*, a later version of the composition in the Metropolitan Museum in New York. See Fontein and Wu, *Unearthing China's Past*, 221–224; Rorex, *Eighteen Songs of a Nomad Flute*.

    I have previously identified the Kitan tribesmen depicted in the four album leaves as "generic versions of barbarians" because they are all dressed alike in long, heavy coats and boots and, in terms of the hairstyles, wear identical short braids behind the ears. The depictions thus show none of the variation seen in tomb wall paintings, where the forehead is sometimes shaved entirely, sometimes a fringe is left along the brow; usually the braids fall in front of the ears and only very rarely behind—to cite an example of the variation in hairstyles alone. Wall paintings also show a variety of male and female dress, not just long coats and boots. See Johnson, "Wedding Ceremony for an Imperial Liao Princess."

6. Steinhardt, *Liao Architecture*, 185.
7. Swann, *Pan Chao*, 83. Ban Zhao is here repeating an ancient maxim.
8. Franke, "Women under the Dynasties of Conquest," 23–24.
9. My admittedly rough count of published reports on Liao excavations in which the sex of at least one of the occupants is recorded showed that out of forty-six tombs, twelve were single female burials and sixteen housed couples or multiple burials that included women. Information on tomb occupants may be incomplete. For example, at Kulunqi tomb number 1, the bones of several individuals were scattered and no analysis of gender was offered in the archaeological report.
10. Kuhn, "Decoding Tombs of the Song Elite," 50–60, 69–78.
11. Tang Tongtian, "Liaodai de mingfu," 4:95–103.
12. One such example is the tomb of Princess Chenguo, discovered in 1984. See Neimenggu zizhiqu wenwu kaogu yanjiusuo, Zhelimu meng bowuguan, *Liao Chenguo gongzhu mu*.
13. Sun Jianhua, "Discovery and Research on the Tomb of the Princess of Chen and Her Husband, Xiao Shaoju," in Hsueh-man Shen, *Gilded Splendor*, 67–74.
14. Ibid., plate 8. See also Hsueh-man Shen, *Gilded Splendor*, passim. Many of the artifacts in this exhibition came from the Princess Chenguo tomb.
15. Neimenggu zizhiqu wenwu kaogu yanjiusuo, Zhelimu meng bowuguan, *Liao Chenguo gongzhu mu*, 25–47.
16. Ibid.
17. So, "Tiny Bottles."
18. Neimenggu zizhiqu wenwu kaogu yanjiusuo, Zhelimu meng bowuguan, *Liao Chenguo gongzhu mu*, 6–24, 48–49.
19. The process is described in Ouyang Xiu, *Xin Wudaishi*, 72:888, and in the *Kitan guozhi* 23:1a–b; see also Wittfogel and Feng, *Liao Society*, 204.
20. Wulanchabu meng wenwu gongzuozhan, "Chayou Qianqi Haoqianying di liuhao Liao

mu qingli jianbao." This tomb's contents were featured in a 2001 exhibition at the Shanghai Museum, "Life on the Grasslands," which I viewed at that time.
21. Kuhn, "Introduction to the Chinese Archaeology of the Liao," 34.
22. *LS, juan* 10.
23. The skeleton of an adult male, face down, was discovered under the doorway to tomb number 1 at Kulunqi. See Jilin sheng bowuguan, Zhelimu meng wenhuaju, "Jilin Zhelimu meng Kulunqi yi hao Liao mu fajue jianbao," 8:5. See also Johnson, "Wedding Ceremony for an Imperial Liao Princess," 111.
24. The four album leaves (*Lady Wen-chi's Return to China*) in the Boston Museum of Fine Arts and the later version (*Eighteen Songs of a Nomad Flute*) in the Metropolitan Museum in New York show various yurt and tent styles used by the Kitan. See Fontein and Wu, *Unearthing China's Past*, 221–224; Rorex, *Eighteen Songs of a Nomad Flute*; Leung, "Frontier Imaginary in the Song Dynasty."
25. Ta La, "Archaeological Excavations."
26. Nancy Shatzman Steinhardt, *Chinese Imperial City Planning* (Honolulu: University of Hawai'i Press, 1990), 123–128.
27. Ta La, "Archaeological Excavations."
28. Di Cosmo, "Liao History and Society," 18.
29. Steinhardt, *Liao Architecture*, 14–15, 17; Steinhardt, *Chinese Imperial City Planning*, 125–126. Steinhardt believes that the location of the palace city was owing to buildings already on the site.
30. Hargett, *On the Road in Twelfth-Century China*, 149.
31. *Zhongguo lishi dituji*, 6:5–7.
32. Twitchett and Tietze, "Liao," 97–98. Initially the Xi had enjoyed a separate but subordinate kingdom in the region of Zhongjing and paid tribute to the Liao. In the latter part of the tenth century the Xi king became a Liao official, and the Xi state's independent status was abolished. Over time the status of the Xi people as the second most preferential group in Liao society declined until the Xi were seen as potential enemies and "barbarized" in the eyes of Kitan elite.
33. Steinhardt, *Liao Architecture*, 17–18; for more information on Liao cities, see also Steinhardt, *Chinese Imperial City Planning*, 122–128.
34. Liu Pujiang, *Liao Jin shi lun*, 38.
35. The term *haner*, literally "sons of Han," occurs in the *Da Jin guozhi* and in other, mainly private or unofficial, sources. The early Liao government had a bureau for "*haner* affairs" that was replaced by the Southern Administration. See Liu Pujiang's *Liao Jin Shi lun* and "Shuo 'hanren,'" 58–63.
36. *LS*, 2:15; Wittfogel and Feng, *History of Chinese Society*, 198.
37. Endicott-West, "Yüan Government and Society," 610. The Liao and Jin legal divisions based on cultural or ethnic identity have been overlooked by previous scholars.
38. Liu, "Shuo 'hanren,'" 59.
39. Standen, *Unbounded Loyalty*.

40. Wakeman, "China in the Context of World History," 35.
41. *JS*, 97:2151.
42. Zhangjiakou shi Xuanhua qu wenwu baoguansuo, "Hebei Xuanhua Xiabali Liao Han Shixun mu."
43. Ibid.
44. See tomb artifacts and wall paintings in Hebei sheng wenwu yanjiusuo Zhangjiakou shi wenwu guanlichu Xuanhua qu wenwu guanlisuo, "Hebei Xuanhua Liao Zhang Wenzao bihua mu fajue jianbao."
45. Ibid., color plate 11.
46. Ibid., color plate 12. The stack of drawers may represent sutra boxes. Similar sutra boxes made of cedar and inscribed in Sanskrit were found in the adjacent tomb, that of Zhang Shigu (d. 1118).
47. Zhangjiakou shi Xuanhua qu wenwu baoguansuo, "Hebei Xuanhua Liao dai bihua mu," color plate facing p. 17.
48. In the celebrated story of the rise of the Jurchen leader Aguda, a pivotal moment occurred when Aguda challenged the Liao emperor Tianzuo at a feast by refusing to dance at the emperor's command. Tianzuo was too drunk to do anything about the insult until the next morning, by which time Aguda had decamped and gone to raise a rebellion that ultimately was successful in overthrowing the Liao state. See Twitchett and Tietze, "Liao," 140; *JS, juan* 3.
49. Hebei sheng wenwu yanjiusuo Zhangjiakou shi wenwu guanlichu Xuanhua qu wenwu guanlisuo, "Hebei Xuanhua Liao Zhang Wenzao bihua mu fajue jianbao," 9:31–39; Zhangjiakou shi wenwu shiye guanlisuo, Zhangjiakou shi Xuanhua qu wenwu baoguansuo, "Hebei Xuanhua Xiabali Liao Jin bihua mu"; Zhangjiakou shi Xuanhua qu wenwu baoguansuo, "Hebei Xuanhua Xiabali Liao Han Shixun mu"; Zhangjiakou shi Xuanhua qu wenwu baoguansuo, "Hebei Xuanhua Liaodai bihua mu."
50. Su Bai, "Guanyu Hebei xichu gumu de zhaji," 61. See the discussion of these ceiling representations in Steinhardt, *Liao Architecture*, 345–347; Kuhn, "Liao Architecture," 344–346.
51. Hebei sheng wenwu guanlichu, Hebei sheng bowuguan, "Liaodai caihui xingtu shi woguo tianwenshi shang de zhongyao faxian"; Hebei sheng wenwu yanjiusuo Zhangjiakou shi wenwu guanlichu Xuanhua qu wenwu guanlisuo, "Hebei Xuanhua Liao Zhang Wenzao bihua mu fajue jianbao."
52. Leung, "Frontier Imaginary in the Song Dynasty." Leung does not cover the *Fan ma* painting because it is not a depiction of the Wenji story nor is it a work of the Song "barbarian" school.
53. Ibid.
54. Fontein and Wu, *Unearthing China's Past*, 221–224; Rorex, *Eighteen Songs of a Nomad Flute*; Leung, "Frontier Imaginary in the Song Dynasty."
55. Hargett, *On the Road in Twelfth-Century China*, 149.

THREE
Jin Women's Daily Lives

1. Sources include Hong Hao, *Songmo jiwen*, and various entries by different authors in Xu Mengxin, *Sanchao beimeng huibian*; see also the translation in Franke, "Chinese Texts on the Jurchen."
2. Hong Hao, *Songmo jiwen*. Information on Jin-dynasty women is also found in the *Jinshi*, *Da Jin guozhi*, and the *Jin wen zui*.
3. Xu Mengxin, *Sanchao beimeng huibian*, 3:1a–2b. See also Franke, "Chinese Texts on the Jurchen," 126, and Hok-lam Chan, *Legitimation in Imperial China*, 53. Franke believes that the reference to yellow hair or eyes suggests some European intrusions. I suggest, however, that the reference to exotic colors is intended to underscore how wild and uncouth these tribal peoples seemed to the Chinese.
4. Xu Mengxin, *Sanchao beimeng huibian*, 3:2b.
5. Sima Qian, *Shiji*, 144.
6. Xu Mengxin, writing—or rather compiling—in the twelfth century, is a contemporaneous but secondary source. His text includes primary materials by observers like Li Shanqing and Hong Hao but not always with careful attention to accuracy, and Xu often inserted extraneous opinions, presumably his own.
7. Fiskesjö, "On the 'Raw' and the 'Cooked' Barbarians of Imperial China."
8. Franke, "Chin Dynasty," 6:216–220; Jing-shen Tao, *Jurchen in Twelfth-Century China*, 3–13.
9. Tillman, "Overview of Chin History and Institutions," 25.
10. Liu, "Shuo 'hanren,' " 64–65.
11. On Yuan social classes, see Endicott-West, "Yüan Government and Society," 610
12. Guo Moruo, "Tan Jin ren Zhang Yu."
13. Xu Mengxin, *Sanchao beimeng huibian*, 3:2a–b; the hairstyle of the early Jurchen is also described by the Russian anthropologist A. P. Okladnikov, "Jurchen State," 242.
14. One of the very few extant paintings showing Jurchen tribesmen is a short Five Dynasties hand scroll in the National Palace Museum in Taiwan, *The Parting of Su Wu and Li Ling*, attributed to Chou Wen-chü [Zhou Wenju]. The title comes from a Han-dynasty event, but the rendition shows the principals Su Wu and Li Ling in typical Kitan costumes. Two servants holding Li Ling's horses, however, have a different appearance; they wear boots and long belted jerkins. Their hair is worn long in locks. One, whose face is visible, has a beard and mustache. Their dress, hairstyle, and facial adornment mark them as Jurchen. The period is one in which some *sheng* Jurchen were captured and reduced to the status of slaves by the Liao. Chinese National Palace Museum, Taiwan, *Chinese Art Treasures*, 44–45.
15. For portraits of the Manchu imperial family, see Spence, *Emperor of China*, and Rawski and Rawson, *China*.
16. Guo Moruo, "Tan Jin ren Zhang Yu," 2.

17. I am indebted to Zhao Zifu for this translation.
18. The last Qing emperor, Puyi, took this painting, along with other ancestral treasures, to Manchuria when he was the Japanese puppet emperor of Manchukuo in the 1930s, which is why the painting is now in the Jilin Provincial Museum, Puyi's former palace. Puyi recognized the Jin as former monarchs of the northeast and forerunners of the Manchus.
19. Beijing shi wenwu guanlichu, "Beijing xia Nongtan Jin mu."
20. Ibid.
21. Heilongjiang sheng wenwu kaogu gongzuodui, "Suibin Yongsheng de Jin dai pingmin mu"; Heilongjiang sheng wenwu kaogu gongzuodui, "Songhuajiang xiayou Aolimi gucheng ji qi zhouwei de Jindai muqun"; Heilongjiang sheng wenwu kaogu gongzuodui, "Heilongjiang pan Suibin Zhongxing gucheng Jin dai muqun"; see also Jilin sheng bowuguan Nong'an xian wenguan suo, "Jilin Nong'an Jindai jiaomu wenwu"; Ning Lixin, "Shanxi Shuo xian Jindai huozang." The archaeologists identify these tombs as Jurchen.
22. Franke, "Chinese Texts on the Jurchen," 138.
23. Heilongjiang sheng wenwu kaogu yanjiusuo, "Heilongjiang Acheng Juyuan Jindai Qi guowang mu fajue jianbao."
24. Zhu Qixin, "Royal Costumes of the Jin Dynasty."
25. Su Bai, *Zhonghua renmin gongheguo zhongda kaogu faxian*, 59.
26. Ibid.
27. For example, Shizong wanted his people to read Jurchen literature. A Jurchen script had been invented early in the dynasty, but predynastic literature existed only in oral form. Therefore, Shizong had the Chinese classics such as the *Classic of Filial Piety* translated into Jurchen script. The Jin people who read such materials imbibed Chinese values, not those of the ancient Jurchen.
28. Hebei sheng wenwu yanjiusuo Zhangjiakou shi wenwu guanlichu Xuanhua qu wenwu guanlisuo, "Hebei Xuanhua Liao Zhang Wenzao bihua mu fajue jianbao."
29. Beijing shi wenwu yanjiusuo, *Beijing Jindai huangling*; Beijing shi wenwu yanjiu Jinling kaogu gongzuodui, "Beijing Fangshan qu Jinling yizhi de diaocha yu fabiao."
30. Beijing shi wenwu yanjiusuo, *Beijing Jindai huangling*, 194–206.
31. Ibid., 52–55, 69–75.
32. Ibid., 69–88.
33. Beijing shi wenwu yanjiu Jinling kaogu gongzuodui, "Beijing Fangshan qu Jinling yizhi de diaocha yu fabiao," 37–39.
34. *JS*, 63:1500–1501.
35. Xu Mengxin, *Sanchao beimeng huibian*, 4:31.
36. *LS*, 4:49; 16:186. But for nearly every law, exceptions were also issued.
37. *JS*, 63:1518.
38. Ibid., 64:1526.
39. Ibid., 1533.
40. *JS*, 63:1509.
41. Ibid.

42. De Pee, "Till Death Do Us Unite."
43. Shanxi sheng kaogu yanjiusuo, Yangquan shi wenwu guanli weiyuanhui, Pingding xian wenwu guanlisuo, "Shanxi Pingding Song Jin bihua mu jianbao."
44. Liu Pujiang, *Liao Jin Shi lun*, 115.
45. Henan sheng bowuguan Jiaozuo shi bowuguan, "Henan Jiaozuo Jin mu fajue jianbao," 8:6–17.
46. Hargett, *On the Road in Twelfth-Century China*, 149.
47. Ibid.; Walton, "Diary of a Journey to the North."
48. Chai Zejun and Zhang Chouliang, *Fanzhi Yanshan si*. The artists' names and the date are preserved in inscriptions at the site.
49. Bush, "Women as Protagonists," 3. Cited with permission of the author.
50. I spent some time observing a full-scale copy of this mural at the Jin Watergate Museum in Beijing, April 2001.
51. Karetzky, "Recently Discovered Chin Dynasty Murals," 248. "Wildflower" was a euphemism for prostitute.
52. Chai Zejun and Zhang Chouliang, *Fanzhi Yanshan si*, 128, plate 68.
53. Bush, "Women as Protagonists."
54. Datong shi bowuguan, "Datong shi Nanjiao Jindai bihua mu."
55. Ebrey, *Inner Quarters*, 265.
56. Wenxi xian bowuguan, "Shanxi Wenxi si di Jin mu."
57. For example, the well-known Song-period tomb at Baisha has a well-preserved and very elegantly painted scene of a couple at a table dated ca. 1196. See Xu Pingfang, "Baisha Song mu," 487. Here, the man in blue and his wife in red are seated at a table on which is a wine pot and cups. Draperies and servants are shown behind them. These scenes of husband and wife amid domestic harmony are not unique to Jin tombs and have been found in some eleventh-century Song tombs.
58. Shanxi sheng kaogu yanjiusuo, "Shanxi Jishan Jin mu fajue jianbao." The tombs are dated to the late Jin period by an epitaph in M 7 by Duan Jieyu (b. 1181) in memory of his parents. In these tombs, men and women are buried, often two or even three women together with a male, in the same coffin.
59. Dated 1196 and 1210, respectively (Yang Fudou, "Houma Jishan Jin mu," 507–509; Shanxi sheng kaogu yanjiusuo, "Shanxi Jishan Jin mu fajue jianbao").
60. On Li Qingzhan, see Kai-yu Hsu, "Poems of Li Qingzhao." On burials, see de Pee, "Till Death Do Us Unite."
61. For a selection of Song poems, see Wu-chi Liu and Irving Yucheng Lo, eds., *Sunflower Splendor: Three Thousand Years of Chinese Poetry* (Bloomington: Indiana University Press, 1975), 297–455.
62. Yang Fudou, "Houma Jishan Jin mu."
63. Ibid.
64. Steinhardt, "Jin Hall at Jingtusi."
65. Ibid., 94–95.

66. On Yuan drama depicted in wall paintings, see Anning Jing, *Water God's Temple of the Guangsheng Monastery*.
67. Presentation by Beijing University professor Zang Jian, "Women in Chinese History," at Michigan State University, October 22, 2002.

FOUR
Sexuality and Marriage

1. *LS*, 52: 863–865; 81:1285–1286.
2. Sun Guoping, "Discovery and Research on the Tomb of the Princess of Chen."
3. *LS*, 52:863–865.
4. Jilin sheng bowuguan, Zhelimu meng wenhuaju, "Jilin Zhelimu meng Kulunqi yi hao Liao mu fajue jianbao."
5. Johnson, "Wedding Ceremony for an Imperial Liao Princess," 125.
6. *LS*, 52:864.
7. Such assemblages of flags, drums, and "officials" are seen in many Kitan depictions, but the identity and functions of the men wearing black hats is still undetermined as of this writing.
8. Wittfogel and Feng, *History of Chinese Society*, 276.
9. *LS*, 52:864; Johnson, "Wedding Ceremony for an Imperial Liao Princess," 126.
10. *LS*, 52:863–865.
11. Jilin sheng bowuguan, Zhelimu meng wenhuaju, "Jilin Zhelimu meng Kulunqi yi hao Liao mu fajue jianbao," 5.
12. De Pee, "Till Death Do Us Unite."
13. Birge, "Levirate Marriage."
14. Because so much useful information comes from the reports of Song observers who could hardly avoid imbuing their reports with familiar Song norms for feminine behavior, it is useful to try to access the degree of prejudice or bias in their reports.
15. Holmgren, "Observations on Marriage and Inheritance Practices," 145–146.
16. Hong Hao, *Songmo jiwen*. Hong was a Song scholar and official who received his *Jinshi* degree in 1128. Hong, 3:5b. See also the translation in Franke, "Chinese Texts on the Jurchen."
17. Hong, *Songmo jiwen*, 16.
18. *Da Jin guozhi*, 250.
19. Hargett, *On the Road in Twelfth-Century China*, 149–150. The gold filaments Fan notes are mirrored in the gold thread woven into the cloth of the clothing of the Prince of Qi and his wife.
20. Chai Zejun and Zhang Chouliang, *Fanzhi Yanshan si*; Karetzky, "Recently Discovered Chin Dynasty Murals."
21. Chai Zejun and Zhang Chouliang, *Fanzhi Yanshan si*.
22. Johnson, "Place of *Qingming shanghe tu*."

23. Ebrey, *Inner Quarters*; Ko, *Cinderella's Sisters*, plate 16.
24. Wittfogel and Feng note that Kitan folkways reveal the persistence of wife stealing. See *History of Chinese Society*, 219–224.
25. *LS*, 71:1201.
26. *Kitan guozhi*, 13:142. *LS*, 8:89, 71:1201. Emperor Jingzong's maternity is not entirely clear. He was the second son of Emperor Shizong. His formal biography in the *Liaoshi* states that his mother was Empress Huaijie, surnamed Xiao. Lady Zhen's biography states, "She was very beautiful . . . and gave birth to Prince Ning. . . . She knew how to manage the household well. When [Shizong] became emperor, he made her his empress. . . . She was killed in the Change rebellion." The future emperor Jingzong had the personal name Xian and the title Prince Ning. As emperor, Jingzong conducted funeral ceremonies for the two empresses, and although the names are not stated, these two women must have been Empress Huaijie and Lady Zhen. Jingzong would have been unlikely to have honored Lady Zhen in this manner if she had not been his mother. The *Kitan guozhi* (13:142) lists Lady Zhen as Shizong's only empress and Emperor Jingzong as her eldest son. Neither source provides her title.
27. *Quan Liao wen*, 371; Holmgren, "Observations on Marriage and Inheritance Practices," 144–145.
28. *Quan Liao wen*, 360.
29. *Da Jin guozhi*, 176.
30. Elliott, *Manchu Way*, 277n197; Shuo Wang, "Manchu Women in Transition." After the girls were selected, the emperor chose the most promising for service at court. Any woman who did not marry among the Manchu elite during the time she served the court would be released. The girls' families were handsomely rewarded for their daughters' service, and girls who were released were much sought after in marriage.
31. Hong, *Songno jiwen*; see also the translation in Franke, "Chinese Texts on the Jurchen."
32. Koumiss, a drink made from fermented mare's milk, was the most common form of alcohol among steppe peoples, including the Kitan, Jurchen, and Mongols, all of whom were known as heavy drinkers.
33. The groom's family would be shamed if the bride's father selected too few horses. If he rejected them all, he could select from among the horses the groom's family and friends rode in on. In return, the bride's family gave gifts to the groom's family based on how many horses had been selected.
34. *Da Jin guozhi*, 553; see the discussion in Holmgren, "Observations on Marriage and Inheritance Practices," 132–133.
35. *Da Jin guozhi*, 28.
36. *JS*, 3:57.
37. Ibid., 61.
38. Ibid., 64.
39. Birge, "Levirate Marriage," 110.
40. Jennifer Holmgren has made extensive studies of Kitan marriage patterns. See *Mar-

riage, *Kinship and Power in Northern China*, especially "Marriage, Kinship and Succession under the Ch'i-tan Rulers of the Liao Dynasty," and "Observations on Marriage and Inheritance Practices," 129–135. She finds similar patterns among the Mongols and other northern peoples.

41. Holmgren, "Marriage, Kinship and Succession."
42. *LS*, 71:1199.
43. Liu Pujiang, in conversation, Beijing University, April 2001.
44. Kane, *Kitan Language and Script*, 5.
45. *LS*, 71:1201.
46. Ibid., 1201–1202.
47. Wittfogel and Feng, *History of Chinese Society*, 208–211; Holmgren, "Marriage, Kinship and Succession," 73–78.
48. Wittfogel and Feng, *History of Chinese Society*, 198–199.
49. Holmgren, "Marriage, Kinship and Succession," 74.
50. *LS*, 107:1472.
51. *LS*, 116:1539; 52:863–865.
52. *LS*, 52:863–865; see also Wittfogel and Feng, *History of Chinese Society*, 275–277.
53. Rudenko, *Frozen Tombs of Siberia*, 191–193. The remains of a woman in Chinese dress was found in the chieftain's tomb together with a four-wheeled carriage, of probable Chinese manufacture, pulled by four horses in quadriga arrangement, with remains of silk and embroidered hangings.
54. Di Cosmo, "Northern Frontier in Pre-Imperial China," 192–193.
55. Yu Yingshi, "Han Foreign Relations," 386–389, 394–398.
56. Wright, "Sui Dynasty," 142.
57. Twitchett, "Hsüan-tsung," 438, 440.
58. Twitchett and Tietze, "Liao," 104, 140.
59. Ibid., 121, 140.
60. Holmgren, "Marriage, Kinship and Succession," 47–48.
61. Ibid., 45–49.
62. *JS*, 1501–1502, 2613.
63. Wittfogel and Feng, *History of Chinese Society*, 211.
64. *Kitan guozhi*, 141. Perhaps an error, an instance where the *Kitan guozhi* as a source must be treated with caution.
65. This marriage pattern is seen in elite marriages between the Yelü and Xiao clans and also pertained among the Jurchen and even in the later Manchu populations. See Wittfogel and Feng, *History of Chinese Society*, 17–18, 206–212. On preferential marriage systems more generally, see Holmgren, "Observations on Marriage and Inheritance Practices," 135–142.
66. Meng Gutuoli, "Qidan zu hunyin tantao."
67. Holmgren, "Marriage, Kinship and Succession," 56–57; Wittfogel and Feng, *History of Chinese Society*, 18, 210.

68. Meng Gutuoli, "Qidan zu hunyin tantao," 58.
69. Neimenggu wenwu kaogu yanjiusuo, Aluke'erqinqi wenwu guanlisuo, "Neimenggu Chifeng Baoshan Liao bihua mu fajue jianbao." Yelü Qinde was an imperial relative, but his marriage is not recorded in the LS.
70. Neimenggu zizhiqu wenwu kaogu yanjiusuo, Zhelimu meng bowuguan, *Liao Chenguo gongzhu mu*; Louis, "Shaping Symbols of Privilege," 96.
71. Holmgren, "Marriage, Kinship and Succession," 4; Wittfogel and Feng, *History of Chinese Society*, 198–199, 207–212.
72. Holmgren, "Marriage, Kinship and Succession," 47–48.
73. Even in Song China, a man might take a younger sister in marriage to replace an elder who had died.
74. *Quan Liao wen*, 238.
75. LS, 4:49; Wittfogel and Feng, *History of Chinese Society*, 211, 255; Holmgren, "Observations on Marriage and Inheritance Practices," 42–43.
76. LS, 71:1205.
77. Ibid., 74:1231–1232; *Liaodai shike wenbian*, 95.
78. Tang Tongtian, "Liaodai de mingfu," 4:96–97.
79. *Quan Liao wen*, 36.
80. *Liaodai shike wenbian*, 516.
81. Virginity was not an issue but pregnancy was.
82. LS, 71:1206.
83. *Quan Liao wen*, 64.
84. Ibid., 64–65.
85. Hargett, *On the Road in Twelfth-Century China*, 154.
86. Hong Hao, *Songmo jiwen*, 19.
87. JS, 8:179.
88. Zhang was a common name among the Bohai and the name of one of the preeminent *haner* families in the Southern Circuit.
89. *Liaodai shike wenbian*, 42.
90. *Da Jin guozhi*, 262–264, 279.
91. LS, *juan* 107.
92. Birge, "Levirate Marriage."

FIVE
Widowhood and Chastity

1. LS, 2:23–24, 71:1200. The emperor died in the eighth month and the body was placed in the funerary temple in the ninth month. The mausoleum complex including the imperial tomb was completed in 927, which is probably when the funeral was held. The funeral is described in the *Kitan guozhi*, 8:139. For a preliminary archaeological report of the site, see Zhongguo shehui de xueyuan kaogu yanjiusuo, Neimenggu kaogu yanjiu di er zuo

gongzuo dui, "Neimenggu Balin Zuoqi Liaodai zuling kaogu fajian de xin shuohuo," *Kaogu*, 2008, no. 2:3–6.
2. *LS*, 71:1200; *Kitan guozhi*, 8:139.
3. Ibid., 139–140.
4. Birge, "Levirate Marriage," 110 ff.
5. Holmgren, "Observations on Marriage and Inheritance Practices" has the most extensive discussion of levirate in Mongol society; see also Birge, "Levirate Marriage"; Ebrey, *Inner Quarters*, 188–203; Elliott, "Manchu Widows"; Shuo Wang, "Manchu Women in Transition," 77–110.
6. Elliott, "Manchu Widows," 33.
7. A case in point is the mother of Chinggis Khan, who was widowed relatively young with small children. She did not remarry. Temujin, who would later become Chinggis Khan, and his brothers grew up in desperate poverty. That the family survived at all was probably owing to the reluctant support of allies. Allsen, "Rise of the Mongolian Empire," 334.
8. *Da Jin guozhi*, 553; Birge, "Levirate Marriage."
9. Elliott, "Manchu Widows," 49–54.
10. Wittfogel and Feng, *History of Chinese Society*, 200.
11. *LS*, 107:1474.
12. Elliott, "Manchu Widows," 40–44.
13. Elliott makes this point emphatically (ibid., 49–54); Holmgren also discusses suicide in "Observations on Marriage and Inheritance Practices"; see also Waltner, "Widows and Remarriage."
14. Holmgren, "Observations on Marriage and Inheritance Practices," 156.
15. Hong Hao, *Songmo jiwen*, 12.
16. *Da Jin guozhi*, 553.
17. Levirate was more repugnant to the Chinese than any other barbarian custom.
18. Xu Mengxin, *Sanchao beimeng huibian*, 17:3b–4a; see also Holmgren, "Observations on Marriage and Inheritance Practices," 174–177.
19. Holmgren, "Observations on Marriage and Inheritance Practices," 151–154.
20. Franke, "Jurchen Customary Law," 228, citing *JS*, 6:14a.
21. *JS*, 5:115.
22. Birge, "Women and Confucianism," 226. The Jin titled the code *Taihe* after the Tang code on which it was based. The Tang code in turn took its title from the Taihe reign period in which it was promulgated. (There was no Taihe reign period in the Jin dynasty.)
23. *JS*, 6:115.
24. The source of this story is the Ming-period *Songshi jishi benmo*, one of the least reliable Chinese sources since it repeats all kinds of slander. See Chen Bangzhan, *Songshi jishi benmo*, 768–769.
25. *JS*, 70:1621.
26. *LS*, 4:9. The imperial dispensation allowed widows and widowers of the Yishi, Pinbei,

and Tugui clans, "who were unable to live alone," to marry. See Wittfogel and Feng, *History of Chinese Society*, 256.
27. *LS*, 15:179.
28. *Liaodai shike wenbian*, 261.
29. Ibid., 511.
30. Birge, "Levirate Marriage," 114–117.
31. Holmgren, "Observations on Marriage and Inheritance Practices," 166.
32. *Quan Liao wen*, 182–183.
33. Ibid., 206.
34. Ibid.
35. *LS*, 81:1285.
36. Ibid.
37. For separation of the sexes in Song China, see Ebrey, *Inner Quarters*, 21–44.
38. *JS*, 3:61.
39. Franke, "Jurchen Customary Law," 227.
40. Ibid., 140.
41. *JS*, 7:164.
42. Shuo Wang, "Manchu Women in Transition."
43. *LS*, 10:109; see also Wittfogel and Feng, *History of Chinese Society*, 258.
44. *LS*, 65:1001; Wittfogel and Feng, *History of Chinese Society*, 266.
45. *LS*, 71:1206.
46. Ibid., 89:1350; Wittfogel and Feng, *History of Chinese Society*, 263.
47. *Da Jin guozhi*, 173.
48. *JS*, 63:1515.
49. *JS*, 17:383; Alutu et al., *Songshi*, 476–477:13817–13850.
50. Dribe, Lundh, and Nystedt, "Widowhood Strategies."

SIX

Warrior Women

1. *LS*, 71:1199.
2. Ibid., 1:3.
3. Ibid., 71:1199.
4. Liu Pujiang, *Liao Jin shi lun*, 55–56.
5. *Kitan guozhi*, 13:138.
6. Liu Pujiang, *Liao Jin shi lun*, 56; see also *JS*, 67:1587.
7. Twitchett and Tietze, "Liao," 97–99.
8. Liu Pujiang, *Liao Jin shi lun*, 56. This ranking by ethnic identity or cultural affiliation in the Liao period and a more formal system in the Jin predates the better-known ethnic stratification of society in the Yuan dynasty.

Notes to Pages 123–128

9. Holmgren, "Marriage, Kinship and Succession," 47–48.
10. Ibid., 46–49.
11. *LS*, 1:6; Ouyang Xiu, *Xin Wudaishi*, 72:886–887. See also Wittfogel and Feng, *History of Chinese Society*, 142. For a brief history of the struggles of the first emperor to establish an imperial tradition, see Holmgren, "Marriage, Kinship and Succession," 45–52.
12. *LS*, 1:6.
13. *LS*, 1:6, 35:401; see also Wittfogel and Feng, *History of Chinese Society*, 549.
14. *LS*, 71:1199.
15. *LS*, 71:1199. The remark that no one could speak the Hui language seems to contradict the *LS* notation that Yingtian's Shulü clan had Huihu origins. If the clan had Uygur connections, members should have been conversant with the Uygur language. If, however, they were Xi, and somewhat removed from Uygur but in the same general language group, the rapid acquisition of the Uygur language makes sense.
16. Wittfogel and Feng, *History of Chinese Society*, 200, 243.
17. Kane, *Kitan Language and Script*.
18. *LS*, 3:27.
19. Ibid., 72:1212–1214; Wittfogel and Feng, *History of Chinese Society*, 416–417.
20. *LS*, 31:363–365; Wittfogel and Feng, *History of Chinese Society*, 543.
21. *LS*, 71:1200.
22. Ibid., 1201–1202.
23. Twitchett and Tietze, "Liao," 87.
24. *Kitan guozhi*, 6:59–60.
25. Ibid.
26. *LS*, 65:986–987, 1001.
27. *Kitan guozhi*, 13:142. The Kitan practice of awarding multiple titles can lead to confusion. Longqing is elsewhere designated Prince of Qin. The third son, Longyu, is consistently identified as the Prince of Qi, but we hear virtually nothing more of him. However, another son, known as the Prince of Chu, was said to have been the son of Hann Derang, not Emperor Jingzong, and yet another child, Diange, who was younger, would therefore also have been Hann's son. See Wright, "*Ambassadors Records*," 29–30. Lu's report was first published in *Cheng Yao Lu*, 4:a–b (1010–1016); see Wright, *From War to Diplomatic Parity*, 183–186.
28. Wright, "*Ambassadors Records*," 29–30.
29. *LS*, 71:1201–1202
30. *Kitan guozhi*, 18:174.
31. Ibid., 175–176.
32. The rebirth ceremony apparently involved spending the night in a tunnel-like tent to emerge with the rising sun. It may be a remnant of an earlier steppe custom. It resembles the Japanese ceremony of the same nature by which a new emperor was deified, which may also have its roots in ancient steppe practices. In Liao terms, the ceremony, which is still not fully understood, seems to have conveyed legitimacy, not deification.

33. The Jin dynasty emperor Shizong reigned for twenty-nine years; only Khubilai Khan, of the Yuan dynasty, had a longer reign (thirty-five years).
34. *LS*, 71:1201–1202.
35. Ibid.; Twitchett and Tietze, "Liao," 90.
36. Twitchett and Tietze, "Liao," 90.
37. Shizong's reign and Hann's various posts and activities are chronicled in *LS*, *juan* 10–15.
38. Lau Nap-yin and Huang K'uan-chung, "Founding and Consolidation of the Sung Dynasty," 264.
39. Wright, *From War to Diplomatic Parity*, 68, 71.
40. *LS*, 71:1201.
41. Ibid.; see 14:167–168 and *juan* 75 passim.
42. Wright, *From War to Diplomatic Parity*, 44–45.
43. Ibid., 105.
44. *Quan Liao wen*, 36; *LS*, 71:1203.
45. *LS*, 71:1203, 72:1285; Wittfogel and Feng, *History of Chinese Society*, 419.
46. Twitchett and Tietze, "Liao," 91; Wittfogel and Feng, *History of Chinese Society*, 200.
47. *Kitan guozhi*, 13:142–143.
48. *LS*, 71:1204.
49. Ibid., 29:342–344.
50. Ibid., 71:1207; *Quan Liao wen*, 6; Wittfogel and Feng, *History of Chinese Society*, 416.
51. Wittfogel and Feng, *History of Chinese Society*, 416.
52. *LS*, 19:225.
53. Ibid., 22:264–265.
54. *JS*, 17:383; Alutu et al., *Songshi*, 476–477:13817–13850. *Songshi jishi benmo*, 976–981; see also Pei-yi Wu, "Yang Miaozhen."
55. Alutu et al., *Songshi*, 476:13821; Franke, "Chin Dynasty," 255–256.
56. Ibid.
57. Alutu et al., *Songshi*, 476:13821. The numbers are surely exaggerated.
58. Pei-yi Wu, "Yang Miaozhen," 139–140.
59. Alutu et al., *Songshi*, 476:13817.
60. Pei-yi Wu, "Yang Miaozhen," 140. Wu argues (147) that Miaozhen was unconventional from the perspective of Han morality, especially in violating widow chastity. But in terms of Jin-dynasty policy on widows, for a widow to take a new husband would also have been a serious violation, although for different reasons, and may be why her liaison with Li Quan was brief.
61. Alutu et al., *Songshi*, 476:13817.
62. Ibid., 477:13849.
63. Ibid., 13829.
64. Ibid.
65. Ibid., 13817–13821.
66. Pei-yi Wu, "Yang Miaozhen," 146.

67. Alutu et al., *Songshi*, 477:13836.
68. Ibid.
69. Ibid., 13837.
70. Franke, "Chin Dynasty," 257.
71. *JS*, 17:383.
72. Alutu et al., *Songshi*, 477:13851.
73. *JS*, 17:383.

SEVEN
Private Affairs

1. Twitchett and Tietze, "Liao," 89.
2. Kitan script has two variations, known as big-character and small-character script, respectively. Most extant inscriptions are in small-character script. See Kane, *Kitan Language and Script*, ix.
3. I inspected a large number of Liao steles and tombstones in the Liaoning Provincial Museum in April 2001. Many appeared to have dual inscriptions, one in Chinese and the opposite in Kitan. Some were inscribed in Chinese only. Another famous example of Kitan script is found on the celebrated blank stele to Empress Wu of the Tang dynasty. The Kitan inscription was added to the stele later, probably in the Jin or early Yuan period. To date, the Liao scripts have not been fully translated.
4. *Quan Liao wen*. Buddhist monks can be identified by the nature of their names and the prefix *shamen* 沙門.
5. *Jin wen zui*, passim.
6. *LS*, 71:1202.
7. On the export of classical books to the Liao, see Talbott Huey, "Chinese Books as Cultural Exports from Han to Ming: A Bibliographic Essay," *Studies on Asia*, ser. 3, 3, no. 1:85–101 (www.isp.msu.edu/studiesonasia/).
8. Standen, *Unbounded Loyalty*, 107–116.
9. K. T. Wu, "Chinese Printing," 448–489.
10. To my knowledge, no books in Kitan script have yet been found, but one would like more information on the books and scrolls found in the Yemaotai tomb.
11. K. T. Wu, "Chinese Printing," 449.
12. *LS*, 107:1471–1472.
13. *Quan Liao wen*, 409.
14. Ibid., 183.
15. *LS*, 71:1206. I earlier expressed some skepticism on the actual authorship of these poems.
16. *Liaodai shike wenbian*, 516; dated 1101.
17. Ibid., 248; *Quan Liao wen*, 125–127.
18. *Liaodai shike wenbian*, 590; dated 1040.

19. Ibid., 76–77.
20. Ibid., 105.
21. Ibid., 567–568; dated 1108.
22. *Quan Liao wen*, 231.
23. Kai-yu Hsu, "Poems of Li Qingzhao."
24. *Quan Liao wen*, 264.
25. Ibid., 105.
26. *Liaodai shike wenbian*, 590.
27. Ibid., 684.
28. Wittfogel and Feng, *History of Chinese Society*, 198.
29. Twitchett and Tietze, "Liao," 92.
30. Wittfogel and Feng, *History of Chinese Society*, 45. According to this source, although Hann Derang and his brothers were appointed to office prior to the institution of an examination system, other members of the Hann family received preferential treatment in examinations.
31. Franke, "Chin Dynasty," 271–273.
32. K. T. Wu, "Chinese Printing," 453–459.
33. *JS*, 51:1129–1130.
34. Ibid., 126:2742.
35. Ibid., 125:2721.
36. Ibid., 126:2735.
37. Ibid., 51:1132–1134.
38. Bol, "Seeking Common Ground."
39. *JS*, 64:1527.
40. For comparison with the Song, see Ebrey, *Inner Quarters*, 21–44.
41. *LS*, juan 1–7. Ceremonies and sacrifices at Mount Muye figure frequently in the annals of the first two Liao emperors. See Wittfogel and Feng, *History of Chinese Society*, 213–215.
42. Steinhardt, *Liao Architecture*.
43. *Quan Liao wen*, 230, 240–245; *Liao Inscriptions*, 288–293.
44. Kuhn, "Liao Architecture."
45. Dunnell, *Great State of White*. Dunnell shows how the Tangut state of Xia depended on Buddhism for its legitimacy.
46. See the plan of the city in Steinhardt, *Liao Architecture*, 7. This point supports Kuhn's contention regarding the contributions of the Han Chinese specialists to Liao Buddhist architecture. See Kuhn, "Liao Architecture."
47. Steinhardt, *Liao Architecture*, 31–56.
48. Steinhardt, "Jin Hall at Jingtusi."
49. Beijing shi wenwu yanjiusuo, *Beijing Jindai huangling*; Beijing shi wenwu yanjiu Jinling kaogu gongzuodui, "Beijing Fangshan qu Jinling yizhi de diaocha yu fabiao."
50. Steinhardt, "Jin Hall at Jingtusi."

51. *Da Jin guozhi*, 276; the inscription is dated 1199.
52. Chai Zejun and Zhang Chouliang, *Fanzhi Yanshan si*, 1.
53. Bush, "Women as Protagonists," 1.
54. Chai Zejun and Zhang Chouliang, *Fanzhi Yanshan si*, photographs of the paintings, 58–177.
55. Bush, "Women as Protagonists," 2.
56. Chai Zejun and Zhang Chouliang, *Fanzhi Yanshan si*, plates 44, 58, 62, 68, 102, 103, 104.
57. Ibid., plates 57, 63.
58. Ibid., plate 97. This mill is similar to one in a Five Dynasties or early Song painting on silk (*Mill on the River*) in the Shanghai Museum, viewed June 2007.
59. Ibid., plate 113.
60. Bush, "Women as Protagonists," 3; Chai Zejun and Zhang Chouliang, *Fanzhi Yanshan si*, 128, plate 68. The cartouche identifies her as *qing yi* 青衣 (Blue Robe)
61. Bush, "Women as Protagonists," 4.
62. *Quan Liao wen*, 360. A date is not given for this work, but it is listed with other works from the reign of Shengzong (983–1031). Unlike later accounts, it does not include the death of the empress and probably dates therefore to her lifetime.
63. *LS*, 82:1289–1291.
64. Ibid.
65. Twitchett and Tietze, "Liao," 90.
66. *LS*, 82:1291.
67. Ibid., 14:167.
68. Ibid., 64:986–988.
69. See the translation in Wright, *From War to Diplomatic Parity*, 186.
70. *Quan Liao wen*, 360. The Prince of Chu was the empress's fourth son. She bore three sons and two daughters to Emperor Jingzong. Jingzong's fourth son listed in the *Liaoshi* was apparently not born of Ruizhi (*LS*, 64:986–987, 1001).
71. *Quan Liao wen*, 360.
72. *Kitan guozhi*, 13:243. The duke of the ancient city of Piyang received this fief from the Han emperor. He was the reputed lover of Empress Lü, widow of Liu Bang, the first Han emperor. See Sima Qian, *Shiji*, 76:2702–2703; Ban Gu, *Hanshu*, juan 43.
73. Wright, *From War to Diplomatic Parity*, 186.
74. Ibid., 233. Liu's account is situated next to an item dated 1005, so it was probably written in that year (*Quan Liao wen*, 360).
75. *LS*, 64:986–987.
76. Wright, "Ambassadors Records," 29–30 (romanization changed to pinyin). This report was published in *Cheng Yao Lu* (dated 1010–1016), 4:a–b (as cited in Wright, "Ambassadors Records," 38).
77. Wright, "Ambassadors Records." In fact, Hann at this time was sixty-five and the empress was fifty-three.

78. Ibid., 38–41.
79. Ibid., 8.
80. Twitchett and Tietze, "Liao," 79–80.
81. Ibid., 81, 84.
82. Holmgren, "Marriage, Kinship and Succession," 63.
83. Wittfogel and Feng, *History of Chinese Society*, 207.
84. On standards for Song women and widows, see Ebrey, *Inner Quarters*; Birge, "Levirate Marriage"; Birge, "Women and Confucianism." See also Birge, *Women, Property, and Confucian Reaction*.
85. Chen Bangzhan, *Songshi jishi benmo*, 147.
86. For Chinese standards in the Ming, see Birge, "Women and Confucianism."
87. The discovery was reported at http://218.25.39.149/74599716460953600/20021231/1047809.shtml (accessed December 2005).
88. Christian Deydier Oriental Bronzes, *L'art et la matière*, items 56–62. These items, dedicated in ceremonies in 1026, include a number of solid-gold and gold-gilt boxes, a gold belt, silver cups, and a solid-gold bowl. They may have been buried in a separate hoard and not inserted in the tomb, which was presumably robbed in antiquity, as were the imperial tombs.

Conclusion

1. Kane, *Kitan Language and Script*, 227–260.
2. Kane lists epitaphs, eulogies, and a curious but lengthy inscription at the grave site of the Tang-dynasty empress Wu, dating from the Jin period.
3. Ibid., 4.
4. Shizong had two empresses, Lady Zhen and a Xiao empress, although whether sequentially or in combination is not clear. He also seems to have had several unnamed concubines. The situation with Muzong, the next emperor, is unclear, but he did not name an empress. Shizong's son, Jingzong, took concubines, and his empress, Ruizhi (later Empress Dowager Chengtian), came to court first as his principal concubine. Shengzong instituted and regularized the old Tang system of ranking concubines. Thus, in terms of concubines, a slow step-by-step development led to increasingly Han customs.
5. Zhongguo shehui de xueyuan kaogu yanjiusuo, Neimenggu kaogu yanjiu de er zuo dui, "Neimenggu Balin Zuoqi Liaodai zuling kaogu fajian de xin shuohuo," 3–6. Abaoji's tomb site has not yet been fully investigated by archaeologists but the elaborate tombs of the Kitan elite from this early date in the 920s resemble Tang-dynasty mausoleums; the same seems to be true for the auxiliary tombs at the *zuling* site. For another tomb of the Yelü elite of the 920s see Neimenggu wenwu kaogu yanjiusuo, Aluke'erqinqi wenwu guanlisuo, "Neimenggu Chifeng Baoshan Liao bihua mu fajue jianbao."
6. One of the great, still-standing pagodas of the Liao period, the Guanyin Pavilion of the Dulesi monastery, not far from modern Beijing, was constructed by Hann Kuangsi, the

father of Hann Derang, who held high office under Emperor Jingzong. (Steinhardt, *Liao Architecture*, 35). Other notable pagodas were located in the Chinese sectors of Liao cities.

7. Ebrey, *Inner Quarters*, 2–37.
8. Standen, *Unbounded Loyalty*.
9. Bush, "Women as Protagonists."
10. Elliott, "Manchu Widows," 40–44.
11. *JS*, 6:144; Franke, "Jurchen Customary Law," 228.
12. *LS*, 71:1207.
13. Standen, *Unbounded Loyalty*, 10, 107–123.
14. Dunnell, *Great State of White*, 16, 71–72.
15. Ibid., 158.
16. Fletcher, "Mongols," 26, 38; George Qingzhi Zhao, *Marriage as Political Strategy*, 57–67.
17. George Qingzhi Zhao, *Marriage as Political Strategy*, 67–69.
18. McGrath, "Reigns of Jen-tsung," 279–289; Davis, "Chaste and Filial Women," 216.
19. Davis, *Wind Against the Mountain*, 61–63 and passim.
20. Segal, "Hōjō Masako" (cited with permission of the author).
21. *Quan Liao wen*, 65–66.

Glossary

Note: characters are given in traditional or simplified format according to the source.

Abaoji (*see* Yelü Abaoji)
Aguda (*see* Wanyan Aguda)
Aizong 哀宗
Alutu 阿魯圖
Aluzhen 阿魯真
Anyang 安阳
Aolimi 奧里米
baiaoli 拜奧禮
baimen 拜門
Baopu (*see* Xing Baopu)
Baoshan 宝山
Baozhi (*see* Xing Baozhi)
Bei, Prince (*see* Yelü Bei)
Beijing 北京
Beishu 北書
Bianzhou 汴州
Bohai 渤海
bu 部

cainü	才女
Cai Yan	蔡琰
Cao *shi*	曹氏
Chang'an	長安
Changbaishan	長白山
Changge (Yelü)	耶律常哥
Changsheng, Prince	常勝
Chanyuan	澶淵
Chaoyang	朝阳
Chen *fei*	宸妃
Chengtian	承天
Chenguo	陳国
Chen *shi*	陳氏
Chen Xing	陳陘
Chu	楚
Chucheng	楚城
Chunqin	淳欽
Chuzhou	楚州
Cui Li	崔立
Da (surname)	大
Da Jin guozhi	大金國志
Daming temple	大明寺
Daozong, Emperor	道宗
Datong	大同
Dawopu	大臥鋪
de	得
Defei	德妃
Deguang, Emperor	德光
Deng	登
Dian *fei*	奠妃
Diange	奠哥

ding ware	定瓷
Dong Jiazun	董家遵
Dongjing	東京
Dongtanguo	東丹國
Duji *shi*	獨吉氏
Dule monastery	獨樂寺
Du *shi*	杜氏
erhu	二胡
Erliben (see Xiao Erliben)	
fan	蕃
Fan Chengda	范成大
Fan *shi*	樊氏
Fanzhi	繁峙
fei	妃
fei	非
Feng Miaozhen	馮妙真
Gaozong, Emperor	高宗
Geng Yanyi	耿延毅
gongzhu	公主
Guanyin	觀音
guifei	貴妃
Guo Anyong	國安用
guojia	國家
guoshi	國史
Hailing *wang*	海陵王
Han	漢
haner	漢兒
Hanlin	翰林
Hann	韓
Hann Derang	韓德讓
Hann Fang	韓昉

Hann Kuangsi	韓匡嗣
Hann Qingmin	韓慶民
Hann Shixun	韩师训
Hann Yanhui	韓延徽
Hann Yu	韓瑜
Hann Zhigu	韓知古
hanren	漢人
Hebei	河北
Heilongjiang	黑龍江
Helong	賀龍
Henan	河南
heqin	和亲
Hong Hao	洪皓
Hou Han	後漢
Houma	侯馬
hu	胡
Huaian	淮安
Huaijie, Empress	懷節
Huai River	淮河
Huanzhou	環州
Hu Gui	胡瓌
Huife	惠妃
Huihu	回鶻
Huining	會寧
Huizong, Emperor	徽宗
Hu Li	胡礪
Jiaguhushan	夾谷胡山
Jianfu	建福
Jiangnan	江南
Jiangsu	江蘇
Jiang Yuan	江淵

Jiaozuo	焦作
jiefu	節婦
Jilin	吉林
Jin (Jurchen)	金
Jin	晉
Jing'an	靖安
Jingzong, Emperor	景宗
Jingzu	景祖
jinshi	進士
Jishan	稷山
Jixian	薊縣
Jizhou	薊州
Kaifeng	開封
kang	炕
Kangxi, Emperor	康熙
Kang Zhuzhu	康住住
Kitan	契丹
Kulunqi	庫伦旗
Lei	雷
Liangxiang	良鄉
Liang Yuan	梁援
Lianshui	漣水
Liao	遼, 辽
Liaoning	遼宁
Liaoyang	遼陽
Liaozhou	遼洲
liefu	列婦
lienü	列女
lienü zhuan	列女傳
Li Fu	李福
Lihu (*see* Yelü Lihu)	

Lintao	臨洮
Li Qingzhao	李清照
Li Quan	李全
Li Shanqing	李善慶
Li *shi*	李氏
Liu Bin	劉斌
Liu Shang	劉商
Liu *shi*	劉氏
Liu Xiang	劉向
Li Yi	李翊
Li Ying	李英
Li Yuanhao	李元昊
Longqing (*see* Yelü Longqing)	
Longxu (*see* Yelü Longxu)	
Longyu (*see* Yelü Longyu)	
Longyun (*see* Yelü Longyun)	
Lü (Han empress)	呂
lu (caitiff)	虜
Lu Zhen	路振
Luan *shi*	欒氏
Luguo furen	魯國夫人
Manchu (Manzu)	滿族
Ma Zhiwen	馬直溫
meng'an	猛安
Ming	明
Ming Huang, Emperor	明皇
Moho	靺鞨
mouke	謀克
Mulan	木蘭
Muye, Mount	木葉山
Muzong, Emperor	穆宗

nan	南
Nanjing	南京
nanren	南人
nei	內
niangzi	娘子
Nie Shunying	聶舜英
Ning, Prince	寧
Nongtan	農坦
Nuolan	挼蘭
Nüzhen	女真
Ouyang Xiu	歐陽修
Penglai	蓬萊
Pinbei	品卑
Pingding	平定
Pingliang	平涼
Pingyuan	平原
pipa	琵琶
Piyang, Duke of	辟陽公
Pucha Alihu	蒲察阿里虎
Pucha Mingxiu	蒲察明秀
Puyi	溥儀
Qi	齊
Qianlong, Emperor	乾隆
Qiguo, Prince of	齊國
Qin	秦
Qinde (see Yelü Qinde)	
Qing	清
qingbai porcelain	青白瓷
Qingming shanghe tu	清明上河圖
Qingzhou	青州
Qin-Jinguo	秦晉國

Qinzong, Emperor	欽宗
Qiu *shi*	仇氏
Rende, Empress	仁德
Renyi, Empress	仁懿
ru	儒
Ruizhi, Empress	睿智
Ruizong, Prince	睿宗
Sahenian	撒合輦
Shaanxi	陝西
Shalizhi	沙里質
shamen	沙門
Shandong	山東
Shangjing	上京
Shanxi	山西
sheng (Jurchen)	生（女真）
Shengzong, Emperor	聖宗
shi	氏
Shilu (see Yelü Shilu)	
Shira Muren	潢河
Shi *shi*	師氏
Shi *shi*	史氏
Shi *shi*	石氏
Shizong, Emperor	世宗
shu	熟
shuguo	屬國
Shulü	述律
Shun	舜
Shushan army	屬珊軍
Sima Qian	司馬遷
Siwen (Xiao) (see Xiao Siwen)	
Song	宋

Songhua River	松花江
sui	歲
Sui	隋
Suibin	绥滨
Suishu	隋書
Sungari River	松花江
Sunjiawan	孙家湾
Suzhou	蘇州
taihou	太后
Taizong, Emperor	太宗
Taizu, Emperor	太祖
Talanabo	撻覽阿鉢
Tang	唐
Taoyuan	桃源
Tian Si	田四
Tianxi, Emperor	天錫
Tianzuo, Emperor	天祚
Toghtō	脫脫離
Tonghe	統和
wai	外
Wang Anshi	王安石
Wang Ding	王鼎
Wang Kui	王逵
Wang Yishen	王義深
Wang Ze	王澤
Wanyan	完顏
Wanyan Aguda	完顏阿骨打
Wanyan Haowen	完顏好問
Wanyan Shulan	完顏素蘭
Wanyan Yan	完颜晏
Wanyan Zhongde	完顏仲德

Wanyan Zhuer	完顏豬兒
Weishao *wang*	衛紹王
Weishu	魏書
Weizhou	濰州
wen	文
Wen *fei*	文妃
Wenji	文姬
Wenji gui Han	文姬归汉
wu	武
Wu, Mount	巫山
Wugulun *shi*	烏古論氏
Wulinda *shi*	烏林荅氏
Wuqimai, Emperor	吳乞買
Wu Zetian (Empress Wu)	武則天
Xi	奚
Xia	夏
Xiabali	下八里
Xian (see Yelü Xian)	
Xian, Prince (see Yelü Xian)	
Xianbei	鮮卑
Xiang Qi	相琪
xiannü	賢女
Xianyu	鮮于
Xianzong	顯宗
Xiao	蕭
Xiao Chuo (Yanyan)	蕭綽（燕燕）
Xiao Chuobu	蕭啜不
Xiao Erliben	蕭訛里本
Xiao *fei*	蕭妃
Xiao Haili	蕭海里
Xiao Hudu	蕭胡覩

218

Xiao Hui	蕭惠
Xiao Shaoju	蕭紹矩
Xiao *shi*	蕭氏
xiaoshi	小事
Xiao Siwen	蕭思溫
Xiao *taihou*	蕭太后
Xiao Wen	蕭溫
Xiao Xiaozhong	蕭孝忠
Xiao Yanyan	蕭燕燕
Xiao Yixin	蕭意辛
Xiao Yulu	蕭裕魯
Xia Quan	夏全
Xijing	西京
Xing Baopu	邢抱朴
Xing Baozhi	邢抱質
Xing De	邢德
Xingzong, Emperor	興宗
Xin Tangshu	新唐書
Xiongnu	匈奴
xiucai	秀才
xiunü	秀女
Xi Xia	西夏
Xizong, Emperor	熙宗
Xuanhua	宣化
Xuanzong, Emperor	宣宗
Xu Guo	許國
Xu Xiji	徐晞稷
Xuzhou	許州
Yan	燕
yang	陽
Yang Aner	楊安兒

Glossary

Yang Anguo	楊安國
Yang *guifei*	楊貴妃
Yang Miaozhen	楊妙真
Yanjing	燕京
Yansage	癌撒葛
Yanshan temple	巖山寺
Yan Tong	閻通
Yanyan (*see* Xiao Yanyan)	
Yan-Yun	燕雲
Yaonian	遙輦
Yelü	耶律
Yelü Abaoji	耶律阿保機
Yelü Bei	耶律倍
Yelü Changge	耶律常哥
Yelü Hongyi	耶律弘益
Yelü Jian	耶律簡
Yelü Lihu	耶律李胡
Yelü Longqing	耶律隆慶
Yelü Longxu	耶律隆緒
Yelü Longyu	耶律隆裕
Yelü Longyun	耶律隆運
Yelü Qinde	耶律勤德
Yelü Ruan	耶律阮
Yelü Shilu	耶律適魯
Yelü Shucheng	耶律庶成
Yelü Tage	耶律撻葛
Yelü Wuzhi	耶律屋質
Yelü Xian	耶律賢
Yelü Xiezhen	耶律斜軫
Yelü Yixin	耶律乙辛
Yelü Zhong	耶律中

Yelü Zhuzhe	耶律朮者
Yemaotai	叶茂台
Yenmujin	巖母堇
Yide, Empress	懿德
Yilayuliye	移剌余里也
yin	陰
Yingtian, Empress	應天
Yin *shi*	尹氏
Yishi	乙室
Yishisji	乙室巳
Yitian, Empress Dowager	儀天
Yizhou	宜州
Youzhou	幽州
Yuan	元
Yuan *fei*	元妃
Yuanshi	元史
Yueguo, Princess	越國
Yue *shi*	藥氏
Yutian	玉田
Yu Yin	虞寅
zaju	雜劇
Zhaitang	斋堂
Zhang Fengnu	張鳳奴
Zhang Guan	張館
Zhang Hui	張滙
Zhangjiakou	张家口
Zhang Jianli	張建立
Zhang Lin	張林
Zhang *shi*	張氏
Zhang Shiqing	张世卿
Zhang Shiyou	张世右

Zhangsu, Emperor	章肅
Zhang Wenzao	张文藻
Zhang Yu	张瑀
Zhangzong, Emperor	章宗
Zhao Liangsi	趙良嗣
Zhao Mingcheng	趙明誠
Zhao Siwen	趙思溫
Zhaosu, Empress Dowager	昭肅皇太后
Zhao Weiyi	趙惟一
Zhen, Lady	甄
Zheng Yande	鄭衍德
Zhiguang	智光
zhiyingsi	祇应司
Zhongjing	中京
Zhongxing	中兴
Zhou	周
zhu shui cao qian xi	逐水草遷徙
zu	族

Bibliography

All transcribed Chinese is in pinyin; Chinese characters are rendered in simplified or traditional format according to the original.

Primary Sources

Ban Gu 班固. *Hanshu* 漢書. Reprint, Beijing: Zhonghua shixue congshu, 1962.

Chen Bangzhan 陳邦瞻 [Ming]. *Songshi jishi benmo* 宋史紀事本末. Reprint, Beijing: Zhonghua shuju chubanshe, 1977.

Da Jin guozhi 大金國志. Yuwen Maozhao 宇文懋照 [Song]. Reprint, Beijing: Zhonghua shuju chubanshe, [1968].

Fang Xuanling 房玄齡, ed. *Jin shu* 晉書. Reprint, Beijing: Zhonghua shuju chubanshe, 1976.

Hong Hao 洪皓 [1088–1155, Song; *jinshi* 1128]. *Songmo jiwen* 松漠紀聞. Reprint, [Changchun shi]: Jilin wenshu chubanshe, 1986.

Hou Hanshu 後漢書. Edited by Fan Wei 范蔚 [398–445]. Reprint, Beijing: Zhonghua shuju chubanshe, 1965–1973.

Jinshi 金史. Compiled and edited by Alutu 阿魯圖 et al. [Yuan]. Reprint, Beijing: Zhonghua shuju chubanshe, 1975.

Jin wen zui 金文最. Compiled by Zhang Jinwu 張金吾 [1787–1829]. Reprint, n.p.: Chengwen chubanshe, 1967.

Kitan [Qidan] guozhi 契丹國志. Ye Longli 葉隆禮 [*jinshi* 1247]. Reprint, Shanghai: Shanghai guji chubanshe, 1985.

Liaodai shike wenbian 遼代石刻文編. Edited by Xiang Nan 向南. Kaifeng: Hebei jiaoyu chubanshe, 1995.

Liaoshi 遼史. Compiled and edited by Toghtō 脫脫離 et al. [Yuan]. Reprint, Beijing: Zhonghua shuju chubanshe, [1974].

Ouyang Xiu 歐陽修. *Xin Wudaishi* 新五代史. Reprint, Beijing: Zhonghua shuju chubanshe, ca. 1974.

Quan Liao wen 全遼文. Edited by Chen Shu 陳述. Beijing: Zhonghua shuju chubanshe, 1982.

Sima Qian 司馬遷. *Shiji* 史記. Reprint, Beijing: Zhonghua shuju chubanshe, 1982.

Songshi 宋史. Compiled and edited by Alutu 阿魯圖 et al. [Yuan]. Reprint, Beijing: Zhonghua shuju chubanshe, 1985–1990.

Xue Juzheng 薛居正. *Jiu Wudaishi* 舊五代史. Reprint, Shanghai: Zhonghua shuju chubanshe, 1927.

Xu Mengxin 徐夢莘 [1126–1207]. *Sanchao beimeng huibian* 三朝北盟會編. Reprint, Shanghai: Shanghai guji chubanshe, 1987.

Secondary Sources

Akiner, Shiren, and Nicholas Sims-Williams, eds. *Languages and Scripts of Central Asia*. London: School of Oriental and African Studies, University of London, 1997.

Allsen, Thomas. "The Rise of the Mongolian Empire and Mongolian Rule in North China." In Franke and Twitchett, *Alien Regimes and Border States*, 321–414.

Bao Jialin 鮑家麟. *Zhongguo funü shi lunji* 中國婦女史論集. Taipei: Daoxiang chubanshe, [1988].

Barfield, Thomas. *The Perilous Frontier*. Cambridge: Blackwell, 1989.

Bernhardt, Kathryn. *Women and Property in China, 960–1949*. Stanford, CA: Stanford University Press, 1999.

Bielenstein, Hans. "Wang Mang, the Restoration of the Han Dynasty, and the Latter Han." In Twitchett and Loewe, *Ch'in and Han Empires*, 223–290.

Birge, Bettine. "Levirate Marriage and the Revival of Widow Chastity in Yuan China." *Asia Major* 8, pt. 2 (1995): 107–153.

———. "Women and Confucianism from Song to Ming." In *The Song-Yuan-Ming Transition in Chinese History*, edited by Paul Jakov Smith and Richard von Glahn, 212–240. Cambridge, MA: Harvard University Press, 2003.

———. *Women, Property, and Confucian Reaction in Sung and Yüan China*. Cambridge: Cambridge University Press, 2002.

Bol, Peter. "Seeking Common Ground: Han Literati Under Jurchen Rule." *Harvard Journal of Asiatic Studies* 47, no. 2 (December 1987): 461–538.

Bray, Francesca. *Technology and Gender: Fabrics of Power in Late Imperial China.* Berkeley: University of California Press, 1997.

Brindley, Erica. "Barbarian or Not? Ethnicity and Changing Conceptions of the Ancient Yue (Viet) Peoples, ca. 400–50 B.C." *Asia Major*, ser. 3, 61, pt. 1 (2003): 1–31.

Bush, Susan. "Five Paintings of Animal Subjects or Narrative Themes and Their Relevance to Chin Culture." In Tillman and West, *China Under Jurchen Rule*, 183–215.

———. "Women as Protagonists in Jin Paintings." Unpublished paper, 2001.

Cai Meibiao 蔡美彪. "Shishuo Liao Yelü shi, Xiao shi zhi youlai" 试说辽耶律氏,萧氏之由來. *Lishi yanjiu* 歷史研究 5 (1993): 53–60.

Cao Xingyuan 曹星原. "Chuan Hu Gui 'Fan ma tu' zuozhe kaolue" 传胡瓌"番马图"作者考略. *Wenwu* 文物, 1995, no. 12:80–89.

Carlitz, Katherine. "The Social Uses of Female Virtue in Late Ming Editions of *Lienu Zhuan.*" *Late Imperial China* 12, no. 2 (1991): 117–148.

Cass, Victoria. *Dangerous Women: Warriors, Grannies and Geishas of the Ming.* New York: Rowman and Littlefield, 1999.

Chan, Hok-lam. *The Historiography of the Chin Dynasty: Three Studies.* Wiesbaden, Ger.: Steiner, 1970.

———. *Legitimation in Imperial China: Discussions Under the Jurchen-Chin Dynasty (1115–1234).* Seattle: University of Washington Press, 1984.

Chinese National Palace Museum and the Chinese Central Museum. *Chinese Art Treasures: A Selected Group of Objects from the Chinese National Palace Museum and the Chinese National Central Museum, Taichung, Taiwan.* Geneva: Skira, 1960.

The Chinese Partnership Research Group, Min Jiayin, Editor in Chief. *The Chalice and the Blade in Chinese Culture: Gender Relations and Social Models.* Translated by Mao Guoxuan. Beijing: China Social Sciences Publishing House, 1995.

Christian Deydier Oriental Bronzes Ltd. *L'art et la matière.* Catalog of an exhibition held at Christian Deydier, Paris, October 2–November 14, 1998. London: Christian Deydier Oriental Bronzes, 1998.

Crossley, Pamela Kyle. *The Manchus.* Malden, MA: Blackwell, 1997.

———. *Orphan Warriors: Three Manchu Generations and the End of the Qing World.* Princeton, NJ: Princeton University Press, 1990.

———. "Thinking About Ethnicity in Early Modern China." *Late Imperial China* 2, no. 1 (1990): 1–35.

Crossley, Pamela Kyle, Helen F. Siu, and Donald S. Sutton, eds. *Empire at the Margins: Culture, Ethnicity, and Frontier in Early Modern China.* Berkeley: University of California Press, 2006.

Davis, Richard L. "Chaste and Filial Women in the Chinese Historical Writings of the Eleventh Century." *Journal of the American Oriental Society* 121, no. 2 (2001): 201–218.

———. *Wind Against the Mountain: The Crisis of Politics and Culture in Thirteenth-Century China*. Cambridge, MA: Harvard Council on East Asian Studies, 1996.

de Pee, Christian. "Till Death Do Us Unite: Texts, Tombs, and the Cultural History of Weddings in Middle-Period China (Eighth through Fourteenth Century)." *Journal of Asian Studies* 65, no. 4 (November 2006): 691–712.

Di Cosmo, Nicola. "Liao History and Society." In Hsueh-man Shen, *Gilded Splendor*, 15–22.

———. "The Northern Frontier in Pre-Imperial China." In Loewe and Shaughnessy, *Cambridge History of Ancient China*, 885–966.

Dong Jiazun 董家遵. "Lidai jiefu, lienü de tongji" 歷代節婦烈女的統計. In *Zhongguo funü shi lunji* 中國婦女史論集, edited by Bao Jialin 鮑家麟, 111–117. Taipei: Daoxiang chubanshe, [1988].

Dribe, Martin, Christer Lundh, and Paul Nystedt. "Widowhood Strategies in Preindustrial Society." *Journal of Interdisciplinary History* 38, no. 2 (Autumn 2007): 207–232.

Drompp, Michael R. "From Qatun to Refugee: The Taihe Princess among the Uighurs." In *The Role of Women in the Altaic World: Permanent International Altaistic Conference, 44th Meeting, Walderberg, 26–31 August 2001*, edited by Veronika Veit, 57–68. Wiesbaden, Ger.: Harrassowitz, 2007.

Dunnell, Ruth W. *The Great State of White and High*. Honolulu: University of Hawai'i Press, 1996.

Ebrey, Patricia Buckley. *Confucianism and Family Rituals in Imperial China: A Social History of Writing about Rites*. Princeton, NJ: Princeton University Press, 1991.

———. *The Inner Quarters: Marriage and the Lives of Chinese Women in the Sung Period*. Berkeley: University of California Press, 1993.

———. *Women and the Family in Chinese History*. New York: Routledge, 2003.

Elliott, Mark C. *The Manchu Way: The Eight Banners and Ethnic Identity in Late Imperial China*. Stanford, CA: Stanford University Press, 2001.

———. "Manchu Widows and Chastity in Qing China." *Comparative Studies in Society and History* 41, no. 1 (January 1999): 33–71.

Endicott-West, Elizabeth. "The Yüan Government and Society." In Franke and Twitchett, *Alien Regimes and Border States*, 587–615.

Feng Jiasheng 馮家昇. *Liaoshi zhengwu sanzhong* 遼史證誤三種. Shanghai: Zhonghua shuju chubanshe, 1959.

Fiskesjö, Magnus. "On the 'Raw' and the 'Cooked' Barbarians of Imperial China." *Inner Asia* 1, no. 2 (1999): 139–168.

Fletcher, Joseph. "The Mongols: Ecological and Social Perspectives." *Harvard Journal of Asiatic Studies* 46, no. 1 (June 1986): 11–50.

Fontein, Jan, and Tung Wu. *Unearthing China's Past*. Boston: Museum of Fine Arts, 1973.

Franke, Herbert. "The Chin Dynasty." In Franke and Twitchett, *Alien Regimes and Border States*, 215–320.

———. "Chinese Texts on the Jurchen: A Translation of the Jurchen Monograph in the *San Ch'ao Pei-meng Hui-pien*." In Franke and Lam, *Studies on the Jurchens and the Chin Dynasty*, 120–177.

———. "Jurchen Customary Law and the Chinese Law of the Chin Dynasty." In *State and Law in East Asia*, edited by Dieter Eikemeier and Herbert Franke, 215–233. Wiesbaden, Ger.: Harrassowitz, 1981.

———. "Notes on Some Jurchen Words in Chinese Orthography." In *Language and Literature—Japanese and the Other Altaic Languages: Studies in Honour of Roy Andrew Miller on His 75th Birthday*, edited by Karl H. Menges and Nelly Naumann. Wiesbaden, Ger.: Harrassowitz, 1999.

———. "A Sung Embassy Diary of 1211–1212: The *Shih-Chin lu* of Ch'eng Cho." *Bulletin de l'École française d'Extrême-Orient* 69 (1981): 171–207.

———. "Women under the Dynasties of Conquest." In *La donna nella Cina imperiale e nella Cina repubblicana*, edited by Lionello Lanciotti, 23–43. Florence, It.: Olschki, 1980,

Franke, Herbert, and Hok-Lam Chan. *Studies on the Jurchens and the Chin Dynasty*. Aldershot, UK: Ashgate, 1997.

Franke, Herbert, and Denis Twitchett, eds. *Alien Regimes and Border States, 907–1368*. Vol. 6 of *The Cambridge History of China*, edited by Denis Twitchett and John K. Fairbank. Cambridge: Cambridge University Press, 1994.

———. "Introduction." In Franke and Twitchett, *Alien Regimes and Border States*, 3–42.

Goldin, Paul Rakita. *The Culture of Sex in Ancient China*. Honolulu: University of Hawai'i Press, 2002.

Gong Shuduo 龔書鐸 and Liu Delin 劉德麟, eds. *Tu shuo Liao, Xi Xia, Jin* 圖說遼, 西夏, 金. Changsha: Jilin Publishing House, 2006. Reprint, Taipei: Knowledge House Press, 2007.

Greenberg, Joseph H. *Grammar*. Vol. 1 of *Indo-European and Its Closest Relatives: The Euroasiatic Language Family*. Stanford, CA: Stanford University Press, 2000.

Bibliography

Guisso, Richard W. L. "The Reigns of the Empress Wu, Chung-tsung and Jui-tsung (648–712)." In Twitchett, *Sui and T'ang China*, 290–332.

Guo Moruo 郭沫若. "Tan Jin ren Zhang Yu de 'Wenji gui Han tu' " 談金人張瑀的 "文姬归汉图." *Wenwu* 文物, 1964, no. 7:1–6.

Hargett, James M. *On the Road in Twelfth-Century China: The Travel Diaries of Fan Chengda (1126–1193)*. Stuttgart: Steiner, 1989.

Hinsch, Bret. *Women in Early Imperial China*. Oxford: Rowman and Littlefield, 2002.

Holmgren, Jennifer. "Marriage, Kinship and Succession under the Ch'i-tan Rulers of the Liao Dynasty (907–1125)." In *Marriage, Kinship and Power in Northern China*, by Jennifer Holmgren, 44–91. Aldershot, UK: Ashgate, 1995.

———. "Observations on Marriage and Inheritance Practices in Early Mongol and Yüan Society, with Particular Reference to the Levirate." In *Marriage, Kinship and Power in Northern China*, by Jennifer Holmgren, 127–192. Aldershot, UK: Ashgate, 1995.

Honig, Emily. *Creating Chinese Ethnicity: Subei People in Shanghai, 1850–1980*. New Haven, CT: Yale University Press, 1992.

Hsu, Kai-yu. "The Poems of Li Qingzhao (1084–1141)." In *Images of Women in Chinese Literature*, edited by Li Yu-ning, 72–95. Indianapolis: University of Indianapolis Press, 1994.

Hucker, Charles O. *A Dictionary of Official Titles in Imperial China*. Stanford, CA: Stanford University Press, 1985.

Jilin sheng bowuguan cangpin zhuanji 吉林省博物馆藏品专辑. *Yi yuan duo ying* 藝苑掇英. Shanghai: Shanghai renmin meishu chubanshe, n.d.

Jing, Anning. *The Water God's Temple of the Guangsheng Monastery: Cosmic Function of Art, Ritual, and Theater*. Boston: Brill, 2002.

Johnson, Linda Cooke. "The Art of the Jurchen Revival: A Court Movement in Chin-Dynasty China." Master's thesis, San Jose State University, 1974.

———. "The Place of *Qingming shanghe tu* in the Historical Geography of Song Dynasty Dongjing." *Journal of Song-Yuan Studies* 26 (1996): 145–182.

———. "The Wedding Ceremony for an Imperial Liao Princess: Wall Paintings from a Liao Dynasty Tomb in Jilin." *Artibus Asiae* 44, no. 2/3 (1983): 108–135.

Judge, Joan. *The Precious Raft of History*. Stanford, CA: Stanford University Press, 2007.

Kane, Daniel. *The Kitan Language and Script*. Leiden, Neth.: Brill, 2009.

Karetzky, Patricia Eichenbaum. "The Recently Discovered Chin Dynasty Murals Illustrating the Life of the Buddha at Yen-shang-ssu, Shansi." *Artibus Asiae* 42, no. 4 (1980): 245–252.

Keightley, David N. *Sources of Shang History*. Berkeley: University of California Press, 1978.
Ko, Dorothy. *Cinderella's Sisters: A Revisionist History of Footbinding*. Berkeley: University of California Press, 2005.
———. *Every Step a Lotus: Shoes for Bound Feet*. Berkeley: University of California Press, 2001.
———. *Teachers of the Inner Chambers: Women and Culture in Seventeenth-Century China*. Stanford, CA: Stanford University Press, 1994.
Kroll, Paul W. "The Life and Writings of Xu Hui (627–650), Worthy Consort, at the Early Tang Court." *Asia Major* 22, pt. 2 (2009): 35–64.
Kuhn, Dieter. "Decoding Tombs of the Song Elite." In *Burial in Song China*, edited by Dieter Kuhn, 11–160. Heidelberg: Würzburger Sinologische Schriften, 1994.
———. "An Introduction to the Chinese Archaeology of the Liao." In Hsueh-man Shen, *Gilded Splendor*, 25–30.
———. "Liao Architecture: Qidan Innovations and Han-Chinese Traditions?" *T'oung Pao*, 2nd ser., 86, no. 4/5 (2000): 325–362.
Lattimore, Owen. *Inner Asian Frontiers of China*. New York: American Geographical Press, 1940. Reprint, Boston: Beacon Press, 1962.
Lau, Nap-yin. "Waging War for Peace? The Peace Accord between the Song and the Liao in AD 1005." In *Warfare in Chinese History*, edited by Hans van de Ven, 180–219. Boston: Brill, 2000.
Lau Nap-yin and Huang K'uan-chung. "Founding and Consolidation of the Sung Dynasty under T'ai-tsu (960–976), T'ai-tsung (976–997), and Chen-tsung (997–1022)." In Twitchett and Smith, *Sung Dynasty and Its Precursors*, 206–278.
Lee, James, and Cameron Campbell. *Fate and Fortune in Rural China: Social Organization and Population Behavior in Liaoning, 1774–1873*. New York: Cambridge University Press, 1997.
Leung, Irene. "The Frontier Imaginary in the Song Dynasty (960–1279): Revisiting Cai Yan's 'Barbarian Captivity' and Return." Ph.D. diss., University of Michigan, 2001.
Li, Qingquan. "Preparing Sutra and Tea: Interpreting Liao Dynasty Tomb Murals at Xuanhua." Paper presented at the Association for Asian Studies Annual Meeting, Chicago, March 31–April 3, 2005, session 129.
Li Dianfu and Sun Yuliang 李殿福,孙玉良. *Bohai guo* 渤海国. Beijing: Wenwu chubanshe, 1987.
Liu Pujiang 刘浦江. *Liao Jin Shi lun* 辽金史论. Liaoyang: Liaoning daxue chubanshe, 1999.

———. "Shuo 'hanren'—Liao Jin shidai minzu ronghe de yige cemian" 说汉人—辽金时代民族融合的一个侧面. *Minzu yanjiu* 民族研究, 1998, no. 6:57–65.

Li Yiyou 李逸友. "Qidan de kunfa xisu" 契丹的髡发习俗. *Wenwu* 文物, 1983, no. 9:15–17.

Loewe, Michael. "The Former Han Dynasty." In Twitchett and Loewe, *Ch'in and Han Empires*, 103–222.

Loewe, Michael, and Edward L. Shaughnessy, eds. *The Cambridge History of Ancient China*. Cambridge: Cambridge University Press, 1999.

Louis, François. "Shaping Symbols of Privilege: Precious Metals and the Early Liao Aristocracy." *Journal of Sung-Yuan Studies* 33 (2003): 71–109.

Mann, Susan. *Precious Records: Women in China's Long Eighteenth Century*. Stanford, CA: Stanford University Press, 1997.

———. "Presidential Address: The Myths of Asian Womanhood." *Journal of Asian Studies* 59, no. 4 (2000): 835–862.

Mann, Susan, and Yu-Yin Cheng, eds. *Under Confucian Eyes: Writings on Gender in Chinese History*. Berkeley: University of California Press, 1991.

McGrath, Michael. "The Reigns of Jen-tsung (1022–1063) and Ying-tsung (1063–1067)." In Twitchett and Smith, *Sung Dynasty and Its Precursors*, 279–346.

Menges, Karl H. *Tungusen und Ljao*. Wiesbaden, Ger.: Steiner, 1968.

Meng Gutuoli 孟古托力. "Qidan zu hunyin tantao" 契丹族婚姻探讨. *Beifang wenwu* 北方文物, 1994, no. 1:51–59.

Murray, Julia. *Mirror of Morality: Chinese Narrative Illustration and Confucian Ideology*. Honolulu: University of Hawai'i Press, 2007.

———. "A Southern Sung Painting Regains Its Memory: *Welcoming the Imperial Carriage (Ying-luan t'u)* and Its Colophon." *Bulletin of Sung-Yuan Studies* 22 (1990–1992): 109–124.

National Palace Museum. *A Special Exhibition of Horse Paintings: Hua ma ming pin te zhan tu lu*. Taipei: Guoli gugong bowuyuan, 1990.

Ng, On-cho, and Q. Edward Wang. *Mirroring the Past: The Writing and Use of History in Imperial China*. Honolulu: University of Hawai'i Press, 2005.

Nienhauser, William H., trans. "The Ballad of Mulan." In *Sunflower Splendor: Three Thousand Years of Chinese Poetry*, edited by Wu-chi Liu and Irving Yucheng Lo, 297–408. Bloomington: Indiana University Press, 1975.

Okladnikov, A. P. "The Jurchen State." In *The Soviet Far East in Antiquity*, edited by Henry N. Michael, 202–280. Toronto: University of Toronto Press, 1965.

Ouyang Xiu. *Historical Records of the Five Dynasties*. Translated by Richard L. Davis. New York: Columbia University Press, 2004.

Powers, Martin. "Love and Marriage in Song China: Tao Yuanming Comes Home." *Ars Orientalis* 28 (1998): 51–57.

Raphals, Lisa. *Sharing the Light: Representations of Women and Virtue in Early China.* Albany: SUNY Press, 1998.

Rawski, Evelyn S. *The Last Emperors: A Social History of Qing Imperial Institutions.* Berkeley: University of California Press, 1998.

Rawski, Evelyn S., and Jessica Rawson, eds. *China: The Three Emperors, 1662–1795.* London: Royal Academy of Arts, 2006.

Rogers, M. C. "The Late Chin Debates on Dynastic Legitimacy." *Sung Studies Newsletter* 13 (1977): 57–66.

Rorex, Robert. *Eighteen Songs of a Nomad Flute: The Story of Lady Wen-Chi, a Fourteenth-Century Handscroll in the Metropolitan Museum of Art.* New York: New York Graphic Society, 1974.

Rossabi, Morris, ed. *China among Equals.* Berkeley: University of California Press, 1983.

Rudenko, Sergei I. *Frozen Tombs of Siberia: The Pazyryk Burials of Iron-Age Horsemen.* London: Dent, 1970.

Segal, Ethan. "Hōjō Masako and the Politics of Gender in Early Medieval Japan." Unpublished paper presented at the Midwest Japan Seminar, DePaul University, Chicago, December 1, 2007.

Shen, Hsueh-man, ed. *Gilded Splendor: Treasures of China's Liao Empire (907–1125).* New York: Asia Society, 2006.

So, Jenny F. "Tiny Bottles: What a Well-Dressed Qidan Lady Wears on Her Belt." *Orientations* 35, no. 7 (October 2004): 75–79.

Spence, Jonathan D. *Emperor of China: Self-Portrait of K'ang-hsi.* New York: Knopf, 1974.

Standen, Naomi. *Unbounded Loyalty: Frontier Crossings in Liao China.* Honolulu: University of Hawai'i Press, 2007.

Steinhardt, Nancy Shatzman. "The Architectural Landscape of the Liao and Underground Resonances." In Hsueh-man Shen, *Gilded Splendor*, 41–53.

———. "A Jin Hall at Jingtusi: Architecture in Search of Identity." *Ars Orientalis* 33 (2003): 77–119.

———. *Liao Architecture.* Honolulu: University of Hawai'i Press, 1997.

Sun, Guoping. "Discovery and Research on the Tomb of the Princess of Chen and Her Husband, Xiao Shaoju." In Hsueh-man Shen, *Gilded Splendor*, 67–74.

Su Xingjun 苏兴钧. "Ji Jin ren 'Wenji gui Han tu juan'" 記金人"文姬归汉图卷." *Wenwu* 文物, 1964, no. 3:34–35.

———. "Zhang Yu 'Wenji gui Han tu'" 张瑀 "文姬归汉图." *Yi yuan duo ying* 藝苑掇英, 45. Shanghai: Shanghai renmin meishu chubanshe, n.d.

Swann, Nancy Lee. *Pan Chao: Foremost Woman Scholar of China*. Introduction by Susan Mann. Ann Arbor: Center for Chinese Studies, University of Michigan, 2001.

Tackett, Nicholas. "The Great Wall and Conceptualizations of the Border Under the Northern Song." *Journal of Song-Yuan Studies* 38 (2008): 99–138.

Ta La. "Archaeological Excavations of the Site of the Liao City of Shangjing, 2001 to 2002." In Hsueh-man Shen, *Gilded Splendor*, 54–59.

Tang Tongtian 唐统天. "Liaodai de mingfu" 辽代的命妇. *Zhongguo shi yanjiu* 中国史研究, 1988, no. 4:95–103.

Tao, Jing-shen. "Barbarians or Northerners: Northern Sung Images of the Khitans." In Rossabi, *China among Equals*, 66–86.

———. "The Jurchen *Chin-shih* Degree in the Chin Dynasty." In *Proceedings of the Third East Asian Altaistic Conference*, edited by Ch'en Hok-lam and Jagchid Sechin, 221–239. Taipei: Guoli Taiwan daxue, 1969.

———. *The Jurchen in Twelfth-Century China: A Study of Sinicization*. Seattle: University of Washington Press, 1976.

T'ien Ju-k'ang. *Male Anxiety and Female Chastity*. Leiden, Neth.: Brill, 1988.

Tillman, Hoyt Cleveland. "An Overview of Chin History and Institutions." In Tillman and West, *China under Jurchen Rule*, 252–238.

Tillman, Hoyt Cleveland, and Stephen H. West, eds. *China under Jurchen Rule: Essays on Chin Intellectual and Cultural History*. Albany: SUNY Press, 1995.

Tsao, Hsingyuan. *Differences Preserved: Reconstructed Tombs from the Liao and Song Dynasties*. Seattle: University of Washington Press, 2000.

Twitchett, Denis. "Hsüan-tsung (Reign 712–56)." In Twitchett, *Sui and T'ang China*, 333–463.

———. "Introduction." In Twitchett, *Sui and T'ang China*.

———, ed. *Sui and T'ang China, 589–906*. Vol. 3, pt. 1. of *The Cambridge History of China*, edited by Denis Twitchett and John K. Fairbank. Cambridge: Cambridge University Press, 1979.

Twitchett, Denis, and Michael Loewe, eds. *The Ch'in and Han Empires, 221 B.C.– A.D. 220*. Vol. 1 of *The Cambridge History of China*, edited by Denis Twitchett and John K. Fairbank. Cambridge: Cambridge University Press, 1986.

Twitchett, Denis, and Paul Jakov Smith, eds. *The Sung Dynasty and Its Precursors, 907–1279*. Vol. 5, pt. 1 of *The Cambridge History of China*, edited by Denis Twitchett and John K. Fairbank. Cambridge: Cambridge University Press, 2009.

Twitchett, Denis, and Klaus-Peter Tietze. "The Liao." In Franke and Twitchett, *Alien Regimes and Border States*, 43–153.

Ulrich, Laurel Thatcher. "Vertuous Women Found: New England Ministerial Literature, 1668–1735." *American Quarterly* 28, no. 1 (1976): 20–40.

Wakeman, Federic E., Jr. "China in the Context of World History." In *Telling Chinese History: A Selection of Essays*, edited by Lea H. Wakeman, 27–43. Berkeley: University of California Press, 2009.

Waldron, Arthur. *The Great Wall of China: From History to Myth*. Cambridge: Cambridge University Press, 1990.

Waltner, Ann. "Widows and Remarriage in Ming and Early Qing China." In *Women in China: Current Directions in Historical Scholarship*, edited by Richard W. Guisson and Stanley Johannesen, 129–146. Youngstown, NY: Philo Press, 1981.

Walton Linda. " 'Diary of a Journey to the North': Lou Yue's 'Beixing rilu.' " *Journal of Sung-Yuan Studies* 32 (2002): 1–38.

Wang, Gungwu. "The Rhetoric of a Lesser Empire: Early Sung Relations with Its Neighbors." In Rossabi, *China among Equals*, 47–65.

Wang, Shuo. "Manchu Women in Transition: Gender, Ethnicity, and Acculturation in 17th and 18th-Century China." Ph.D. diss., Michigan State University, 2002.

Wang, Yi-t'ung, trans. " 'The Lamentation' of Ts'ai Yen." In *Sunflower Splendor: Three Thousand Years of Chinese Poetry*, edited by Wu-chi Liu and Irving Yucheng Lo, 36–39. Bloomington: Indiana University Press, 1975.

Watson, Rubie S., and Patricia Buckley Ebrey, eds. *Marriage and Inequality in Chinese Society*. Berkeley: University of California Press, 1991.

Wechsler, Howard. "The Founding of the Tang Dynasty, Kao-tsu Reign (618–626)." In Twitchett, *Sui and T'ang China*, 150–187.

White, Richard. *The Middle Ground: Indians, Empires, and Republics in the Great Lakes Region, 1650–1815*. New York: Cambridge University Press, 1991.

Wittfogel, Karl A., and Feng Chia-sheng. *The History of Chinese Society: Liao (907–1125)*. Philadelphia: American Philosophical Society, 1940.

Wright, Arthur. "The Sui Dynasty, 581–617." In Twitchett, *Sui and T'ang China*, 48–149.

Wright, David Curtis. *"The Ambassadors Records": Eleventh-Century Reports of Sung Embassies to the Liao*. Papers on Inner Asia, no. 29. Bloomington: Research Institute for Inner Asian Studies, Indiana University, 1998.

———. *From War to Diplomatic Parity in Eleventh-Century China: Sung's Foreign Relations with Kitan Liao*. Leiden, Neth.: Brill, 2005.

Wu, K. T. "Chinese Printing under Four Alien Dynasties (916–1368 A.D.)." *Harvard Journal of Asiatic Studies* 13 (December 1950): 447–523.

Wu, Pei-yi. "Yang Miaozhen: A Woman Warrior in Thirteenth-Century China." *Nan nü* 4, no. 2 (2002): 137–169.

Yang, Xiaoneng. "Unearthing Liao Elite Art and Culture: An Empire in Northern China from the 10th to the 12th Century." *Orientations* 35, no. 7 (October 2004): 66–74.

Yang Xin, Richard M. Barnhart, Nie Chongzheng, James Cahill, Lang Shaojun, and Wu Hung. *Three Thousand Years of Chinese Painting*. New Haven, CT: Yale University Press, 1997.

Yu Yingshi. "Han Foreign Relations." In Twitchett and Loewe, *Ch'in and Han Empires*, 377–462.

Zang, Jian. "Women and the Transmission of Confucian Culture in Song China." In *Women and Confucian Cultures in Premodern China, Korea, and Japan*, edited by Dorothy Ko, Jahyun Kim Haboush, and Joan R. Piggott, 123–141. Berkeley: University of California Press, 2003.

Zhang Bangwei 张邦炜. "Liao, Song, Xixia, Jin shiqi shaoshu minzu de hunyin zhidu yu xisu" 辽,宋,西夏,金时期少数民族的婚姻制度与习俗. *Shehui kexue yanjiu* 社会科学研究, 1988, no. 6:120–124.

Zhang Hongxing. *The Qianlong Emperor: Treasures from the Forbidden City*. Edinburgh: NMS, 2002.

Zhao, George Qingzhi. *Marriage as Political Strategy and Cultural Expression: Mongolian Royal Marriages from World Empire to Yuan Dynasty*. New York: Lang, 2008.

Zhongguo lishi dituji 中国历史地图集. Edited by Tan Qixiang 谭其骧. Vol. 6, *Song-Liao-Jin* 宋辽金. Beijing: Ditu chubanshe, [1990].

Zhu Guochen 朱国忱 and Wei Guozhong 魏国忠, eds. *Bohai shigao* 渤海史稿. Heilongjiang: Heilongjiang sheng wenwu chubanshe, 1984.

Zhu Qixin. "Royal Costumes of the Jin Dynasty." *Orientations* 21, no. 12 (December 1990): 59–64.

Electronic Sources

Announcement of the discovery of the tomb of Yelü Nu and his wife, Lady Xiao. http://www.ylwh.com/ylwh/qd/4.htm (accessed October 17, 2007).

"Another Kind of 'Return.'" Information on the Liao-dynasty wooden log burial chamber at the Liaoning Museum; pictures of the interior paintings. 15 April 2003. CHW weekly observation of 01/09/2001. http://www.culturalheritagewatch.org/01/001.html (accessed April 15, 2003).

"Emperor's Tombs of the Liao Dynasty." http://www.218.25.39.149/745997164609536 00/20021231/1047809.shtml. Discovery of the tombs of Yelü Bei, Yelü Yu (Emperor Shizong), Yelü Xian (Emperor Jingzong), Xiao Yanyan (Empress Dowager Chengtian), and the famous minister Yelü Longyun (Hann Derang) (accessed March 16, 2003).

"Liao Dynasty," 8. 7 July 2003. http://www.uglychinese.org/liao.htm (accessed September 16, 2003).

Archaeological Reports

Beijing shi Haidianqu wenhuawenwuju 北京市海淀区文化文物句. "Beijing shi Haidian qu Nanxinzhuang Jin mu qingli wenbao" 北京市海淀区南心庄金墓清理文报. *Wenwu* 文物, 1988, no. 7:56–65.

Beijing shi wenwu guanlichu 北京市文物管理处. "Beijingshi Tongxian Jin dai muzang fajue jianbao" 北京市通县金代墓葬 掘简报. *Wenwu* 文物, 1977, no. 11:9–14.

———. "Beijing xia Nongtan Jin mu" 北京下农坛金墓. *Wenwu* 文物, 1977, no. 11:9–14.

Beijing shi wenwu shiye guanliju, Mentougou qu wenhua bangongshi 北京市文物事业官局,门头沟区文化办公室. "Beijing shi Zhaitang Liao bihua mu fajue jianbao" 北京市斋堂辽壁画墓发掘简报. *Wenwu* 文物, 1980, no. 7:23–32.

Beijing shi wenwu yanjiu Jinling kaogu gongzuodui 北京市文物研究金陵考古工作队. "Beijing Fangshan qu Jinling yizhi de diaocha yu fabiao" 北京房山区金陵遗址的调查与发表. *Kaogu* 考古, 2004, no. 2:26–40.

Beijing shi wenwu yanjiusuo, ed. 北京市文物研究所. *Beijing Jindai huangling* 北京金代皇陵. Beijing: Wenwu chubanshe, 2006.

Chai Zejun 柴择俊 and Zhang Chouliang 张丑良, eds. *Fanzhi Yanshan si* 繁峙巖山寺 (山西). Beijing: Wenwu chubanshe, 1990.

Changzhi shi bowuguan 长治市博物馆. "Shanxi Changzhi shi Guzhang Jin dai jinian mu" 山西长治市故漳金代纪年墓. *Kaogu* 考古, 1984, no. 8:737–743.

Chen Shu 陈述. "Ba Jilin Da'an chutu Qidan wen tongjing" 跋吉林大安出土契丹文铜镜. *Wenwu* 文物, 1973, no. 8:36–40.

Chifeng shi bowuguan kaogudui, Aluke'erqinqi wenwu guanlisuo 赤峰市博物馆考古队,阿鲁科尔沁旗文物管理所. "Chifeng shi Aluke'erqinqi zu Wenduoeraoruishan Liao mu qingli jianbao" 赤峰市阿鲁科尔沁旗温多尔敖瑞山辽墓清理简报. *Wenwu* 文物, 1993, no. 3:57–67.

Datong shi bowuguan 大同市博物馆. "Datong shi Nanjiao Jin dai bihua mu" 大同市南郊金代 壁画墓. *Kaogu xuebao* 考古学报, 1992, no. 4:511–527.

Fang Xiongfei 方雄飞 (Liaoning sheng wenwu kaogu yanjiusuo, 辽宁省文物考古研究

所). "Liao Qinguo taifei Jinguo wangfei mu zhikao" 辽秦国太妃晋国王妃墓志考. *Wenwu* 文物, 2005, no. 1:88–96.

Feng Yongqian 冯永谦. "Yemaotai Liao mu chutu de taociqi" 叶茂台辽墓出土的陶瓷器. *Wenwu* 文物, 1975, no. 12:40–48.

Hebei sheng wenwu guanlichu, Hebei sheng bowuguan 河北省文物管理处,河北省博物馆. "Liaodai caihui xingtu shi woguo tianwenshi shang de zhongyao faxian" 辽代彩绘星图是我国天文史上的重要发现. *Wenwu* 文物, 1975, no. 8:40–43.

Hebei sheng wenwu yanjiusuo Zhangjiakou shi wenwu guanlichu Xuanhua qu wenwu guanlisuo 河北省文物研究所,张家口市文物管理处,宣化区文物管理所. "Hebei Xuanhua Liao Zhang Wenzao bihua mu fajue jianbao" 河北宣化辽张文藻壁画墓发掘简报. *Wenwu* 文物, 1996, no. 9:14–46.

Heilongjiang sheng wenwu kaogu gongzuodui 黑龙江省文物考古工作队. "Cong chutu wenwu kan Heilongjiang diqu de Jin dai shehui" 从出土文物看黑龙江地区的金代社会. *Wenwu* 文物, 1977, no. 4:27–39.

———. "Heilongjiang pan Suibin Zhongxing gucheng Jin dai muqun" 黑龙江畔绥滨中兴古城金代墓群. *Wenwu* 文物, 1977, no. 4:40–50.

———. "Songhuajiang xiayou Aolimi gucheng ji qi zhouwei de Jindai muqun" 松花江下游奥里米古城及其周围的金代墓群. *Wenwu* 文物, 1977, no. 4:56–62.

———. "Suibin Yongsheng de Jin dai pingmin mu" 绥滨永生的金代平民墓. *Wenwu* 文物, 1977, no. 4:50–55.

Heilongjiang sheng wenwu kaogu yanjiusuo 黑龙江省文物考古研究所. "Heilongjiang Acheng Juyu Jindai Qi guowang mu fajue jianbao" 黑龙江阿城巨源金代齐国王墓发掘简报. *Wenwu* 文物, 1989, no. 10:1–10.

Henan sheng bowuguan Jiaozuoshi bowuguan 河南省博物馆,焦作市博物馆. "Henan Jiaozuo Jin mu fajue jianbao" 河南焦作金墓发掘简报. *Wenwu* 文物, 1979, no. 8:1–17.

Ji Chengzhang 吉成章. "Haoqianying di liuhao Liao mu ruogan wenti de yanjiu" 豪欠营第六号辽墓若干问题的研究. *Wenwu* 文物, 1983, no. 9:9–14.

Jilin sheng bowuguan, Zhelimu meng wenhuaju 吉林省博物馆,哲里木盟文化局. "Jilin Zhelimu meng Kulunqi yi hao Liao mu fajue jianbao" 吉林哲里木盟库伦旗一号辽墓发掘简报. *Wenwu* 文物, 1973, no. 8:2–18.

Jilin sheng bowuguan cangpin zhuanji 吉林省博物馆藏品专辑. *Yi yuan duo ying* 藝苑掇英, no. 6 [1980]. Shanghai: Shanghai renmin meishu chubanshe, [1980].

Jilin sheng bowuguan Nong'an xian wenguansuo 吉林省博物馆农安县文官所. "Jilin Nong'an Jindai jiaomu wenwu" 吉林农安金代窖墓文物. *Wenwu* 文物, 1988, no. 7:74–81.

Liaocheng diqu bowuguan 聊城地区博物馆. "Shandong Gaotang Jindai Yu Yin mu fajue jianbao" 山东高唐金代虞寅墓发掘简报. *Wenwu* 文物, 1982, no. 1:49–51.

Liaoning sheng bowuguan, Liaoning Tieling diqu wenwuzu fajue xiaozu 辽宁省博物馆, 辽宁铁岭地区文物组发掘小组. "Faku Yemaotai Liao mu jilue" 法库叶茂台辽墓记略. *Wenwu* 文物, 1975, 12:26–36.

Liaoning sheng bowuguan wenwu gongzuodui 辽宁省博物馆文物工作队. "Liao dai Yelü Yanning mu fajue jianbao" 辽代耶律延宁墓发掘简报. *Wenwu* 文物, 1980, no. 7:18–22.

Liaoning sheng wenwu kaogu yanjiusuo 辽宁省文物考古研究所. "Fuxin Liao Xiao He mu fajue jianbao" 阜新辽萧和墓发掘简报. *Wenwu* 文物, 2005, no. 1:33–50.

Li Fangyu 李方玉 and Long Baozhang 龙宝章. "Jin dai Yu Yin mushi bihua" 金代虞寅墓室壁画. *Wenwu* 文物, 1982, no. 1:52–53.

Ma Xigui 吗希桂 and Beijing shi wenwu guanli chu 北京市文物管理处. "Beijing Xianyitan Jin mu" 北京先衣坛金墓. *Wenwu* 文物, 1977, no. 11:91–94.

Neimenggu wenwu kaogu yanjiusuo, Aluke'erqinqi wenwu guanlisuo 内蒙古文物考古研究所, 阿鲁科尔沁旗文物管理所. "Neimenggu Chifeng Baoshan Liao bihua mu fajue jianbao" 内蒙古赤峰宝山辽壁画墓发掘简报. *Wenwu* 文物, 1998, no. 1:73–95.

Neimenggu wenwu kaogu yanjiusuo, Chifeng shi bowuguan, Aluke'erqinqi wenwu guanlisuo 内蒙古文物考古研究所, 赤峰市博物馆, 阿鲁科尔沁旗文物管理所. "Liao Yelü Yüzhi mu fajue jianbao" 辽耶律羽之墓发掘简报. *Wenwu* 文物, 1996, no. 1:14–32.

Neimenggu wenwu kaogu yanjiusuo, Zhelimu meng bowuguan 内蒙古文物考古研究所, 哲里木盟博物馆. "Neimenggu Kulunqi bahao Liao mu" 内蒙古库伦旗八号辽墓. *Wenwu* 文物, 1987, no. 7:74–84.

Neimenggu zizhiqu wenwu kaogu yanjiusuo, Zhelimu meng bowuguan 内蒙古自治区文物考古研究所, 哲里木盟博物馆. *Liao Chenguo gongzhu mu* 辽陈国公主墓. Beijing: Wenwu chubanshe, 1993.

Ning Lixin 宁立新. "Shanxi Shuo xian Jindai huozang" 山西朔县金代火葬. *Wenwu* 文物, 1987, no. 6:82–86.

Shanxi sheng kaogu yanjiusuo 山西省考古研究所. "Shanxi Jishan Jin mu fajue jianbao" 山西稷山金墓发掘简报. *Wenwu* 文物, 1983, no. 1:45–63.

———. "Shanxi Xinjiang Nanfan zhuang, Wuling zhuang Jin Yuan mu fajue jianbao" 山西新绛南范庄, 吴岭庄金元墓发掘简报. *Wenwu* 文物, 1983, no. 1:64–71, plates 59–60.

Shanxi sheng kaogu yanjiusuo, Jindongnan gongzuozhan 山西省考古研究所, 晋东南工作站. "Shanxi Changzi xian Shizhe Jin dai bihua mu" 山西长子县石哲金代壁画墓. *Wenwu* 文物, 1985, no. 6:45–54.

Shanxi sheng kaogu yanjiusuo, Shanxi sheng Wenxi xian bowuguan 山西省考古研究所, 山西省闻喜县博物馆. "Shanxi sheng Wenxi xian Jindai zhuandiao bihua mu"

山西省闻喜县金代砖雕壁画墓. *Wenwu* 文物, 1996, no. 12:36–46; includes unpaginated plates.

Shanxi sheng kaogu yanjiusuo, Yangquan shi wenwu guanli weiyuanhui, Pingding xian wenwu guanlisuo 山西省考古研究所, 阳泉市文物管理委员会, 平定县文物管理所. "Shanxi Pingding Song Jin bihua mu jianbao" 山西平定宋金壁画墓简报. *Wenwu* 文物, 1996, no. 5:4–18; includes color plates.

Shanxi sheng Pingding kaogu yanjiusuo. 山西省平定考古研究. "Shanxi Pingding Song Jin bihua mu jianbao" 山西平定宋金壁画墓简报. *Wenwu* 文物, 1996, no. 5:4–15.

Su Bai 缩白, ed. *Zhonghua renmin gongheguo zhongda kaogu faxian* 中华人民共和国重大考古发现. Beijing: Wenwu chubanshe, 1999.

Sun Guoping 孙国平, Du Shouchang 杜守昌, and Zhang Lidan 张丽丹. "Liaoning Chaoyang Sunjiawan Liao mu" 辽宁朝阳孙家湾辽墓. *Wenwu* 文物, 1992, no. 6:12–16.

Sun Jianhua 孙建华. "Baoshan Liao bihua mu" 宝山辽壁画墓. In Su Bai, *Zhonghua renmin gongheguo zhongda kaogu faxian*, 492.

——. "Yelü Yuzhi mu" 耶律羽之墓. In Su Bai, *Zhonghua renmin gongheguo zhongda kaogu faxian*, 495.

Torii Ryūzō. *Sculpted Stone Tombs of the Liao*. Beiping: Harvard-Yenching Institute, 1942.

Wang Jianqun 王健群 and Chen Xiangwei 陈相伟. *Kulun Liaodai bihua mu* 库伦辽代壁画墓. Beijing: Wenwu chubanshe, 1989.

Wang Zeqing 王泽庆. "Kulunqi yi hao Liao mu bihua chutan" 库伦旗一号辽墓壁画初探. *Wenwu* 文物, 1973, no. 8:30–35.

Wenxi xian bowuguan 闻喜县博物馆. "Shanxi Wenxi si di Jin mu" 山西闻喜寺的金墓. *Wenwu* 文物, 1988, no. 7:67–73.

Wulanchabu meng wenwu gongzuozhan 乌兰察布盟文物工作站. "Chayou Qianqi Haoqianying di liuhao Liao mu qingli jianbao" 察右前旗豪欠营第六号辽墓清理简报. *Wenwu* 文物, 1983, no. 9:1–8.

Wu Yugui 吴玉贵. "Neimenggu Chifeng Baoshan Liao mu bihua 'Ji jin tu' kao" 内蒙古赤峰宝山辽墓壁画"寄锦图"考. *Wenwu* 文物, 2001, no. 3:92–96.

Xi'an shi wenwu baohu kaogusuo 西安市文物保护考古所. "Xi'an beizhou Liangzhou Sabao shi jun mu fajue jiangbao" 西安北周凉州萨保市君暮发掘简报. *Wenwu* 文物, 2005, no. 3:4–33.

Xu Pingfang 徐苹芳. "Baisha Song mu" 白沙宋墓. In Su Bai, *Zonghua renmin gongheguo zhongda kaogu faxian*, 486–488.

Yang Fudou 杨富斗. "Houma Jishan Jin mu" 侯马稷山金墓. In Su Bai, *Zhonghua renmin gongheguo zhongda kaogu faxian*, 507–510.

Yang Renkai 杨仁恺. "Yemaotai Liao mu chutu guhua de shidai ji qita" 叶茂台辽暮出土古画的时代及其它. *Wenwu* 文物, 1975, no. 12:37–39.

Yan Yu 雁羽. "Jinxi Dawopu Liao Jin shidai hua xiang shi mu" 錦西大臥鋪辽金时代画象石墓. *Kaogu* 考古, 1960, no. 2:29–33.

Zhangjiakou shi wenwu shiye guanlisuo, Zhangjiakou shi Xuanhua qu wenwu baoguansuo 张家口市文物事业管理所, 张家口市宣化区文物保管所. "Hebei Xuanhua Xiabali Liao Jin bihua mu" 河北宣化下八里辽金壁画墓. *Wenwu* 文物, 1990, no. 10:1–17.

Zhangjiakou shi Xuanhua qu wenwu baoguansuo 张家口市宣化区文物保管所. "Hebei Xuanhua Liao dai bihua mu" 河北宣化辽代壁画墓. *Wenwu* 文物, 1995, no. 2:4–27.

———. "Hebei Xuanhua Xiabali Liao Han Shixun mu" 河北宣化下八里辽韩师训墓. *Wenwu* 文物, 1992, no. 6:1–28.

Zhao Pingchun 赵评春. "Jin Qi guowang mu" 金齐国王墓. In Su Bai, *Zhonghua renmin gongheguo zhongda kaogu faxian*, 504–506.

Zhao Xiaohua (Liaoning sheng bowuguan) 赵晓华(辽宁省博物馆). "Liaoning sheng bowuguan zhengji rucang yitao Liao dai caihui muguo" 辽宁省博物馆征集入藏一套辽代彩绘木椁. *Wenwu* 文物, 2000, no. 11:63–71.

Zheng Shaozong 郑绍宗. "Xuanhua Liao bihua mu" 宣化辽壁画墓. In Su Bai, *Zhonghua renmin gongheguo zhongda kaogu faxian*, 501–503.

Zhongguo shehui kexueyuan kaogu yanjiu suo Neimenggu de er gongzuo dui Neimengu kaogu yanjiu suo 中国社会科学院考古研究所 内蒙古 第二工作队内蒙古 文物考古研究所, "内蒙古巴林左旗 辽代祖陵考古发掘的 新收获." 考古 *Kaogu*, 2008, no. 2:3–6.

Index

Abaoji, Liao emperor, xi, xvii, 42, 97–98, 106, 121, 123–125, 160, 166, 168; mausoleum of, 106–107, 124
abduction, xxv, xxvi, 97; abduction marriage, 54, 85, 86, 89, 104. *See also* marriage
acculturation, 14–15, 61, 66–67, 71, 79, 93, 113, 143, 163, 176
adultery, 6, 113–117, 118, 161–162
afterlife, 33, 169. *See also* religion
agency, of women, xix, 5, 15, 22, 24, 34, 41, 120, 124, 139–140, 175–179; in finances, 34, 133, 138, 150–153, 163, 174; in marriage, xviii, 135, 138, 145; in warfare, xviii, 15, 34, 123–124, 129–138
Aguda, Jin emperor, xii, xxxii, 56–57, 66, 91, 97, 102–103, 109, 192n48
Aizong, Liao emperor, xii, 17, 18, 67
alcohol, consumption of, 31, 39, 44, 62, 75–76, 81, 90, 192n48, 197n32. *See also* koumiss
Altaic language group, xxiii, 96, 108, 120
Aluzhen, xii, 17, 21–23, 170
animism, 53, 84. *See also* religion
archaeologists, 13, 50, 61, 81, 84, 168
archaeology: archaeological discoveries, xxviii, xxx, 15, 40, 81, 84, 96–98, 108, 162–163, 167–169, 187n24, 188n38, 190n9;

archaeological sites: Abaoji mausoleum, 106–107, 124; Baoshan, 99; Jin imperial tombs, xxix, 63–65; Kulunqi, xxix, 37, 81–85; Prince Qi, 54, 61–64; Princess Chenguo, 33–38
aristocracy, xvii, xxiii, 139, 169. *See also* nobility

Ban Zhao, 33, 178
Barbarian Horses, 27–30. *See also* Fan Ma
barbarians, xix, 10, 16, 44, 76, 86–87, 91, 96, 109, 113, 124, 161, 173; barbarization, xxii, 40, 72, 78–79, 87, 173, 178; as characterized by Sima Qian, xx, xxi, 56, 178, 184n15; in Jin Wenji painting, xxviii, 139, 143, 171; Song perceptions of, 37, 52, 146, 161, 176
beards, 55, 56, 57, 82
Bei, Liao prince, 15, 40, 106–107, 125, 160, 184n28
Beijing (modern city), xxix, xxxi, 40, 43, 56, 60, 63, 78, 174, 186n50
betrothals, xxix, 54, 85, 90–92, 96, 104, 111, 119, 142, 148, 156; of Xiao Yanyan and Hann Derang, 154, 156–157, 159, 160–161, 165, 168
Birge, Bettina, 22, 91, 112

Index

Bohai, state of, xxiv, xxxii, 26, 39–40, 56, 97, 125, 184n28; Bohai culture, xxiii, 10, 14, 42, 57, 66, 110, 143, 163, 172, 175; intermarriage with, xxv, 66, 93, 97–98, 103, 119, 152, 177; surnames, 3, 16, 18–19, 23, 170
bride-price marriage, xxiv, 90–91, 96, 108, 173, 177–178. *See also* dowry; marriage
Buddhism, xix–xx, xxvii, xxx, 10–11, 72–73, 79, 81, 87, 112, 141–147, 149–154, 166, 174–175, 205n45; Buddhist burial customs, 13, 38–39, 44, 49, 50–55, 68, 84, 151, 166; Buddhist piety, 11, 16, 23, 152, 163, 174, 178–179; donor lists, xxx, 34, 142, 150–151, 163, 174, 177; retreat for widows, xxix, 104, 108, 111–112, 118, 120, 173, 178; temples, 14, 53, 72–73, 141, 152–153, 174–175, 205n46. *See also* tea
burial customs, xxii–xxiii, xxix, 3, 14, 33, 35, 37–38, 41, 49, 54, 60, 150, 162, 168–169, 172; Chinese and *haner*, 63, 68; Jin practices 60, 61–62, 64–65, 68, 171; Jurchen burials, xxix, 55, 60, 152, 174; Liao practices, 33, 35, 38, 41, 50, 84, 162, 174; predynastic Kitan, xxix, 38, 174; single and joint burials, 7, 34, 50–51, 68, 77, 98, 190n9. *See also* funerary customs; tombs
Bush, Susan, xxvii, 73, 152–153, 177, 185n36

Cai Yan. *See* Wenji
cainü, 12
camels, camel carriages, xxv, 29–30, 37, 41, 44, 69, 81, 84, 169, 171
celebrations, 39, 49, 52, 76, 94, 153
Central Circuit, Central Capital (Zhongzing): Jin, 174; Liao, xxxii, 39, 41, 123. *See also* Beijing; Zhongjing
Changge. *See* Yelü Changge
Chanyuan, battle of, ix, xviii, xxxii, 121, 129, 131, 155
chastity, xxix, 3, 21, 24, 107, 118; Chinese norms for, 104–105, 139, 161; premarital, 88, 107, 139, 161; preservation of, 2, 19, 21, 118, 122; widow chastity, xx, 9, 25, 109, 111–113, 118–120, 161, 163, 170, 178, 203n60. *See also* widows, widowhood
Chen, Lady, xi, xxvii, 4–5, 9–10, 24, 48, 143, 167, 171, 187n10
Chen *fei*, 103–104
Chengde, 40
Chengtian, Liao empress dowager, xi, xx, 119, 139, 140, 172, 180; burial of, 161–162; as Empress Ruizhi, xviii, 93, 126–127, 130, 154–155, 158, 167; as regent, xviii, 121, 126–132, 140, 167, 180; romance of, xxx, 113, 119, 130, 154–164; as warrior, xviii, xxii, xxix, 34, 126, 129, 130, 138, 140, 175. *See also* betrothals
Chenguo, Liao princess of, xi, xix, 99; tomb of, 35–38, 133, 149, 168, 179
children, 12, 45–47, 48, 73, 92, 101, 103, 105, 107, 181, 187n33; education of, xix, 111–112, 120, 144, 146–147, 148; as emperors, 180; in levirate marriages, 104, 108, 120
Chinese. *See* Han Chinese population
Chinese (Han) culture, xviii, xix, xxii–xxiv, xxx, xxxii, 5, 12–15, 23, 33, 40, 48–49, 52, 56, 89, 120, 133, 163, 168–169, 174–175, 178; among the Bohai, 143, 152, 184n28; *haner* conservation of, 49, 51, 53, 74. *See also* sinicization
Chinese language, xviii, 170–171; literacy in, xxiv, 6, 10, 12, 13, 129, 140, 142–144, 147, 149, 166, 178; script, use of in Liao and Jin, 13, 142, 167, 170; spoken, xx, xxiii, 63, 166, 170, 173, 175. *See also* Liao Chinese (language)
Chinese surnames, 16, 20, 23, 25
Chinggis (Genghis) Khan, xxxiii, 132, 180, 200n7
chronology, xii, 165, 169
Chu, Liao prince of, 127, 156–159, 202n27, 206n70
Chun, Liao prince (Emperor Tianxi), xii, 131, 132

242

Index

Chunqin, Liao empress. *See* Yingtian, Liao empress dowager
cities: Jin, xxi, 56, 60, 61, 68, 87, 170 (*see also* Huining; Nanjing; Shangjing; Zhongjing); Liao, xxix, xxxiii, 14–15, 41, 99, 123, 146, 151, 155 (*see also* Dongjing; Nanjing; Shangjing; Xijing; Zhongjing). *See also* Kaifeng
civil government, civil affairs, xviii, xx, xxxi, xxxii, 4, 11, 25, 106, 127–128, 140, 143, 155, 168, 172
class, social, xxix, 3, 4, 11, 12, 21, 23, 25, 46, 48–49, 53, 62, 66, 68–69, 78, 81, 84, 92, 139, 153, 193n14; clothing as signifier, 48, 49, 53, 62–63, 78
clothing, xxiii, 6, 17, 33, 172, 175; Chinese styles, 25, 47, 69, 71, 72, 158, 171; class status indicated by, 46, 48–49, 53, 78, 81, 172; Han and *haner*, 46, 75, 171, 175; Jurchen, xxvi, 57–58, 61–63, 68, 69, 72, 78, 153, 170–171, 193n14; Kitan, 12, 27, 28, 35, 36–37, 44–47, 48, 53, 167, 190n5, 193n3. *See also* hairstyles
collaboration, collaborators, 5, 42, 43
concubinage: concubines (in general), xvii, 3, 18, 67, 89, 93, 94, 96, 102, 116, 130, 133, 156, 173, 207n4; concubines (individuals), 18, 100, 101, 103, 118; imperial concubines, 2, 11, 23, 34–35, 66, 67, 89, 93–94, 100, 121, 126, 132, 148, 174; as institution, 94, 99–104, 174
Concubine Xiao, xxiv, xxviii, 11, 12, 24. *See also* Xiao *fei*
Confucian classics, 2, 4, 5, 6, 10–11, 23, 66, 105, 139, 141–142, 143–147, 163, 173, 178, 194n27
Confucian culture, xxviii, 2, 6, 167; education, xviii, xxiv, 4, 105, 143–149, 173
Confucian ethics: ideals, virtues for women, xix, xx, xxiv, xxx, 3, 6–11, 16–19, 21–25, 65–67, 102, 111–112, 115, 139, 163–164, 166, 168–169, 171, 175, 176, 178;

patriarchy, 134, 178, 179. *See also* filial piety; loyalty
Confucianism, as philosophy, xviii, xxv, 15, 60, 149, 161, 163, 164, 169
conquest dynasties, xv, xviii–xxi, 105, 122, 128, 133, 142, 149, 156, 176
Cui Li (rebellion), 17, 18, 20
cultural mediation, negotiation, xx, xxii, xxiv–xxv, 12, 14, 163–164, 171, 174
culture: culture, Bohai, 66, 143, 152, 171; culture-bearers, xviii, 5, 9–10, 24, 49–50, 66, 143, 167, 171, 173, 177; definition and uses of, xix–xxi, xxiv–xxv, xxviii, 12, 14, 24, 163–164, 166, 168–169, 171, 174; Han Chinese, xix, 5, 16, 33, 40, 49, 171, 178; *haner*, 44, 48, 49–53, 68, 74, 176; Jin 71, 73, 77; Jurchen, xix, xxxii, xxxiii, 55–57, 61, 66, 68, 77, 140, 142, 169, 170, 174; Kitan, xix, 15, 24, 37, 39, 52–53, 140, 167; Liao, 41, 68, 168; Song 38, 71, 75

Da Jin guozhi, 54, 86, 109
daily life, xxviii, 26, 31, 52, 63, 67, 72, 75, 77, 78, 84, 153, 163, 165, 179; among Han Chinese, *haner*, 41, 49, 51, 68–76, 78, 79; Jin, 60–65, 77; among Kitan, 27–41, 52; *sheng* Jurchen, 54–60, 65–66, 77
Datong (Xijing), Western Capital, xxxii
Deguang, Liao emperor, xi, 52, 93, 106–107, 124, 159–160, 168
divorce, 67, 100, 104, 117–118, 119
Dongjing, Eastern Capital, xxxi, 14, 40, 184n28
Dongtanguo, 14–15, 40. *See also* Bei, Liao prince
dowry, xxiv, xxv, 54, 86, 91, 92, 96, 104, 105, 108, 152

Eastern Circuit, xxxi, 40, 184n28. *See also* Dongjing
Ebrey, Patricia, 75, 176, 184n27

243

education: academies, 5, 147; examinations and degrees, 25, 146–147, 187n10; Jin education system, 147–148; *jinshi* degree, 86, 145, 146; schools, 10, 23, 143, 147, 148; women's education, xviii, xx, xxviii, 2, 4, 6, 10–11, 15, 23–24, 96, 101, 115, 139, 141–149, 162–164, 167, 172, 173, 178, 179, 181

Eleanor of Aquitaine, 180

Elliott, Mark, 108

Empress Wu, Tang. *See* Wu Zetian

epitaphs, xxviii, 6–7, 11, 13, 15, 99–100, 112, 130, 144, 145, 146

Erliben. *See* Xiao Erliben

ethnicity, xxiii–xxiv, 16, 23, 42, 57, 184n25, 191n35, 201n8

Fan Chengda, 72, 78–79, 87–88, 102, 113, 171

Fan Ma (Barbarian Horses), 27–32, 33, 35, 51

Feng Chia-sheng, 93, 99, 108, 160

filial piety, xxviii, 1, 4, 6–7, 8, 9, 16, 19, 20–24, 55, 56, 67, 139, 145–146, 168, 169, 173, 178; *Classic of Filial Piety*, 61, 66. *See also* Confucian ethics

following in death, xviii, xx, xxix, 2, 7–8, 11, 18–24, 104, 106–107, 108, 109, 111, 112, 118, 119, 120, 124, 154, 166–167, 169, 173, 177, 178, 180. *See also* widows; Yingtian

foot binding, xxx, 88, 176

Franke, Herbert, xx, 116, 183n8

frontiers, xxi, xxii, 10, 23–25, 52, 111, 142, 176–177, 178, 179

funerary customs, 12, 14, 30, 38, 39, 44, 49, 60, 61, 64, 68, 80, 84–85, 125, 174, 197n5, 199n1; funerary masks, 13, 35, 38, 41, 60, 188n38. *See also* burial customs; tombs

gender, xvii, xix, xx, 31, 46, 176; gender divisions, 33, 51, 53, 60, 73, 113, 115, 150, 177; separation of sexes, 33, 73, 104, 113, 115, 148, 176, 201n37

generation-gap marriage, 98–99, 112, 126, 160, 173, 178. *See also* marriage

geography, xxi, xxx–xxxiii, 56, 158, 177–178, 179. *See also* frontiers

Great Wall, xxi, 184n17

Hailing *wang*, Jin emperor, xii, 63, 67, 103, 110, 118

hairstyles, xxiii; in general, 52, 78, 112, 171; Jurchen, 55–56, 57, 62, 171, 193n14; Kitan, 28, 30–33, 37, 46, 52–53, 81, 190n5; queue, 53, 69, 175; of women, 32, 46, 48, 53, 72–73, 74, 171. *See also* beards

Han Chinese population, xix, xxii, xxv, xxxii, 20, 26, 40, 78, 79, 111, 151, 173, 178; under Jin, 20, 55, 68–77, 93, 109, 138, 147, 148, 151, 161, 171, 178; under Liao, 41–51, 68, 88–89, 93, 167, 177–178; surnames of, xxix, 3, 15, 16, 18, 19, 25, 42, 151, 174, 177; women, xvii, xxv, xxviii, 2, 4, 15, 22, 41, 51, 68–76, 78, 89, 93, 104, 118–119, 138–139, 145, 151, 166, 170–171, 174–175, 177, 180

Han culture: cultural values, xix, xxi, xxiv, 3, 19, 24, 33, 55, 68, 78, 89, 163, 166, 176; influence of in Liao and Jin, xvii, xxviii, 5, 15, 16, 23–25, 48–49, 51–53, 55, 61, 63, 67, 71, 77, 89, 91, 118–119, 138, 140–143, 166, 168–169, 171–173, 177

Han dynasty, xxi, xxv, xxvii, 1–2, 58–59, 60, 96, 149, 157, 183n11. *See also Wenji gui Han*

haner, hanren, xvii, xxi, xxii, xxiii, xxix, 15–16, 26, 40–55, 63, 68, 76–77, 78, 91, 99, 102, 109, 111–112, 118–119, 127, 145–148, 174, 175, 177, 191n35; division by ethnic identity, 57; women, 15, 26, 41, 47–48, 49, 50, 53, 55, 68–76, 77, 105, 112, 118, 139, 165, 166, 171, 175

Hann Derang, xi, xxx, 5, 99, 113, 119, 127–130, 141, 154–162, 168, 202n27, 205n30. *See also* Chengtian; Yelü Longyu

Hann family elite status, xxxi, 16, 42, 44, 48, 93, 100, 155

Hann Kuangsi, 151, 155

Hann Shixun (tomb of), 44–46, 172

244

Index

Hann Yanhui, 100, 143
Hann Zhigu (tomb of), 155
Hebei province, xxxi, xxxii, 26, 40, 63, 147, 151
Heilong (Amur) River, 55
Heilongjiang province, xxxii, 26, 61
Henan province, xxxii, 69
heroism, heroine, xix, xx, xxv, xxvii, xxix, 8, 10, 19, 21, 59, 107, 119, 121, 131, 133, 139, 163, 171, 181
histories, privately written. See *Da Jin guozhi*, *Kitan guozhi*
history: Chinese dynastic histories, xvii, xviii, xxii, xxv, xxviii, xxx, 1–2, 3, 9, 10, 11, 23, 26, 54, 66, 86, 94, 212, 122, 123, 133, 146, 149, 150, 163. See also *Hou Hanshu*; *Jinshi*; *Liaoshi*
Hōjō Masako, 180
Holmgren, Jennifer, 86, 93, 94, 99, 159
Hong Hao, 54, 86, 87, 90, 102, 144, 186n47
horses, horseriding, xi, xvii, xxvi, 9, 12, 13, 26, 33, 35–37, 44, 49, 95, 125, 139, 148, 167, 168, 177; horsemanship, 7, 13, 35, 57, 131, 135, 165, 178
Hou Hanshu, xxv, 1, 2, 3, 9
hu. See pastoralist, pastoralism
Hu Gui, 27, 189n4
Huai River, xxxii, 138
Huihu clan, xxii, 92, 122, 202n15
Huining, Jin capital, 56, 60, 61, 63
Huizong, Song emperor, 68
hunting, xxvii–xviii, xxx, 12, 13, 14, 15, 29, 33, 34, 35, 41, 52, 53, 54, 55, 86, 89, 126, 127, 132, 139, 156, 168, 169; hunting for girls, 89, 156. See also abduction

identity: cultural, xvii–xviii, xix, xx, xxii, xxiv, xxviii, 6, 9, 14, 22, 42, 52, 104, 140, 163, 176–179, 191n37; ethnic, xxiv–xxviii, 23, 42, 57, 191n37; Han, 51, 167; Jurchen, 21, 61, 67, 78–79, 170; Kitan, 9, 37, 43, 123, 167

incest, 20, 109
indigenous culture, lifestyles, xvii, xix, xxi–xxii, 10, 56, 166, 174
inner Asia, xvii, xxi, xxiii, 180
Inner Mongolia, 26, 35, 39, 99
intermarriage, 42, 52, 93, 99, 122, 177. See also marriage

Japan, xxi, 180, 194n
Jilin province, 26, 61
Jin, state of, xii, xiii, xvii, xix, xx–xxi, xxiv, xxvii, xxx–xxxiii, 16–17, 25–26, 56, 59, 60, 65, 68, 77, 79, 104, 113, 132, 133, 143, 148, 153, 174, 179
Jin culture, xxvii, 17, 19, 23–52, 57, 69, 71–72, 76, 100, 109–110, 170, 172, 181
Jin society, xxiv, xxvii, 3, 7, 10, 20, 22, 25, 54, 61, 65–66, 79, 86, 88, 100, 104–105, 109, 112, 133, 134, 148–149, 163, 171–172, 181
Jin wen zui, 142
Jing, Anning, 76
Jingzong, Liao emperor, xi, 39, 89, 93, 99, 126–129, 130, 154–155, 157, 159–160, 162, 167, 197n26, 202n27, 207n4
Jinshi, xvii, xxiv, 1–4, 16, 21, 23, 24, 54, 55, 65, 102, 110, 123, 133, 147, 148, 170, 172, 185n44
Jurchen, state, people, xii–xiii, xxi–xxv, xxvii, xxxii, 56, 57–58, 60–61, 68, 94, 97, 117, 133, 142, 148, 170, 173–174, 192n48; culture, 55–63, 66–67, 69, 70–72, 76, 77, 78, 89, 90, 97–99, 120, 140, 142, 170, 175; language, script, xxiii, xxxi, 10, 22–23, 63, 142, 166, 173, 194n27; society, 24, 54, 57–58, 107, 118, 139, 147, 175; women, xviii, xix, xxiii, xxix, 2–3, 16–18, 21–22, 24, 54, 57–58, 98–99, 105, 110, 118, 139, 147, 163, 166, 169–170, 172, 175, 178
Jurchen language, xxiii, 22–23, 61, 143, 170, 171
Jurchen revival. See revival of Jurchen culture

Index

Jurchen tribes, xvii, xxi–xxiii, 3, 26, 55–57, 66, 77, 93, 148, 152, 193n14; wild or *sheng* Jurchen, xxvii, 55–60, 61–63, 171

Kaifeng, Song capital, xxvi, xxvii, xxxii, 6, 56, 68, 72, 88, 147, 152
Kane, Daniel, xxiii, 6, 49, 92, 167, 173
Khubilai Khan, 128, 180, 203n33
kidnapping, xxvii, 89, 90. See also abduction
Kitan, state, population, xvi, xvii, xxi–xxii, xxv, xxviii, 26, 37–41, 42, 59, 97, 122–123, 127, 132, 149
Kitan-Chinese, 49, 142. See also Liao Chinese
Kitan culture, society, xxiii, 3–13, 23–24, 28–33, 37–41, 44–49–55, 65, 76, 81, 84–85, 90–91, 93, 98–99, 109, 115, 120–122, 143, 146, 149, 151, 155–156; tribesmen, xvii, xviii, xxi, xxvi, 28–33, 37, 176. See also pastoralist, pastoralism
Kitan guozhi, 86, 88, 106, 107, 121, 123, 127, 128, 131, 155, 157, 197n26
Kitan language, script, xxii–xxiii, xxx, 49, 92–93, 124, 129, 142–143, 166–168, 173, 175
Kitan women, xxix, xx–xxii, xxiv, xxix, xxx, 2–16, 33–39, 50–52, 54, 78, 80–85, 87, 89, 90, 92–94, 97–98, 102, 105–106, 121–132, 141–164, 165, 167–169, 172–175, 177–178. See also Chengtian; Xiao *fei*; Yingtian
Korea, Koryŏ, xxi, xxii, 184n28
koumiss, 44, 49, 90, 94, 172, 197n32. See also alcohol
Kulunqi tomb site, xxix, 37, 81–83, 99, 149, 169, 190n9, 191n23

language, significance of, xxi, xxiii, 6, 22, 49, 78, 142; Altaic and Tungusic language groups, xxiii. See also Altaic language group; Chinese language; Jurchen language; Kitan language; Liao Chinese
Latter Jin state, xxiii, xxv, xxxi, 40

Latter Tang state, xxv, xxvii, 4–5, 14, 89, 93, 167
Lattimore, Owen, xxi, 183n11
levirate marriage, xx, xxiv, 20–21, 56, 86, 90, 104, 108–111, 112, 116, 119–120, 154, 160, 163, 173, 177, 184n26
Li Hu, *See* Yelü Lihu
Li Qingzhan, Song poet, 76
Li Quan, 133–138, 203n60
Liang, Xi Xia, empress dowager, 179
Liao, state of, xvii, xviii, xx–xxii, 36, 39–41, 42–43, 56, 57, 97, 106, 116, 132, 143, 151; relations with Song, xviii, xix, xxii, xxxii–xxxiii, 97, 121, 123, 126–128, 129–130, 132, 157–158
Liao Chinese (language), xxiii, 6, 49, 142, 167, 173. See also Kitan-Chinese
Liao River, xxi, 26, 55, 184
Liao society, customs, xxv, xxivv, 7, 11, 14, 21, 22, 25, 26–34, 37, 38–43, 49, 50, 52–53, 57, 75, 78, 80–84, 86, 90, 92, 99, 100, 104–105, 108, 111, 112, 117–119, 139–140, 143, 145, 147, 156, 163–164, 168, 172–175, 178–179
Liaoning province, 14, 26, 144
Liaoshi, xvii, xxii, 9, 185n44
Liaoyang, xxxi, 14, 40. See also Dongjing; Eastern Circuit
lienü, xxiv, 1–4, 9–10, 23–24, 86, 146, 163, 175, 188n47; Jin *lienü*, 16–23, 65, 119, 133, 138, 170; Liao *lienü*, 4–11, 15–16, 23, 104, 108, 119, 120, 144, 169, 175
Liu, Song empress dowager, 180
Liu Bin (Song author), 154, 156–159, 161
Liu Pujiang, 92, 123, 184n20
Liu Xiang (Han writer), 2–3
Longqing. *See* Yelü Longqing
loyalty, xix, xxv, xxvi–xxvii, 2–3, 5, 7, 21, 22, 42–43, 79, 129, 139, 154, 171, 178; as a Confucian virtue, xxvii, 3, 7, 168, 173, 178; as an indigenous value, 2, 23, 24, 169, 178
lu (caitiff), xxi, 159

Index

Lü (Han empress), 157, 206n72
Lu Zhen (Song envoy), 157–159, 161, 167, 186n47

Manchuria, xxi, xxii, xxiii, xxxii, 26–27, 184n28, 194n18
Manchus, xvi, xxi, xxiii, xxv, xxxiii, 43, 60, 69, 89, 99, 109, 116–117, 158, 193n15, 197n30, 198n65
marriage, xix, xxi, xxv, 7, 19, 21–24, 35, 42, 54, 56, 68, 80–105, 108, 116, 117, 122–123, 142, 145, 159–161, 165, 172, 173, 177, 179; companionate marriage, 78; marriage ceremonies, xxv, 80–85, 94–96; marriage customs, xix, xx, 22; marriage diplomacy, 96–98; secondary forms of marriage, 99–104. *See also* abduction, abduction marriage; adultery; bride-price marriage; dowry; generation-gap marriage; levirate marriage; remarriage of widows
material culture, artifacts, costume: Jin, 55–60, 65, 68–76, 78, 86–88, 152, 192n44; Liao, xxiv, xxv, xxix, 12–15, 26, 27, 30, 31, 33, 35–37, 38–39, 54, 60–65, 77, 78, 81, 96, 162, 167–168, 169, 172, 175, 188n43
military, martial affairs: by women, xvii, xviii, xix, xx, xxiv, xxv, xxviii, 2–4, 11, 17, 21–23, 24, 30, 34, 54, 65, 79, 121–140, 162, 164, 165–166, 170–171, 172, 176, 179, 180
Ming dynasty, xx, xxi, xxix, 1, 11, 23, 24, 64, 68, 133, 161–162, 170, 181
Möngke khan (Yuan), 180
Mongolia, xxi, xxii. *See also* Inner Mongolia
Mongols, xvii, xix, xx, xxi, xxiii, xxv, xxxiii, 17–19, 21, 26, 39, 47, 79, 86, 89, 91, 104, 108, 109, 121, 132, 134–138, 170, 173, 178, 180; language, xxiii; women, xx, 86, 89, 109, 132, 139, 180. *See also* Yuan dynasty
morality. *See* Confucian ethics
Mulan, xxv, 133

Nanjing (Jin city), 56. *See also* Kaifeng
Nanjing (Liao city), xxxi, 40–41, 155. *See also* Beijing; Southern Capital; Yanjing
nobility, 139; Bohai, 66, 98, 103; Jin, 62, 66, 102, 148; Kitan, xxxii, 3, 6, 13, 31, 37, 40, 83, 89, 92, 122, 146, 150, 160, 187n31
Northern administration (Liao), 26, 40, 43, 80, 123, 155
Northern Capital (Liao). *See* Shangjing
Nuolan. *See* Xiao Nuolan
Nüzhen, xxii. *See also* Jurchen

Ögödai khan, Yuan, 180

painting: extant scroll paintings, xxix, 12–14, 167, 169, 171; Jin, xxvi–xxvii, 56–60, 62, 63, 68–69, 71–73, 75, 171–172, 185n36; Liao, xxiv, 12–14, 30, 31, 33–39, 44–47, 49, 81–85 (*see also* Chenguo; Kulunqi); significance of, xxii, xxviii, xxix, xxxiii, 26, 27, 31, 33, 37, 39, 43, 44, 47–48, 52–53, 60, 62, 68, 71–73, 78, 79, 84, 152–153, 170, 175. *See also Wenji gui Han*; Yanshan temple
pastoralist, pastoralism, xix, xxi–xxv, xxvi, xxvii–xxviii, xxxii, 3, 10, 14, 26, 27–41, 43–44, 45, 48, 49, 50–53, 55, 60, 68, 81, 84, 85, 95, 96, 111, 118–119, 120, 122, 151, 166–169, 173, 174, 177, 183n11, 190n5
Pazyryk (archaeological site), 96
de Pee, Christian, 76, 84
Persia, xxii, xxviii
pets, household, 44, 48, 49, 68, 75, 79
philosophy. *See* Confucianism as philosophy
Piyang, duke of (Han dynasty), 157, 206n47
poetry, by women, xxiv, xxvii, 5, 6, 10–12, 141, 142, 144, 148, 163, 169
premarital sexuality, xxix, 79, 85–88, 90, 138, 161. *See also* sexuality
printing, 143, 147
prostitution, 2, 21, 102, 118, 153, 170, 195n49

Qi, prince of, 54, 57–58, 60–62, 63, 77, 170, 171
Qianlong, Qing emperor, 57, 60, 64, 194n18
Qin, Liao prince, 158, 202n27
Qin dynasty, xxi, 101, 144
Qin-Jinguo, prince and princess of, 11, 127
Qing dynasty, 1, 43, 57, 60, 64, 89, 109, 116, 117, 176, 177. See also Manchus
Quan, Song empress, 180
queue, 53, 69, 175. See also hairstyles

rape, 9, 10, 18, 19, 20, 88, 90, 120. See also abduction, abduction marriage
Raphals, Lisa, 3, 188n47
religion, xxi, xxiii, xxix, 73, 141, 162. See also animism; Buddhism
remarriage of widows, xxix, 2, 3, 19–22, 25, 91, 92, 107, 110–111, 117–119, 120, 154, 163, 170, 176
Renyi, Liao empress, xxviii, xix, 100, 131
Renzong, Song emperor, 180
revival of Jurchen culture, xxxii–xxiii, 22–23, 60, 62, 68, 170–171, 194n27. See also Shizong, Jin emperor
romanization principles, xxx

sacrificial offerings, 38, 39, 83–84, 85, 149, 169, 174, 205n41. See also animism
schools. See education
script: Jurchen, 10, 23, 61, 173; Kitan, 10, 142–143, 173. See also Kane, Daniel
sedentary agriculture, lifestyle, xix, xxiii, 26, 52, 56
separation of sexes. See gender, gender divisions
sexuality, xix, xx, xxviii, xxx, 79, 86–87, 92, 94, 105, 113, 133, 138, 142, 154, 161, 163–164, 168, 177, 179, 181. See marriage; premarital sexuality
Shalizhi, 16–17, 21, 22, 170
shamanism, 38–39, 45, 55, 84, 95, 149, 174. See also animism

Shandong province, xix, xxxiii, 133, 135–137, 145, 154
Shangjing, Jin capital, 56, 61, 81. See also Huining
Shangjing, Liao capital, xxxi, xxxii, 39–41, 52, 125, 129, 151
Shanxi province, xxxi, xxxii, 5, 68, 69, 72, 73, 75, 76, 152
Shengzong, Liao emperor, xi, xviii, 5, 39, 41, 80, 94, 121, 126–130, 157, 158, 160, 162, 167–168. See also Yelü Longxu
Shizong, Jin emperor, xii, xxiii, xxxii–xxxiii, 22, 43, 57, 61–64, 67, 68, 109, 110, 116, 118, 147, 170, 174–175, 194n27. See also revival of Jurchen culture
Shizong, Liao emperor, xi, xxviii, 66, 89, 93, 98, 125, 159, 197n26, 207n4. See also Zhen, Lady
Shulü clan, 92–93, 122–123, 125, 166, 202n15. See also Yingtian, Liao empress dowager
Silk Road, 36, 69
Sima Qian, xx, xxi, 56, 178, 183n11
sinicization, xxx, xxxiii, 23, 43, 62, 68, 113, 117, 143, 148, 166, 169, 171, 172. See also acculturation
Sixteen Prefectures, xxi, xxiii, 40, 89, 186n50
social class. See class, social
Song state, xxii, xxxii, 16, 26, 40, 42–43, 97, 118, 180; comparison with Liao and Jin, xx, xxiv, xxx, 41, 57, 65–66, 72, 78, 79, 88, 90, 109, 113, 118–119, 122, 133, 161, 162, 171, 179; customs, culture, 22, 33, 34, 37, 39, 48, 52, 68, 71–72, 75, 76, 88, 108, 145–146, 147, 148, 152, 161, 163, 176, 177; embassy to Liao, 157–160, 163, 167; literature, language, xxvi, xxx, 1, 6, 39, 72, 76, 86, 141, 143, 157; wars against Jin, xix, xxxii–xxxiii, 19, 68, 121, 133–138; wars with Liao, xviii, xxxii, 34, 97, 121–130, 132, 154, 155
Songhua (Sungari) River, 55–56

Sorghaghtani-Beki (Yuan), 180
sororate, 95, 96, 99–100, 109, 173
Southern Capital. *See* Nanjing
Southern Circuit, xxiii, xxxi, xxxii, 26, 40, 43, 80, 93, 143
Standen, Naomi, 42, 178
Steinhardt, Nancy, 14, 30, 76, 150
steppe culture, xiv, xix, xxiv–xxv, xxix, 2–3, 9, 15, 18–19, 21, 24, 34, 41, 53, 90, 99, 104, 106, 108, 120, 139, 140, 166, 168–169, 171, 173, 174, 175, 178
surnames for women, xxxi, 15, 16, 89, 92, 93, 100, 122, 123, 150, 170, 177

Tang dynasty, xxii, xxxi, 1, 12, 13, 31, 33, 34, 35, 40, 41, 48, 55, 97, 104, 139, 149, 150, 151, 174, 176, 179, 184n28
Tanguts, 26. *See also* Xi Xia
tea, xxix, 44, 49, 90, 171, 172; Buddhist connotations of, 44, 46, 49, 79
temples, xix, xxix, 14, 18, 34, 35, 38, 53, 64, 72, 73, 76, 136, 151, 152, 163. *See also* Yanshan temple
theater, theatricals, xxix, 68, 76–78, 79. *See also zaju* drama
Tianxi, Liao emperor, xi, 132. *See also* Chun, Liao prince
Tianzuo, Liao emperor, xi, 101, 115, 117, 131, 144, 192n48
Tietze, Klaus-Peter, 141, 142, 156
tombs: Jin, 60–65, 68–77, 78, 151, 152, 174, 175; Liao, xxiv, xxv, xxix, 7, 12–15, 26–28, 30–39, 41, 43–46, 48–51, 52–53, 81–85, 151, 162, 167–169, 171–172, 173, 174, 175, 177, 179. *See also* archaeology; burial customs
Töregene (Yuan), 180
tribesmen: Jurchen, 57–59, 148, 185n38, 193n14; Kitan, xvii, xxi, xxvi, 28–30, 33, 35, 37, 45, 52, 88, 190n5. *See also* clothing; hairstyles
tribute, xxii, xxiv, 56, 130, 184n18, 191n32

Twitchett, Denis, 141–142, 156

urban, xix, xxiii, 40, 41, 52, 75, 120. *See also* cities
Uygur, xxi, 122, 123, 124, 176, 202n15

virginity, 85, 86, 90, 94, 101, 104, 161
virtue, xxiv, 1–4, 8–11, 15–16, 20, 23, 24, 25, 130, 132, 139, 171. *See also* Confucian ethics; Confucianism as philosophy

Wakeman, Frederic, 43
Wang Anshi, xxvi
Wang Kui, 72
Wanyan Aguda. *See* Aguda, Jin emperor
Wanyan clan, 16, 17, 97
Wanyan Haowen, 147
Wanyan Yan. *See* Qi, prince of
war, warfare, xix, xxiii, 34, 55, 63, 97, 110, 127, 129, 132, 138, 147, 180. *See also* Song state, wars against Jin, wars with Liao
warriors, xviii, xxxiii, 56, 60–62, 132, 171; myth of, xxi; warrior women, xviii, xxi, xxvii, xxix, xxx, 16, 18, 92, 112, 119, 121–140, 154, 161, 163, 165, 166, 167, 170–171, 175, 176, 177, 180, 181
Wen *fei*, 101–102, 132, 144, 180
Wenji, Lady (Han heroine), xxv–xxvi, 5, 16, 49, 89, 97, 143, 171, 175, 185nn36–37
Wenji gui Han (Jin painting), frontispiece, xv, xxvi–xxvii, xxviii, 54, 57–63, 69, 77, 79, 139, 171, 172, 175
Western Capital. *See* Datong; Xijing
widows, widowhood, xix, xxiv, xxix, xxx, 3, 7, 9, 20, 21–22, 56, 85, 91, 104, 106–120, 127, 130, 142, 150, 152, 157, 160–161, 163, 170, 172, 174, 177, 178, 179, 180, 181; widow alternatives, xviii, xx, xxviii, xxix, 141, 154, 163, 173, 176; widow suicide, 8, 24, 120, 166–167, 169. *See also* chastity; following in death; levirate marriage; remarriage of widows

Wittfogel, Karl, 93, 99, 108
women: status of in Liao and Jin society, xxx, 23, 41, 52, 75, 96, 104–105, 147, 172, 175, 187n33
Wu, Tang empress. *See* Wu Zetian, Tang empress
Wu, K. T., 143
Wu, Peiyi, 134, 136, 138
Wu Zetian, Tang empress, 34, 139, 151
Wuchimai, Jin emperor, 56
Wugu tribes, xxii
Wugulun *shi*, 17, 19, 22
Wulinda *shi*, 118, 170

Xi tribes, xxi, xxv, xxxi, 26, 39, 41, 42, 57, 92–93, 97, 98, 160, 191n32; ancestry of Empress Yingtian, 123–124, 125, 202n15
Xi Xia, xxxiii, 26, 97, 151, 179
Xia Quan, 135–138
Xianbei, xxi, xxvi, 16, 97
xiannü, 4–5, 9
Xiao, surname, clan, xxix, xxxii, 4, 7–10, 23, 53, 89, 92–93, 97, 98, 144, 155, 166; Kulunqi cemetery of, 37, 81, 178; as marriage clan, 23, 66, 92–93, 98–99, 100, 117, 122, 123
Xiao Chou (Yanyan). *See* Chengtian, Liao empress dowager
Xiao Erliben, 8–10, 169
Xiao *fei*, 11–14, 24, 179
Xiao Hunjan, 126, 131
Xiao Nuolan, 8, 9–10, 169, 187n24
Xiao Shaoju, 35, 99
Xiao Siwen, 126
Xiao *taihou*, 131–132, 180
Xiao Xiaozhong, 80–81, 84, 99
Xiao Yixin, 7–8, 9, 10, 169
Xie, Song grand dowager empress, 180
Xijing (Western Capital), xxxii, 131
Xingzong, Liao emperor, xii, xix, 115, 130, 131, 168
Xiongnu, xxi, 56, 96, 178, 183n11, 185n32

Xu Mengxin, 55, 56, 57
Xuangzong, Jin emperor, xii, 66, 104
Xuanhua archaeological site, 43, 45, 50, 63

Yan-Yun prefectures, xxi, 25, 26, 37, 186n50
Yang Miaozhen, xix, xx, xxiv, xxix, 79, 113, 119, 121, 126, 133–138, 139, 140, 163, 170, 172, 175, 177, 179
Yanjing, xxi, 40, 56, 155, 186n50. *See also* Southern Capital
Yanshan temple, 71–74, 78, 87, 88, 152, 153, 171
Yanyan. *See* Chengtian, Liao empress dowager
Yaonian clan, 13, 92, 100, 157, 166
Yelü Changge, xix, xxviii, 5–7, 9, 10, 12, 24, 94, 104, 111, 149, 168–169, 171, 172, 173
Yelü Chucai, 173
Yelü Lihu, 107, 125
Yelü Longqing, 35, 89, 127, 156, 158–159, 202n27
Yelü Longxu, 126, 137, 154–157. *See also* Shengzong, Liao emperor
Yelü Longyu, 127, 156, 202n27
Yelü Longyun, 155, 156, 162. *See also* Hann Derang
Yelü Nu, 7–8
Yelü Ruan, 125. *See also* Shizong, Liao emperor
Yelü Xiezhen, 126, 127, 155, 163
Yelü Yixin, 6–7, 113–115, 144
Yemaotai, lady of, xxix, 12–14, 143, 167, 169, 172, 173; tomb, 12–14
Yide, Liao empress, 6, 113–114, 144, 180
Yingtian, Liao empress dowager, xi, xviii, xx, xxix, 7, 34, 92–93, 97–98, 106–107, 120, 121, 122–126, 127, 138, 139, 140, 143, 144, 159, 166–167, 172, 175, 179
Yuan dynasty, xviii, xx, xxiii, xxix, 1, 11, 19, 21, 22, 23, 42, 57, 64, 77, 112, 113, 122, 128, 136, 143, 167, 170, 173, 176; historians of, xx, 2, 3, 7, 132

250

Index

Yuan *fei*, 148
Yueguo, Liao princess, 80, 84, 99
yurts, 29, 30; yurt-shaped tombs, 33, 35

zaju drama, 76
Zhang family elites, 16, 42, 44–45, 48, 50, 93, 155
Zhang Fengnu, 21, 170
Zhang *shi*, 50–51
Zhang Shiqing, 47, 50
Zhang Shiyou, 50
Zhang Wenzao, 45, 50

Zhang Yu, 185n37
Zhangzong, Jin emperor, 67, 103, 104, 148, 152
Zhao Siwen, 107
Zhen, Lady, xxvii, 49, 89, 93, 98, 143, 159, 167, 171, 197n26
Zhenzong, Song emperor, 129, 180
Zhongjing, Jin capital, xxxii
Zhongjing (Central Capital): Liao, xxxii, 39, 40–41, 52, 56, 63, 123, 157, 158, 191n32. *See also* Central Circuit
Zodiac, 50–51, 53

About the Author

Linda Cooke Johnson, professor of history at Michigan State University, studied Chinese art history with Professor Michael Sullivan at Stanford University and received her M.A. and Ph.D. in Chinese history from the University of California in a combined program with Santa Cruz and Berkeley. She is the author of *Shanghai: From Market Town to Treaty Port, 1074–1858* (1995) and editor of *Cities of Jiangnan in Late Imperial China* (1996). Her seminal article "The Place of *Qingming shanghe tu* in the Historical Geography of Song Dynasty Dongjing" was published in the *Journal of Song-Yuan Studies* 26 (1996). Her work has been translated and published in China and Japan. She is affiliated with the Gu Wei Hui institute at Beijing University.

Production Notes for Johnson | *Women of the Conquest Dynasties*
Cover design by Julie Matsuo-Chun
Text design and composition by Publishers' Design and Production Services, Inc.
　with display type in Berhnard Modern and text type in Adobe Jensen Pro
Printing and binding by Edwards Brothers, Inc.
Printed on 60# Arbor, 444 ppi